Faithful Revolution

Faithful Revolution

*How Voice of the Faithful Is
Changing the Church*

TRICIA COLLEEN BRUCE

OXFORD
UNIVERSITY PRESS

OXFORD
UNIVERSITY PRESS

Oxford University Press, Inc., publishes works that further
Oxford University's objective of excellence
in research, scholarship, and education.

Oxford   New York
Auckland   Cape Town   Dar es Salaam   Hong Kong   Karachi
Kuala Lumpur   Madrid   Melbourne   Mexico City   Nairobi
New Delhi   Shanghai   Taipei   Toronto

With offices in
Argentina   Austria   Brazil   Chile   Czech Republic   France   Greece
Guatemala   Hungary   Italy   Japan   Poland   Portugal   Singapore
South Korea   Switzerland   Thailand   Turkey   Ukraine   Vietnam

Copyright © 2011 by Oxford University Press, Inc.

Published by Oxford University Press, Inc.
198 Madison Avenue, New York, New York 10016

www.oup.com

Oxford is a registered trademark of Oxford University Press.

Library of Congress Cataloging-in-Publication Data
Bruce, Tricia Colleen.
Faithful revolution : how Voice of the Faithful is changing the church / Tricia Colleen Bruce.
   p.   cm.
Includes bibliographical references.
ISBN 978-0-19-538584-7
1. Voice of the Faithful (Organization) 2. Laity—United States—History—21st century.
3. Laity—Catholic Church—History—21st century. 4. Church renewal.
5. Catholic Church—History—21st century. I. Title.
BX809.V65B78   2011
267'.18273—dc22   2010017468

9 8 7 6 5 4 3 2 1

Printed in the United States of America
on acid-free paper

For my family

Contents

Faithful Revolution

Introduction

I was abused by the prefect, the priest who was second in command at the seminary. He was the priest to see when you got in trouble. You didn't want to see the prefect. My abuse came under the guise of medicine, in the infirmary. He acted as though he had extensive medical training, although he hadn't. I developed a rash down there in September of my freshman year. I wasn't sure what it was, thinking perhaps I had brushed against poison ivy. I was told to see the doctor in town that took care of all of us. He said that I did have a rash due to poison ivy on my arms, but that the other was a kind of jock itch. He prescribed a lotion for my arms, and another kind of lotion medication for the jock itch. When the prescriptions came, I was instructed to pick them up from the infirmary. Upon my arrival, the arm lotion was there with a note that said I would have to pick up the other lotion from the prefect . . . something about me being under 18 and unable to have the medication in my own possession. So I went to pick it up in the prefect's office (a room which doubled as his living quarters). He had the lotion, and told me that due to me being a minor, he would have to apply the lotion. I was confused and knew that didn't seem right, but he insisted. So that's how it started.

—"Will," a victim/survivor of abuse by a
Catholic priest at the age of 14[1]

In January 2002, two dozen lay Catholics gathered in a parish basement near Boston, Massachusetts, to lament new revelations of clergy pedophilia and growing evidence that bishops had knowingly transferred abusive priests from parish to parish. Uncertain how to react, the small group from St. John the Evangelist reached out to neighboring Catholics and invited them to join in expressing feelings of pain, frustration, and anger collectively in the wake of the crisis. In time, the crowd in the basement grew, filling with Catholics trying to reconcile scandal in their church. They gained public attention and saw the need to organize. Rallying around the motto, "Keep the Faith, Change the Church," Voice of the Faithful (VOTF) spread throughout a country of Catholics reeling from daily media exposures of abuse within the U.S. Catholic Church.

This book examines how the collective of a few spawned a nationwide movement of lay Catholics urging reform from within the Catholic Church. What began as a direct response to the abuse of children by clergy evolved into a social movement promoting support for victims, support for nonabusing priests, and structural change in the church that might prevent future abuse and increase lay participation in decision making. In its attempt to open the governance of the Catholic Church to meaningful participation for lay Catholics, VOTF became increasingly politicized in the face of critiques from church authorities. What was to some a fulfillment of decades-old promises for lay participation was to others a liberal threat to Catholic faith and authority. Though VOTF's predominately older, educated, middle- to upper-class and white demographic did not mirror that of U.S. Catholics at-large, it nonetheless laid claim to a mainstream and centrist Catholic identity that could proffer a collective voice for meaningful lay participation in the U.S. Catholic Church. The movement invites broader reflection on the very meaning of a religious identity within the context of an institutional space.

Voice of the Faithful also offers important insight into the study of social movements. Specifically, VOTF reveals the unique character of movements that aim to change institutions from the inside. As scholars have begun to explore social movements operating within institutions such as churches, schools, and corporations, we are left with an increasing need for a name for and better understanding of these internal movements. This book helps to meet this need by defining and characterizing *intrainstitutional social movements* (IISMs). How are IISMs different from movements that target the state or society at-large? How does the insider status of movement participants shape the form, strategies, and collective identity that the movement adopts? These are among the questions that *Faithful Revolution* helps answer.

Historicizing Abuse in the U.S. Catholic Church

Though VOTF mobilized in the wake of revelations of child sexual abuse by clergy and institutional cover-ups made public in early 2002, the problem of abuse in the church (and media attention surrounding it) was, in fact, not new. The movement's emergence, then, must first be understood within the context of this longer history.

The Catholic Church is the largest Christian denomination in the United States, with more than 67.5 million adherents (Yearbook of American and Canadian Churches 2008). Nearly 11,000 children reported having been abused between the years 1950 and 2002 by more than 4,000 U.S. Catholic priests (John Jay College of Criminal Justice 2004, 2006). This number understates the full extent of abuse, particularly given the large number of allegations that surfaced after 2002. In January of that year, investigative reporting at the *Boston Globe* set off a wave of revelations regarding the prevalence of abuse among clergy and the accompanying complicity of U.S. bishops in assuring victims' silence and transferring accused priests from parish to parish. The *Globe* ran some three hundred stories about clergy sexual abuse in the four months that followed (Investigative Staff of the *Boston Globe* 2002:viii). Stories related to scandal in the church ranked numbers one, two, four, and five in the Religion Newswriters Association list of top ten religion news stories in 2002 (see table 0.1). Emergent groups of lay Catholics including VOTF ranked fifth, appearing more frequently than stories about Supreme Court rulings on the words "under God" in the Pledge of Allegiance and religious opposition to a U.S. invasion of Iraq.

Widespread media coverage, along with changes in legal statutes of limitations, led to an exponential increase in allegations of abuse against clergy. Public allegations against clergy, seminarians, and religious men and women in 2002 numbered in the thousands, an immense increase from previous years. A third of all accusations to date were made public in 2002. Figure 0.1 reveals this sharp rise in allegations, catalyzed in early 2002.[2] A much wider scope of abuse emerged than previously predicted.

Although allegations of sexual abuse by clergy peaked after 2002, the abuse itself was more likely to have occurred decades earlier. A study conducted by the John Jay College of Criminal Justice in 2004 revealed that the reported *occurrence* of abuse by members of the Catholic clergy in the United States increased gradually after 1950 before peaking in early 1980s. More than one-third of victims (35.5 percent) reported that their abuse began in the 1970s, regardless of the number of years that passed prior to making an allegation.

TABLE O.I. Top Five Religion News Stories, 2002

#I	A sexual abuse scandal in the Catholic Church begins in January and continues throughout the year with allegations that bishops moved priests who allegedly molested children from parish to parish. In some cases, they keep settlements with victims secret from parishioners.
#2	Cardinal Bernard Law of the Archdiocese of Boston resigns December 13 after continued protests by laypeople and priests over how he handled accusations against abusive priests. Faced with millions of dollars in lawsuits, the archdiocese considers filing for bankruptcy protection.
#3	Evangelicals such as Franklin Graham and Jerry Vine of the Southern Baptist Convention cause controversy with their remarks about Islam. Graham calls it an "evil and wicked" religion and Vine brands the faith's main prophet, Muhammad, a "demon-possessed pedophile." The Bush administration distances itself from the remarks.
#4	At a June meeting in Dallas, U.S. Catholic bishops adopt rules that require the immediate removal from public ministry of any priest who has abused a child. The Vatican later requires that the bishops amend the rules by allowing for procedures for priests to state their cases in tribunals.
#5	The clergy sexual abuse scandal in the Catholic Church gives rise to new lay organizations, such as Voice of the Faithful, that demand greater decision-making roles for parishioners.

Source: Religion Newswriters Association.

Fewer than one in ten allegations cite a starting date for the abuse after 1990. This pattern of accusations is depicted in figure 0.2.

Media coverage of issues related to clergy pedophilia has ebbed and flowed in the past two decades, but no other period has surpassed the intense media attention that incited the moral panic of 2002. Sexual abuse cases involving Catholic clergy first began to draw widespread media attention in 1984. At that time, Father Gilbert Gauthe, indicted in Louisiana on thirty-four counts of sex crimes against children, was set to be the first pedophile priest ever brought to trial in the United States. Admitting to having had sexual contact with boys in every church in which he had served since his 1971 ordination, Gauthe ultimately accepted a plea deal and served ten years of a twenty-year prison sentence. It was during Gauthe's case that lawyers revealed, portentously, the first indication that church leaders had passed priests from parish to parish despite known allegations of abuse.

The June 7, 1985, issue of the *National Catholic Reporter* headlined with criticism of the U.S. bishops' lack of policy response toward victims and abusive priests. Other national newspapers followed suit, sparking widespread media coverage of the issue. Gauthe's lawyer, Ray Mouton, subsequently collaborated with Frs. Michael Peterson and Thomas Doyle to create a ninety-two-page report detailing the civil, canonical, and psychological aspects of child sexual abuse by priests. U.S. priests and bishops convened conferences in 1985 and

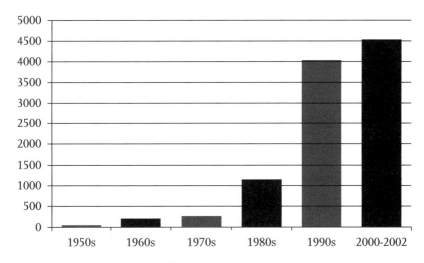

FIGURE O.I. Number of reports of child sexual abuse by priests or deacons, by decade.

Source: John Jay College of Criminal Justice (2004)

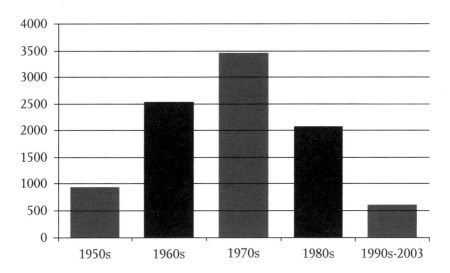

FIGURE O.2. Date alleged abuse began, by decade.

Source: John Jay College of Criminal Justice (2004)

1986 to address the rising incidence of priests abusing young children (Friendly 1986; Isely and Isely 1990). Abuse victim Barbara Blaine founded the Survivors Network of Those Abused by Priests (SNAP) in 1989.

Accusations against the Reverend James Porter in 1992 brought clergy abuse into public view once again, this time bordering the Boston area. Father Porter allegedly abused twenty-eight children in Fall River, Massachusetts, a neighboring diocese to Boston. In a statement printed in the *Fall River Herald*

News, the accused priest was quoted as saying that "it was the church that sent me from one parish to another" and was thus to blame for his repeated abusive behavior (Franklin 1993). The *Chicago Tribune* ran an editorial cartoon in October 1992 after Sinead O'Conner notoriously tore up a picture of the pope during her appearance on NBC's *Saturday Night Live*, alluding to the prevalence of abuse among Catholic clergy.

It was around the time of accusations against Father Porter that Bishop Sean O'Malley, who in 2003 would become Boston's archbishop, was appointed to lead the Fall River Diocese in southeastern Massachusetts. With his diocesan installation in mid-1992, O'Malley announced that he would respond as best as possible to the concerns of those who had been abused (Aucoin 1992). Cardinal Bernard Law, who occupied the top position in the Boston Archdiocese from 1984 to 2002, then echoed O'Malley's commitment to respond appropriately. Law publicly denounced priests who had abused children, while also criticizing the media for focusing on the problem (Hart 1992).

In June 1992, Chicago's Cardinal Joseph Bernardin initiated reforms to his own archdiocese's policies for dealing with accused priests, soon after learning that an accused priest he reassigned had abused again. Bernardin's reforms called for the identification and removal of high-risk priests in active ministry, a review of rehabilitation procedures, and the inclusion of victims and laypeople in committee investigations of allegations. Reforms did not include any legal obligation to notify civil authorities of abuse. Inadvertently, however, the cardinal's reference to twenty incidents of sexual misconduct by priests sparked an investigation by the Illinois state attorney's office. The state attorney subsequently filed grand jury subpoenas. Bernardin's refusal to comply ignited an ironic debate in which the cardinal evoked legal justification for confidentiality while the state attorney evoked moral justification for public reporting. In November 1992, a county judge granted the Chicago Archdiocese's request to quash the subpoenas, ruling that internal proceedings were covered by clerical privilege. A subsequent appeal was denied.

The Chicago reforms became somewhat of a model for diocesan response to allegations of abuse, marked by an emphasis on internal control over external accountability. The National Conference of Catholic Bishops (now the U.S. Conference of Catholic Bishops [USCCB]) insisted that they did not have the authority to adopt a formalized response to the problem of abusive clergy on a national level. At their annual conference in late 1992, the U.S. bishops identified five principles for handling cases of sexual abuse of minors by clergy (USCCB 2002). In the following year, Archbishop William H. Keeler, then president of the National Conference of Catholic Bishops, announced the formation of a committee of bishops to study the issue (Berry and Fox 1993).

By then, Pope John Paul II himself had openly referred to the increasing prevalence of child abuse by clergy as "a public scandal" (Stammer 1993:1).

The ad hoc committee of bishops formed in 1993 produced three reports analyzing diocesan policies on sexual abuse, released between 1994 and 1996 under the title "Restoring Trust." The documents, which would later frame the bishops' 2002 response, emphasized individual diocesan policies that would suspend accused priests, care for victims, cooperate with civil investigations, and "deal with the matter as openly as possible, given the circumstances" (Kinney n.d.). Five years later (in the spring of 1998), the committee sponsored a symposium on abuse by clergy in conjunction with a meeting of the USCCB (USCCB 2002).

Thus the moral panic of 2002 was not the first time that sexual abuse by priests had entered the public consciousness. Lawsuits and settlements against dioceses had already cost the church millions of dollars. Media coverage spurred by the *Boston Globe* did, however, unleash a scandal of new proportions. The year was a tipping point for greater recognition and an organized response to the problem of abuse and its (now more widely known) cover-up. Intense attention paved the way for an unprecedented number of allegations and lawsuits. By five years later (2007), dioceses/eparchies[3] and religious institutes had paid some $498,678,858 in allegation-related costs (USCCB 2008), bringing the total cost to that point to more than $2.3 billion. Seven dioceses (Davenport, Iowa, Fairbanks, Alaska, Portland, Oregon, San Diego, California, Spokane, Washington, Tucson, Arizona, and Wilmington, Delaware) have sought protection from the bankruptcy court since 2002, and numerous parishes have closed throughout the country.[4] Austin Diocese Bishop Gregory Aymond, Chair of the U.S. Bishops' Committee for the Protection of Children and Young People, referred to this period in the church as "our 9/11" (Aymond 2007). Catholic historian John McGreevy has asserted that, "all told the sexual abuse crisis and its ripple effects have become the single most important event in U.S. Catholicism since the Second Vatican Council" (2004:136).

Given the public outcry over the scandal in 2002, it should come as less of a surprise that this was also the year that lay Catholics angered by abuse and corruption within their own church would mobilize an internal movement for reform. The primary aims of the movement that came to be known as *Voice of the Faithful* were to support victims of abuse by priests, support priests who had not abused, and—the goal that would prove most amorphous in intention— change the very structure of the church to promote greater accountability and lay participation. VOTF's struggle to earn and retain legitimacy as a group of authentic and faithful Catholics, rather than marginalized extremists, tested the limits of a Catholic identity and its ties to the institution. The movement awakened promises heard decades before regarding the full participation of the laity in church life, giving voice to an aging cohort of "Vatican II" Catholics desiring to leave behind a more participatory church. VOTF would challenge assumptions about the very meaning of being Catholic and, in so doing, reveal the difficulties that go along with forging a faithful revolution.

Defining a Movement

This analysis of VOTF is founded on the premise that a definition of "social movement" may not be confined to only those collectives targeting the state or society at-large. While some would disqualify as a social movement any mobilization occurring within the Catholic Church or similarly bounded institutional context,[5] this excludes the intersection of authority and its challenges in such diverse settings as schools, churches, and corporations—tensions convincingly revealed by numerous scholars (e.g., Katzenstein 1998; Raeburn 2004; Scully and Creed 1999; Taylor and Raeburn 1995). Recent scholarship on social movements has emphasized by its diversity the need to locate authority in a much broader realm of understanding (see Myers and Cress 2005; Van Dyke, Soule, and Taylor 2004); social realities likewise mandate this shift.

Social movements must, therefore, be more broadly conceptualized as "collective challenges to systems or structures of authority" (Snow 2004). This wider lens provides the theoretical foundation needed to explore and explain the dynamics of social movements emerging from *within* institutional contexts. In recognizing that a link to the political realm is not a necessary condition of social movements, we can begin to more seriously consider the ways authority is contested within alternative cultural contexts, including religious institutions. To this conversation, careful examination of the VOTF movement has much to offer.

Voice of the Faithful must also be situated within a larger body of social movements and organizations that have aimed to change the Catholic Church from within. Numerous lay-oriented, "pro-change" (Dillon 1999) groups have formed around doctrinal or institutional issues to promote reform while remaining Catholic. Lay and religious women have mobilized for greater rights in their church participation (Katzenstein 1998). Religious orders have historically instigated change while promoting unity, rather than fostering the schismatic approach more common among Protestant sects (Finke and Wittberg 2000). These groups, operating within the institutional space of the Catholic Church, provide a useful framework for examining the complex and contradictory manifestations of religion in social movements. With some exception, religious IISMs have received little consideration from scholars of social movements, whose attention has been overly focused until recently on political movements targeting the state.

Lost also in this myopia is a recognition of the vast and influential role that culture—here manifested in religion—plays in shaping the form, identity, and tactical repertoire of social movements. This book explores the complexity of religious identities within religious IISMs, offering evidence that culture matters as much as structure in shaping a movement. Within the religious institutional sphere, religion itself—operating as identity, resource, cultural code, and structure—becomes subject to contestation in a battle over what constitutes legitimate religious expression, ownership, and authority. Findings from this study of VOTF raise important questions regarding the meaning, resilience, and institutional ties of a collective religious identity.

Faithful Revolution helps to fill the gap that a narrow conceptualization of social movements has created. It builds upon the foundational work of scholars including Mary Katzenstein (1998), who paved the way for the study of internal movements by examining feminist activism within the Catholic Church and U.S. military. It improves our understanding of movements operating inside institutions by providing a much-needed name and definition for them. Using the extensive case example of VOTF, I illustrate how the institutional context which bounds a movement has significant influence over that movement's form, collective identity, and strategy selection. The embeddedness that characterizes movements in intrainstitutional settings provides an existing repertoire of movement resources, along with a heightened awareness of boundaries surrounding movement behavior. Accompanying this embeddedness is the notable risk of replicating the very structure an internal movement wishes to change.

This research is based on three years of field observation of VOTF in a variety of U.S. settings. It draws extensively from fifty in-depth interviews with movement founders, leaders, staff, and participants from dozens of local VOTF groups (called affiliates). Among my interviewees are individuals who were present at the initial gatherings that spawned the movement, victims/survivors of abuse by clergy, participating priests (both active and laicized), and VOTF activists who had disaffiliated with the movement (or the Catholic Church) by the time of the interview. Reflecting the relatively homogeneous racial demographic of the movement, nearly all of my informants identify as white. Their ages at the time of the interviews ranged from twenty-six to seventy-three years, with an average age of fifty-eight years. More than half (58 percent) are female. I supplement interviews and field observations with an analysis of movement literature (including websites, brochures, press releases, and media reports).

Wherever possible in relaying the movement story of VOTF, I use an emic approach, presenting events and emotions in the words of those involved.

[handwritten margin note:] of sample at affiliate level

Unless otherwise noted, all quotations come from recorded interviews or, in a few instances, from handwritten field notes. Interviewees' names are generally excluded or altered to protect the anonymity of my sources. The appendix presents a more detailed explanation of my methodology and accompanying challenges, along with additional specifics regarding the demographic characteristics of my informants.

In the chapters that follow, I have combined a chronological, geographic, and thematic presentation of findings. I begin with an in-depth look at VOTF's emergence and development in its first three years as a movement. Chapter 1 introduces the VOTF movement as it emerged in a suburban community near Boston, Massachusetts. Chapter 2 describes the banning of the movement in several U.S. dioceses. It also formally defines an IISM, noting the unique challenges that movements of this type face. Chapters 3 and 4 detail the local context and negotiations within several grassroots VOTF affiliates, comparing and contrasting the strategies employed, successes and failures encountered, and interactions with church authorities. Affiliates demonstrate three possible outcomes for encountering institutional authorities: institutional integration, parallelism, and independence.

Intimately shaping the mobilization of VOTF is the movement's Catholic identity, the character of which is detailed in chapter 5. This chapter raises the question of just whose voice the VOTF movement represents, exploring the demographics of the movement through the lens of generation, gender, race, and class. The relevance of the Second Vatican Council in the movement story is also evident here. Chapter 6 draws attention to debates over collective identity, including the very meaning of being Catholic and the ways in which movement participants actively communicate their religious identities. We see how VOTF articulated and monitored its voice as a movement of authentic Catholics pushing for change from within the church, strategically navigating questions of faith and form.

Chapter 7 emphasizes the salience of culture in intrainstitutional social movements. This and chapter 8 reveal the ways in which discourse, form, and tactics within IISMs are largely bound by the cultural code of the movement. These boundaries result in an adopted movement repertoire and an increased risk of replicating the very institution that an IISM seeks to change. Chapter 9 considers the implications of VOTF for how we think about social movements, institutions, and religion. It provides a characterization and description of movements operating within institutional spaces, including the ways that this positioning impacts a movement's form, tactics, and identity. The book's conclusion considers the lasting impact of VOTF on the Catholic Church and on the meaning of Catholic identity in public discourse.

I

The Beginning

At 8 A.M. on Sunday, January 6, 2002, Joe[1] sat down for his morning cup of coffee. As was his routine, he had already stepped into the cold of a New England winter morning to retrieve the newspaper. His family had subscribed to the *Boston Globe* for years, accustomed to its edgy coverage of issues relevant to the urban New England city and its smaller outliers, including Joe's own town of Wellesley, Massachusetts. Particularly given that more than half of the greater Boston population identifies as Catholic, it was no surprise that the paper would cover the upcoming trial of Father John Geoghan. Geoghan had been accused of sexually abusing a ten-year-old boy while pastor at St. Julia's in nearby Weston. But it was the front page headline that caused Joe to pause.

CHURCH ALLOWED ABUSE BY PRIEST FOR YEARS

Aware of Geoghan record, archdiocese still shuttled him from parish to parish

In shock, Joe read that Boston's Cardinal Archbishop Bernard Law had knowingly transferred Father Geoghan from parish to parish despite more than 130 allegations of abuse toward children, mostly young boys. It was a revelation that rocked Joe's fifty-eight years as a Catholic.

When Joe's wife came downstairs that Sunday morning, his first words to her were: "You're not going to believe this. This is just like

Watergate." The two had vivid memories of the assault on values and collapse of a presidency that had stigmatized the time surrounding their early professional lives. That such moral offense had now touched their own church was almost too much to contemplate. It seemed a disintegration of the legitimacy they had entrusted to their Catholic leaders for years.

Outrage at the news of their bishop's complicit behavior followed the couple to Sunday morning's Mass at St. John the Evangelist Catholic Church in Wellesley. The air was suffused with feelings of shock, disbelief, and betrayal. Said Joe of that morning, "of course it was the buzz. Everybody was talking about it. There was shock, and the priests were shocked, and sister was shocked. And kind of bewildered at the same time. So there was a lot of, just, disbelief." Parishioners were searching for a rubric through which to comprehend news of abuse and years of cover-up within their diocese.

The subsequent week carried with it a deluge of disclosures, bringing to light evidence that Geoghan's case was not an anomaly. There were other priests, other dioceses, and other bishops who had contributed to a potentially systemic enabling of pedophilia within parishes throughout the United States. The revelations transformed the shock of many St. John the Evangelist parishioners into a desire to vocalize anger toward their bishop, toward a system that had disempowered them to such an extent that they felt unable to protect their own children.

Many in Joe's Wellesley parish instinctually solicited support and solace from each other in the wake of the crisis. One woman at the parish described her initial encounter with the news of abuse in this way:

> I remember listening on the radio when the news broke and feeling
> quite shocked and dismayed about this. Because this was something
> I did not expect. And I wanted to disbelieve it; it was earth-shattering.
> So, I really didn't know how to respond to it. And my first reaction
> was to find other members of my church, to talk to them and try to
> understand what's going on.

Another parishioner looking to share reactions collectively was Jim Muller,[2] someone quite familiar with mobilizing people for a cause. A fellow St. John's parishioner later described Muller as an "incomparable visionary," boasting credentials including a jointly earned Nobel Peace Prize. Muller had cofounded International Physicians for the Prevention of Nuclear War, a group whose efforts had earned the Nobel Peace Prize in 1986 along with the recognition of President Ronald Reagan and endorsement of Pope John Paul II.

Acting on desires to voice reactions to clergy abuse and its cover-up, Muller and two other regular parishioners of St. John's asked the pastor for permission to gather as a parish community to discuss the scandal. At the time, the parish was in the early stages of collective conversation regarding how the nationwide priest shortage would require the laity to assume more substantial leadership roles. These discussions provided a fertile context for emerging lay leadership in St. John's surrounding the scandal. The pastor described the conversations around lay empowerment that laid the groundwork for VOTF:

> We [in the parish] wanted to encourage people to begin assuming responsibility, in a broader sense then had been done before. Looking ahead at some of the changes, the structural changes, that are coming in the church—we felt it was important to make people aware of how important their involvement was going to be. And that as the church evolved into the coming century, it was going to be necessary for the voice of the members to be heard.

Thus when news of sexual abuse among Catholic clergy broke, the requests percolating among St. John's parishioners to vocalize a lay response resonated with lay leadership opportunities already initiated within the parish.

Muller and the pastor agreed that holding informal, open microphone sessions after each Mass on the coming weekend would help meet the parishioners' need to collectively react to the ongoing stream of news regarding abuse

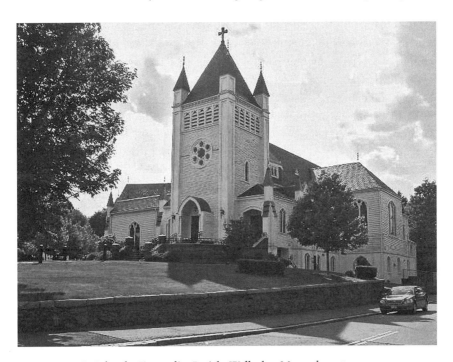

FIGURE I.I. St. John the Evangelist Parish, Wellesley, Massachusetts

in the church. Others later described the pastor's willingness to give members of the parish this opportunity to speak as significant in empowering the laity to respond:

> It was a big move on [the pastor's] part to do it. He was trying to be responsive. [Archdiocesan leaders] had given him no information. They had left him hanging. So, he was dealing with it both as a pastor and as a member of the clergy.

That Sunday, parishioners of St. John's held their first post-Mass sharing session. Those gathered found great meaning in being able to assemble and speak freely as lay Catholics without the formal leadership or instruction of the pastor. One described the significance of their initial gathering in this way:

> I was at the very first meeting, when the pastor of our church invited us to speak after Mass. Which was, if you know anything about the Catholic Church, sort of groundbreaking. To stay put, within the church itself, and to discuss. And to start talking. And it was lay led. [The Pastor] didn't, you know, he could have started the conversation himself and handed the microphone over to fellow parishioners. But that, in itself, set the tone.

To most of those gathered, the post-Mass discussion was simply an out-pouring of emotion relating to revelations of abuse. It was not, in their minds, the start of a movement. One parishioner admitted that the allure of free donuts is what had beckoned him and his daughter to stay after the service. But during the post-Mass sharing sessions, many sensed the gravity of the scandal emerging in their church and the significance of the brewing lay response. One parishioner recounted her own perception of this:

> We were asked to express our feelings about what was happening . . . We hardly knew what words to use. I was so angry. I said something to the effect of, that this problem is systemic in the church. It's not about a few instances. And we didn't know the numbers back then, of abused. I said, it goes all the way to Rome. I suggested that if Cardinal Law were to leave, he should take the pope with him.

She recalled how her sharp criticism of the church had filled the room unlike any words she had uttered previously within church walls. As she put it, "This is my church. There's my pastor whom I love, the retiring monsignor whom I have always adored, sister, who was a gift to the church. And I'm saying these very incensed statements like that. But, they asked."

Finding comfort and like-minded sentiments through sharing, Muller and a handful of additional emergent leaders arranged another sharing session Monday evening to welcome the reactions of those who had not been in attendance at weekend Masses. The follow-up meeting brought several dozen people to the basement of the church, including the pastor and many who had already participated in a post-Mass session. All felt compelled to continue sharing and listening to what other parishioners were feeling. The circle of chairs created an atmosphere of informality and openness. A simple question guided the evening: "What brings you here tonight?"

Responses ranged from sadness to embarrassment to outrage. From around the circle came stories of sons and nephews who had been abused in situations that seemed anomalous at the time. Some spoke of allegations against priests who had been appointed to churches just a few miles away. Said one about the gathering, "Suddenly, there was this sense that this is a lot closer than we ever imagined." The realization carried with it a feeling of a breach in trust. After more than two hours of sharing in the basement of St. John the Evangelist parish, the group agreed that there was still more to be said. They decided to meet once again on the following Monday.

The Voice of the Faithful

Word began to spread to neighbors and members of nearby parishes that something was happening at St. John's on Monday evenings. Catholics dealing with the news found solace in sharing their reactions to the scandal openly and collectively. As meetings continued and the number of attendees increased, shared conversations began to reveal trends in interest and the possibility for collective action. Accordingly, individuals concerned with a particular aspect of the scandal divided themselves into smaller groups to explore each issue and consider ways to address it. Early "working groups" were devoted to understanding the underpinnings of abuse, reaching out to those who had been abused, contemplating how to help nonabusive priests who had been unjustly vilified, and praying for everyone impacted by the scandal.

With gatherings now composed of more than just parishioners from St. John's, attendees felt the need to identify themselves by a name reflecting the dynamic of listening and their desire as laity in the church to be heard. Drawing upon the Latin term *sensus fidelium* ("sense of the faithful") emphasized in the documents of the Second Vatican Council, the group selected the name "Voice of the Faithful." Although they considered using the Latin (*vox fidelium*), they felt that the English translation better reflected their composition of everyday lay Catholics rather than evoking connotations of a pre-Vatican II authority structure.

The newly named "Voice of the Faithful" group next identified a key public event during which they could express their ideas and desire for reform to the Archbishop of Boston, Cardinal Bernard Law. Saturday, March 9, 2002, was the date of the "Cardinal's Convocation," an annual event for the leader of the Boston Archdiocese to meet with area parish representatives. The agenda for this convocation was typically predetermined by the cardinal's office. Less than two weeks prior to the gathering of nearly 3,000 of Boston's lay leaders, however, the archdiocese announced that in light of concerns of abuse in the church, they would suspend the scheduled agenda and instead devote the entire day to "listening sessions." Each of six sessions would be attended by a bishop who would listen to the concerns of area Catholics.

The pastor of St. John the Evangelist handed all of his parish's allotted tickets to the group of parishioners who had been meeting in the basement on Monday evenings. Wanting to maximize this opportunity, Voice of the Faithful (VOTF) decided to draft a statement to read at the convocation. Just six weeks old as a movement, nine women and four men from VOTF arrived at the World Trade Center in downtown Boston on March 9. Tickets in hand and adorned in red to symbolize the Holy Spirit, they walked through scores of individuals leafleting and holding signs reading things like "Shame!"

When the time came, one woman from the group of thirteen, poised in her red dress, stepped up to the microphone and read the following statement:

We are the church.

We speak on behalf of a group of committed Catholics from St. John the Evangelist parish in Wellesley. In our pain, outrage, and sense of betrayal we came together six weeks ago to speak out about the crisis in our church. Strong feelings of anger, anguish, faith, and love of church moved us to put aside an hour after each Mass on two consecutive weekends to address the pedophilia crisis.

Led by parish members, the listening sessions were a powerful indicator of the faithful's need to be heard individually and as a church, and of our need to speak out and to demand accountability and reform. Hundreds of parishioners participated in these sessions and a weekly ninety-minute session has been initiated on Monday nights. Our number grows and those from other parishes who need a place to have their voices heard have joined us. We call ourselves Voice of the Faithful.

Voice of the Faithful seeks consensus in order to effectively respond to this scandal threatening our church. We are sadly aware that pedophilia is a problem not only here, but in other cities and countries. The culture of secrecy and abuses of power that produced this crisis must end. The overriding concerns that have emerged from our discussions are: the desire to be fully responsive to the victims of pedophilia and their families and to ensure that appropriate measures are taken to preclude future occurrences; to support clergy of integrity tarnished by this scandal; and to seek correction of the institutional structures of the Catholic Church that resulted in a gravely flawed response to this terrible betrayal of children.

We urge other parishes to consider this new model of Spirit-driven dialogue. Our weekly sessions are a model for consensus built on mutual respect, genuine listening, and a commitment to act. The gospel of Jesus Christ demands our action in support of the most vulnerable among us. We expect archdiocesan leadership to hear us today and to provide channels for lasting communication and genuine collaboration.

Today, we raise our voices to claim our place at the table.

We are the church. Come join us.

The clarity with which the group of thirteen presented their statement got the attention of others in the session. It motivated the exiting crowd to point a curious media (who had been denied access to the convocation) to their red-clad group. On the following day, the *Boston Globe* coverage referenced "a group of women from Wellesley" who were dressed in red (Paulson 2002a). VOTF had been given a public face.

A Movement Within

It was clear from the cardinal's convocation and its aftermath that Catholics from St. John the Evangelist parish might be on the verge of a social movement inside the Catholic Church. One VOTF member who had attended the convocation described this realization as follows:

The opinions that our fledgling group, Voice of the Faithful, found so daring and scary to express in our "declaration" turned out to be— relative to the opinions of other participants—relatively conservative.

Many convocation participants were, in fact, WAY ahead of us—registering disapproval in stronger terms, calling for Cardinal Law's resignation, etc. Their outspokenness said to me that discontent and disillusionment were archdiocese-wide, and not confined to our small, suburban, red-blazered band. It also said to me that Voice of the Faithful had a potential movement on our hands. That realization turned out to be prophetic.[3]

Consequently, public awareness of the Monday evening meetings at St. John's grew. VOTF flyers found their way into the hands of one couple at the cardinal's convocation who later described their reaction: "We were so happy that somebody had organized that as we were driving home, we said, 'Yes, of course! *This* is the response!' There *should* be some group movement . . . why don't we talk about it as a group? So we went to the next meeting, that Monday night."

As more area Catholics learned about VOTF, the growing crowds at the St. John's meetings piqued the interest of journalists. Newcomers to a meeting following the convocation stepped into debates over if and how much media should be allowed into group meetings. Although many in attendance felt as though exposure was essential to spreading their message to Catholics everywhere, others feared manipulation of their identity and purpose. One participant described the group's hesitation about media intrusion into the comfortable space for sharing they had created at St. John's:

> We were afraid that [the media] were going to exaggerate, or cut and paste, and somehow not faithfully reflect what was going on. What was going on was—and I don't say this lightly—what was going on was very spiritual for people. They were hearing people say things that were coming really right from their hearts. That they would never have said publicly. They were saying it in a setting in which they felt safe. And the fear was, if we let the TV cameras in, it's not going to be a safe place anymore.

Although media coverage could be read as a measure of success, it also carried the threat of stifling access and the freedom to voice dissent from within the church. VOTF was creating a comfortable space in which Catholics could express their frustration with the church while remaining loyal to it. How would outsiders to the institution understand this contradictory commitment? How could VOTF publicly portray loyalty and a collective identity as "good Catholics" while also exposing their agenda for change? Such questions led the group to hesitate in welcoming media coverage, illuminating a common struggle for social movements desiring media attention but fearful of message manipulation.

As a compromise, VOTF decided to invite two media representatives: the local cable station (whose policy it was to air videotaped sessions unedited), and religion writer Michael Paulson of the *Boston Globe* (whose reporting helped reveal the initial news of abuse). While the selective exposure helped build the group's trust in the media, it also meant declining offers from other well-known national media outlets.

By the end of the month, nearly eight hundred people had visited a rudimentary VOTF website. The exponential growth of Monday night meetings indicated to those present that this was not a passing sentiment. What began as a church basement gathering of St. John the Evangelist parishioners had attracted hundreds of interested Catholics from the area. When the group exceeded the 185-person capacity of the church basement, they moved to the adjascent 400-person capacity school basement. When they exceeded the basement's capacity, facilitators led meetings in both spaces. Attendees described meetings as energetic, possessing a momentum similar to that of a political campaign.

The driving force of the Monday meetings continued to be listening. Each session began with an invitation for newcomers to share why they had come. One facilitator emphasized how she welcomed the honest reactions to what was happening in the church:

> I want to hear people feel comfortable, see them feel comfortable
> talking about how they feel about the church. Asking questions that
> they are not afraid to ask. And insisting on answers that they deserve
> to get.

At one meeting, this openness made it possible for a survivor of abuse by clergy to share his own story of abuse. For many gathered, it was the first time they had heard such an account firsthand from a survivor of abuse. Two in attendance shared their reactions to hearing this man's story:

> It was very moving. We weren't expecting this. Yes, we supported
> victims, but we weren't thinking one would come and stand up and,
> in effect, admit he was a victim and tell a story which was heart-
> wrenching. But later, we realized that these people had nobody to talk
> to. By and large, they were ignored, certainly by the large masses.

> It was such a powerful moment, because I think it touched all of us.
> We realized that this man had worked all by himself to try and build

awareness. To try and make the church respond . . . It was clear that what we needed to do was to bring to thousands of other Catholics the experience of talking with a survivor.

The survivor shared that it was the first group of Catholics that had ever invited him to tell his story. VOTF had created a discursive space within the Catholic Church in which such stories of abuse could be told and received, and where survivors could take steps toward healing.

Organizing a Movement

Growth within the nascent VOTF movement intensified the need for organization and clarification in mission. About forty VOTF participants volunteered to be on an ad hoc steering committee. They possessed an impressive skill set—among them were lawyers, writers, professors, social workers, theologians, financiers, information technology (IT) experts, and teachers. The collage of experience reflected the affluence of the area; the dominant age (older than fifty-five) reflected the age demographic of the growing lay movement.

The steering committee immersed itself in the process of defining the identity and aims of VOTF. In its desire to avoid replicating the hierarchical model of the church, which they felt left them with no voice, the committee opted to operate under a model of complete consensus. Jim Muller, whose initiative had sparked the first gathering, assumed the role of president. Volunteers formalized leadership roles for addressing issues such as responding to victims, protecting children, communicating with the cardinal, handling church finances, soliciting leadership from area parishes, interacting with media, and managing administrative tasks.

In creating a mission statement and goals, the VOTF movement was guided in large part by their identity as a movement inside of the Catholic Church. Participants had come to agree that their collective purpose should supersede the immediate effects of the scandal, addressing also the underlying factors contributing to its occurrence. Just how to articulate this was a matter of contention however, given the group's desire to reform church structures while being seen as faithful, committed Catholics. They sought to change the church from within, so identity management was critical in this early stage. VOTF finalized their mission statement and proposed goals at a meeting in early April 2002, achieving consensus around the following mission statement:

To provide a prayerful voice, attentive to the Spirit, through which the faithful can actively participate in the governance and guidance of the Catholic Church.

The three goals read as follows:

1. To support those who have been abused.
2. To support priests of integrity.
3. To shape structural change within the church.

Both the mission statement and goals reflected an intentional presentation of an intrainstitutional, Catholic identity. In addition to change-oriented language, they evoked both the cultural discourse of Catholicism ("prayerful voice," "Spirit," "the faithful") as well as clear ties to the institutional church ("guidance of the Catholic Church," "support priests").

Earlier iterations of VOTF's mission and goals, such as the statement read at the convocation and initially posted on the VOTF website, enunciated a more normative assessment of the current context of abuse. Goal three, for example, had been previously drafted as "to seek a correction of the institutional structures that resulted in a gravely flawed response to this betrayal of children." The wording of the final version adopted less inflammatory language, reflecting an important compromise resulting from the movement's positioning within the Catholic Church. The mission statement and goals needed to project the desire among participants to foster relationships with, not create distance from, church leaders.

As a way to acclimate new and regular attendees to VOTF's mode of reform, facilitators began reading the mission and goals at the start of each meeting. Consensus around the three goals helped confer upon the movement a sense of identity and direction for participants as well as for others attentive to VOTF's progression. One early VOTF participant later described the mission as being the result of "divine intervention" that "absolutely stood the test of time."

With the mission and goals of the movement set, one member boldly proposed to mobilize support among Catholics from all over the United States and North America in the wake of the scandal, not just those Boston Catholics who'd heard about the St. John's gatherings. The motivation behind hosting a "Continental Congress of Catholics" was fourfold: it would sustain media attention, coordinate the efforts of grassroots activism beyond VOTF, create an organizational structure for the movement, and forge relationships across dioceses. The original description for the proposed event read as follows:

It is proposed that VOTF sponsors a Continental Congress of Catholic[s] (CCC) for the purpose of developing a Constitution through which the laity may have democratic representation to select and empower their voice in the Roman Catholic Church. The Congress would be held in Boston sometime this year with delegates invited from the United States, Mexico, and Canada. The goal would be for attendance of over 5,000 individuals representing all parts of North America.

The pedophilic priest scandal and the church cover-up of the crimes indicate that the voice of the faithful is needed to correct these errors of the Catholic Church and promote its growth. This voice cannot be effectively expressed by individual laity—a structure through which the opinions of the laity are refined, prioritized, and forcefully expressed is needed. This structure will not replace the existing clerical hierarchy—it will function alongside it as a buttress, leading to a stronger church.

Over 200 years ago, the people of Boston led the world in creating a representative government to express the will of the people. This solved the problem of taxation without representation—a solution must now be found for the contemporary Catholic dilemma of donation without representation. The Catholics of Boston must offer help by adding a democratic structure to the global Catholic Church. We call on Catholics from throughout the continent to send representatives to this Boston Congress through which the representative structure will be created.

Voice of the Faithful would extend an invitation to Catholic laity worldwide, aiming to bring in 3,500 attendees from greater Boston and 1,500 from elsewhere. Likening Catholic laity to the early settlers in the United States ("donation without representation"), the proposal suggested a rather substantial change to the very operation of the church: a parallel representative structure through which the laity could express their opinions. It was a proposal to democratize the Catholic Church. Although seemingly antithetical to centuries of Catholic tradition and culture, the proposal nonetheless affirmed VOTF's commitment to the church—the additional lay structure would "function alongside it as a buttress, leading to a stronger church."

Offering his own money for the cause, the member who formulated the idea also reserved the only Boston venue large enough to hold such a crowd with a Saturday date available that summer: the Hynes Convention Center. His announcement of this at St. John the Evangelist was met with excitement and astonishment:

> [He] came back to the next week's meeting and said "there was only one date, at one venue, and I put my own money down." And everybody went, "Ahhh!" And he's a young guy! It was just astonishing! That was heart-stopping . . . and what did we have, two months to pull this off?

Planning began for a VOTF convention.

The Response of the Faithful

On July 20, 2002, a sold-out crowd of 4,200 people arrived at the Hynes Convention Center for the inaugural VOTF convention entitled "The Response of the Faithful." They came from thirty-seven states and seven countries (although more than two-thirds were from Massachusetts), each paying $20 and filling every seat in the auditorium. One organizer spoke of his amazement at seeing people continue to file into the convention center:

> It was interesting to see how many people were still coming in . . . you could see that the convention floor itself had filled up. I was just looking up at the balcony, amazed to see these people, almost antlike, come from the entrance, across and sit down. And fill each section, including places where we knew the sight lines were impossible to see! But they didn't care—they just came in and sat down everywhere. It was an incredible experience.

Like the demographics of the founding group, the crowd consisted mostly of middle-aged and older Catholics. Reporter Margery Eagan of the *Boston Herald* described the gathering as "the radicalizing of the gray-haired and sensibly shod, of middle-aged and older white, suburban, bred-in-the-bone Catholics from well-heeled parishes in Newton and Wellesley, Winchester and Hingham, Lexington and Medfield" (Eagan 2002:4).

Workshops featured talks on creating safe parishes, shaping the church's future, and finding ways for the laity to participate in church governance. Speeches by theologians, priests, and scholars of religion highlighted connections to the Second Vatican Council, noting that the incidence of an overly powerful hierarchy and culture of clericalism had been percolating for some time. The sacrament of baptism and documents from the Second Vatican Council, speakers emphasized, had in their intention a far greater role for laity in the church. It was finally time, in the wake of the crisis, to assume this more complete role.

untruly voices

Numerous moments throughout the convention attested to VOTF's desire to project a mainstream Catholic identity. Founding President Muller told those gathered that "the Voice of the Faithful is designed to speak for the majority of Catholics" and that "a critical element in creating a valuable organization will be to convince Catholics of conservative, moderate, and liberal views that the organization is of value." More than half of attendees signed a "Declaration to the Pope" stating that VOTF participants "commit individually and collectively to realize fully the renewal of the Church and the role of the laity envisioned by the Second Vatican Council." Participants identified themselves in the pledge as "loving members of the Catholic Church, the People of God, called to fulfill the mission of Christ in the Church and in the world."

Among the speakers addressing the large Hynes Center crowd was a survivor of clergy abuse. His inclusion was somewhat last minute; he had previously criticized VOTF and lay Catholics generally for their unwillingness to interact genuinely with survivors. One organizer who advocated for his inclusion at the VOTF convention said that it was important to have him speak because "he didn't hold back at all. He was very, very forthright about his dissatisfaction with the church." VOTF organizers' only request to him during planning had been that he not "incite to riot."

As expected, the survivor's talk at the convention offered an untempered prospective on the Catholic Church from a victim of abuse. At the end of his speech he invited everyone at the convention to walk with him in protest to Boston's cathedral, about a mile away. One attendee recalled the emotional invitation:

> He expressed his anger. He was extremely angry. He said, "You have
> this closely scripted convention, you think everything is alright. But it
> isn't alright, because we're the ones who are suffering through all of
> this." He said, "If you really cared, you'd walk with me to the cathedral
> to make a demonstration." And off he walked, off the stage. It was such
> a critical moment. It had been a day when there were 4,000 people
> there who had felt hopeful, and this was a real downer. And the only
> thing that was planned after that was a Mass. And so off he walked.

Nearing the door, the survivor stopped. He decided to delay the walk to the cathedral until the end of the Mass that would conclude the VOTF convention, even though he had not attended a Catholic service himself in years. After the Mass, the survivor and the VOTF leader who had invited him to speak started to walk to the cathedral together. She described their journey:

After Mass, he and I just walked out. We didn't even turn around.
Walked down the stairs and walked to the cathedral, which was a
mile or so. We dared to turn around, and there were a lot of people
behind us. We kept walking. And we turned around, and more
people. We were so surprised when we got there. Many people
gathered around him. It was such a high. He didn't know what to
say and I didn't know what to say. And somebody looked at him and
said "You have to say something, because you had said that at the
meeting." And so, he just turned around to all these people and put
his arms in the air and said "Thank you!" It was really quite
beautiful.

Nearly 500 convention attendees walked from the Hynes Convention Center to
the cathedral that day, where Boston's Archbishop Cardinal Law frequently offered Mass. It was among the largest street demonstrations of lay Catholics in
the city's history.

Conclusion

In the wake of an unfolding scandal of child abuse and institutional cover-up
within the U.S. Catholic Church, the initiative of a handful of Catholic laity
from St. John the Evangelist spawned a social movement. With time and increasing numbers, their emotional responses shifted into an organized desire to
support victims of abuse, to support nonabusive clergy, and to change the
structure of the Catholic Church to better reflect the lay participation emphasized in the documents of Vatican II. In airing their demands for change,
VOTF simultaneously voiced a desire to remain within the church—to be seen
as active, faithful, and committed Catholics.

The movement's chosen name conjures economist Albert Hirschman's
(1970) description of responses to failure in organizations. Facing an organizational lapse, customers or other organizational players may respond by leaving
(exit), expressing dissatisfaction (voice), or remaining loyal to the organization
(loyalty). Hirschman describes the "voice" option as follows:

Voice is here defined as any attempt to change, rather than to escape
from, an objectionable state of affairs, whether through individual or
collective petition to the management directly in charge, through
appeal to a higher authority with the intention of forcing a change in
management, or through various types of actions and protests,
including those that are meant to mobilize public opinion. (p. 30)

Voice is not independent of loyalty or exit, Hirschman argues. On the contrary, the likelihood of voice actually increases with loyalty: "loyalty holds exit at bay and activates voice" (p. 78). The characterization of voice in Hirschman's trilogy describes well the response of St. John's parishioners in the wake of abuse revelations.

The positioning of VOTF within the Catholic Church would be consequential in shaping the mobilization and emergence of the movement. From the start, VOTF participants asked permission of a parish priest to gather, formulated a mission statement and goals that balanced both institutional commitment and change, and affirmed their Catholic identity in the public forum of their first convention. Even as a nascent movement for change, VOTF nonetheless acknowledged the authority of the church and the boundaries it posed around the formation of their movement. They instigated discussion around church leaders' handling of abuse while simultaneously affirming the authority of the institutional church.

The next chapter offers a specific definition for this type of social movement operating within an institutional context. It also explores how the paradoxical positioning of VOTF led the group's identity as mainstream and faithful Catholics to be questioned, compelling some bishops to ban gatherings of VOTF in diocesan parishes.

2

Banned

The VOTF movement emerged from a handful of dismayed parishioners in a suburban Boston parish into a growing movement of lay Catholics. They mobilized around the shared goals of supporting survivors, supporting priests of integrity, and shaping structural change in the Catholic Church. This chapter identifies the VOTF movement as a specific type of social movement: one operating within an institutional space. It also begins to explore the consequences of this intrainstitutional positioning; namely, the public banning of VOTF meetings in several dioceses. This action highlights the complex identity negotiations of a movement operating inside of an institution.

Intrainstitutional Social Movements

A primary distinguishing characteristic of VOTF as a social movement is its positioning within an institution. St. John's parishioners identified with and expressed commitment to the Catholic Church while also communicating their desire to "seek correction of the institutional structures of the Catholic Church." They chose not to find a separate public forum or organization through which to voice their desire for change; rather, they held meetings in their parish and presented their first substantial protest statement at an institutionally sanctioned event: the Cardinal's Convocation.

Because of this embeddedness, VOTF constitutes a movement within an institution, or what I have termed an *intrainstitutional social movement* (IISM). I define this category of social movements as follows:

> Intrainstitutional social movements are movements that target a specific, bounded institution (rather than the state or society at-large), primarily drawing participants from the institution's own established base (e.g., employees, adherents, or members).

I use the term *institution* rather than the more restrictive term *organization* in order to emphasize the notion that an institution (such as the Catholic Church) may be comprised of a multitude of internal organizations, all operating under the umbrella of the larger institution.[1] The institutional context of IISMs may be large or small; a social movement may emerge within a single religious congregation or high school, for example, and still be classified as an IISM. Although the bounds may be narrow or broad, the definition of institutions I employ here is limited to those with at least some degree of formalized boundaries on inclusion.

Intrainstitutional social movements are not only unique in that the *target* of collective action is an institution rather than the state or society at-large, but also in that their *participants* are themselves affiliated in some way with the institution. Participants thus have a sort of "insider" status,[2] although this is not (necessarily) to be interpreted as having a position of power within the institution. This is consequential for the collective identity, form, and tactics that the movement will take.

The insider status of movement participants also means that their very mobilization has the potential to disrupt the institution. They might draw public attention for exposing the failings of the institution and its leaders, threatening the reputation and longevity of the institution. For this reason, institutional resistance to IISMs might be expected. On the other hand, institutional insiders are more likely to temper their demands and tactics in a way that acknowledges their commitment to (and protection of) the institution of which they, too, are a part.

Having emerged from within the church and from among committed Catholics, VOTF initially perceived collaboration between the movement and leaders in the hierarchy of the Catholic Church to be possible, even expected. Most in the burgeoning movement were already active in their parishes and as lay leaders in the church.[3] One participant described that she "expected that hierarchy would in some way appreciate the point of view that we had. And at least want to, for even political reasons, have a working relationship with us." Many parish priests had welcomed newly forming affiliates of VOTF in their parishes; individual VOTF members exercised their Catholic networks to build support for collaboration in the wake of the crisis. In his speech to convention attendees, founding VOTF President Jim Muller shared his sense from personal conversations that "the bishops of the Archdiocese of Boston are unanimous in their support of the ongoing conversations" between archdiocesan and VOTF leadership.

Along with the VOTF convention, however, came early indicators that their movement from within would not be readily accepted by all church leaders. Convention organizers, for example, encountered difficulty when planning for a Catholic Mass. A handful of Boston priests who openly supported VOTF's emergence nonetheless discouraged movement organizers from planning a convention Mass without the express consent of Boston's cardinal Archbishop Law. And despite their support for the lay movement, none of the priests that organizers asked were willing to preside over a VOTF Mass.

Though facing this resistance, an organizer from the original St. John's group refused to give up on the idea of celebrating Mass for Catholics gathered at the convention. VOTF embraced a Catholic faith and identity in its mission; how could its participants be told not to express their faith through the celebration of Mass, a ritual so central to Catholicism? Her own commitment unrelenting, this VOTF conference organizer described her response to the opposition:

> I just dug in my heels. Four-thousand Catholics meeting, and we're
> not going to have the Eucharist? And we say this is the center? I had
> done homework. I knew the liturgical documents. I had to tell
> people, "Yes, we say Mass through the power of the Bishop." . . . If
> the cardinal wants to stop us, that's a fight I would like to have. Can
> you see that headline? "Cardinal says Catholics can't go to Mass." But
> when it came time to find a priest that would say the Mass—a lot of
> priests were in the audience that day—no one wanted to say it.

The situation highlighted the complexity of the intrainstitutional positioning of VOTF: in order to be true to the church and the movement's Catholic identity, VOTF needed to have a priest offer Mass at their convention. Catholic Canon Law prevented them from doing it themselves, without the compliance of a willing, ordained leader in the church. And yet because VOTF was challenging the institution, even those priests supportive of the movement were unwilling to partake in a public measure of perceived resistance to the church. The reticence of area priests to associate themselves with VOTF made it clear to movement participants that they would have to go out of their way to present themselves as authentic, faithful, and mainstream Catholics. Their ability to make change from within necessitated acceptance by church leaders and access to the decision-making structures of the institution.

Voice of the Faithful organizers ultimately found a willing college chaplain, a diocesan priest,[4] to offer Mass at the VOTF convention. Demonstrating his own open views on lay participation in the church, the priest even invited VOTF attendees to join him in reading the Gospel (a role typically reserved for the ordained). The convention Mass signaled for VOTF both adherence to the most central ritual in the Catholic faith as well as a newfound authority in their status as nonordained members of the church. They were willing to relinquish neither their faithfulness to the tradition nor their lay voice.

The days following the VOTF convention brought additional signs that VOTF's acceptance by church leaders would be challenged and difficult to secure. Of particular note was the launching of a financial contribution campaign organizers called the Voice of Compassion fund. VOTF leaders initiated the fund in response to declining contributions to the cardinal's annual fundraising appeal in light of the scandal. Boston's archdiocesan fundraising had amounted to about half of what was raised in the year prior to the scandal. In response, VOTF created an alternative fund to encourage Catholics to contribute by alleviating concerns about archdiocesan use of funds postscandal. The Voice of Compassion fund would be administered by a Catholic foundation and managed transparently by laypeople. It would provide money directly to Catholic programs and ministries that had suffered from reduced contributions to the Cardinal's Appeal.

Voice of the Faithful organizers urged Boston Catholics to contribute, particularly those who would not otherwise give to the archdiocesan fund because of dissatisfaction with church leadership. As one of the Voice of Compassion fund's organizers said, it was a way to build accountability:

> We were saying, we don't want to support the chancery. We want to support the hospitals, or individual groups. So we, VOTF, are going to show the archdiocese how it should be done. We are going to set up another group to give to [the archdiocese]. It's now tax deductible to us, and they are going to help us, with our advice and consent, directly write checks to each of the subgroups that is really doing the work.

Voice of the Faithful hoped that a separate fund would encourage Boston's lay Catholics to contribute financially rather than depriving charities of needed funds because of the scandal.

Two days after the VOTF convention, a spokeswoman for the Boston Archdiocese announced that they would not accept Voice of Compassion funds raised by Voice of the Faithful. The official statement contended that the VOTF fund undermined the Cardinal's Appeal, the traditional means of financial support for the archdiocese. Moreover, it criticized VOTF for failing to "recognize the role of the Archbishop and his responsibility in providing for the various programs and activities of the Church." The archdiocesan statement concluded with the following reprimand regarding "the proper relationship between a bishop and the faithful":

> While the archdiocese and any of its entities are ready to receive contributions from individuals designated for any of the works of the church, it feels obliged to take the position stated above as sign of a ~recent~ sincere effort to maintain the proper relationship between a bishop ~fund~ and the faithful entrusted to his pastoral care in addressing the ~raising~ necessary works of the church. Catholic Cerly of acct.
> Q VOF 2010

Aligned with this official response, other Catholic organizations, including Catholic Charities, also agreed to decline any funds offered by VOTF.

The public refusal of VOTF's contributions was both disappointing and demoralizing to movement participants. The archdiocese did not recognize the legitimacy of VOTF's role as Catholic laity responding collectively to the needs of the church during this time. Some VOTF participants were not surprised by the archdiocese's refusal to accept the funds. One VOTF leader said that although she thought that probably they would not accept it, "that didn't mean that we shouldn't do it, or shouldn't work to try to get them to accept it." She speculated that the overarching reason why the archdiocese may have refused funds raised by VOTF was based in the historical locus of authority in ordination:

> The history of our church has monarchical roots to it, and that form of internal governance still predominates in all aspects of church life. When it comes to theology, I think that's an entirely appropriate way for the church to act. When it comes to administration, I think it's not a good way for our church to act. And yet the culture is all in this monarchical tradition, in a way that any help offered by people *not* clerical and part of that culture is perceived as a threat to the institutional power structure.

By accepting this fund, she reasoned, archdiocesan leaders would be relinquishing some of their own authority and power in the church. The efforts of VOTF reflected an understanding of a church that contained separate spheres for spirituality and administration, faith and form: the movement could work to change one without touching the other. Boston's archdiocesan leaders did not agree.

About a month after the archdiocese refused money from the Voice of Compassion fund, VOTF's then president James Post[5] made a public plea to Boston's Cardinal Law to reconsider. In a *Boston Globe* editorial that ran on August 8, Post wrote:

> We ask the Cardinal to reconsider his position on the Voice of Compassion and accept the offering of the laity seeking to help the needy. Such a response, born of generosity of spirit and genuine concern for others, is truly worthy of his great office. On the other hand, a sharp rejection based on dubious grounds only engenders the bitterness and mistrust we all want to avoid.

No change came about as a result of VOTF's public appeals and persistent offering to the archdiocese. Many in VOTF read the cardinal's refusal of funds as a clear signal that church leaders did not accept VOTF as a legitimate, faithful voice for Catholic laity. As one VOTF participant put it, the message from Cardinal Law was clear: "Don't mess with the money." Another explained how he sensed then that their lay movement would not be welcomed by the Catholic hierarchy:

> I knew right then, as we all did, that they were going to try to paint us into a corner as being anti-Catholic, against the church, bad people. And sure enough, within the next two months, it started to happen. Long Island, New Jersey, Connecticut—up and down the East Coast—bishops were banning VOTF. And then in October, we [in Boston] were banned.

Indeed, in the months following the VOTF convention and Voice of Compassion initiative, bishops began refusing to allow groups that gathered under the VOTF name to meet on church property.

It began in Long Island, New York, on August 9, 2002, one month after the VOTF convention. Bishop William Murphy of the Rockville Centre Diocese instructed the pastors in his diocese to bar VOTF groups from meeting in parishes. He said that parishioners with concerns should instead turn to already-sanctioned venues such as parish councils. Even though a handful of Long Island priests had already welcomed VOTF groups in their parishes, these groups were forced to find new places to meet. Some turned to public spaces such as libraries; others went to neighboring Protestant churches that saw no problem with hosting a banned Catholic group. Another consequence of the ban was the overwhelming turnout for subsequent meetings: hundreds of lay Catholics responded to the Long Island ban by joining VOTF.

Similar restrictions followed in Bridgeport, Connecticut, Newark, New Jersey, and Camden, New Jersey, and in early October 2002, VOTF was banned in its founding archdiocese of Boston, Massachusetts. Although individual pastors varied in their willingness to let VOTF affiliates meet at their parishes, these were among the first restrictions issued by bishops. The ban in Boston began with a letter from an auxiliary bishop to a pastor in North Andover, Massachusetts. The pastor himself had expressed no prior qualms with having the group's 135 members meet at the parish. His own sister-in-law was actually one of the original St. John the Evangelist VOTF founders and current leaders. Nevertheless, citing his vow of obedience to the bishop, the pastor requested that the VOTF group find an alternate meeting place.

Two weeks later, however, the North Andover group's place in the parish was reinstated when Boston's Cardinal Law further specified that the ban applied to only newly forming VOTF affiliates. Affiliates already meeting in parishes could continue to do so. VOTF leaders were relieved that existing groups could continue meeting in parishes, but in a public statement posted on the VOTF website, VOTF's executive director expressed confusion and frustration regarding the "banning of future VOTF affiliates within the same archdiocese, particularly since we as Catholics have every right within church teaching to assemble for the good of our church."

A week after Boston leaders restricted VOTF from meeting in Boston, Archbishop Myers of Newark, New Jersey, instituted a public ban on VOTF in his archdiocesan paper through a piece titled "A Voice Not Rooted in Faith." Myers' critique of the lay movement "whose motives are decidedly in conflict with basic Catholic teaching and tradition" included the following:

> At the same time that it seeks to ignore the real progress and contributions that lay people have made in the church since Vatican II, Voice of the Faithful offers itself as an umbrella group for numerous causes that are divisive within the church and that encourage open disregard for our discipline and teaching. Married clergy, ordination of women, abolition of the tradition of celibacy, altering church teaching on sexual morality, and defiance of the apostolic authority that has guided the church since its founding 2,000 years ago by Our Lord Jesus Christ, have all found a place in the ranks of Voice of the Faithful. These desires form an agenda that I, as spiritual leader of this archdiocese, cannot permit to adulterate the faith and practice of the people of the Church of Newark.

... Through its word and deeds, we believe that this organization has
as its purposes: to act as a cover for dissent with the faith; to cause
division within the church; and to openly attack the church hierarchy.

Voice of the Faithful had, Archbishop Myers wrote, "used the current crisis
in the Church as a springboard for presenting an agenda that is anti-Church
and, ultimately, anti-Catholic." His statement concluded by saying that "the
group is not permitted to use any Archdiocesan or parish property, facility
or assets."

Voice of the Faithful participants reacted strongly to bans instituted by
bishops. Active lay Catholics, with a stated desire to preserve and improve their
own church, had been officially told they could not meet on parish property.
One VOTF participant likened the ban to abandonment:

They can't meet in their own church! They're meeting at other
churches that are bringing them in. That's an abandonment! That's a
form of abuse! It's, "you don't exist." And yet, they go to Mass on
Sunday. But they're not allowed to meet there. I can't imagine that!
It's pretty brave to be in VOTF. You're juggling your faith beliefs,
your emotional beliefs.

Indeed, accusations of being antichurch and anti-Catholic struck at the heart of
the collective identity VOTF espoused. A VOTF leader spoke to the magnitude
of the ban within the young movement:

The banning of Catholics from meeting on church property was a
terribly painful act. It's like, it's official sanctioning. Saying that,
officially, you're doing bad things. Or, maybe you're bad people. And
boy, there were a lot of people who just kinda hunkered down after
that. They didn't want to be out, they didn't want to be challenging
anymore. Just wanted to go back to being people in the pews. So, that
was a psychological challenge to people. To not only operate outside
of a sanctioned process, but now to in fact be identified as some kind
of dissenter or person who's not worthy to meet on church property
to talk about your issues.

The ban signified to those in and out of the movement that VOTF participants
were not, by virtue of their mobilization for change in the church, true Catholics worthy of meeting within the church.

One VOTF member tried to ease the situation by contacting a diocesan
leader with whom he had worked closely in the past. Despite their prior positive
working relationship, the diocesan leader did not respond to this member's

requests for a meeting in his new VOTF capacity. The VOTF member described this encounter:

> Well I know how the church works, so I think I was realistic but hopeful also. I gave [the church leader] a call and said I'd like to speak to him about it and I tried to make an appointment to visit with him and he just kind of brushed me aside, which was actually quite surprising because he and I had an extremely close relationship. But it was clear—there was a clear message that came back from that that my involvement with VOTF made me sort of persona non grata with him. And a number of bishops have had that reaction to VOTF very publicly. And a number of others have said it privately but not publicly.

In this VOTF participant's mind, this subtle rejection was another indication that the movement had become a signal for dissent within the church, a threat to the existing leadership structure.

Significantly, the rejection of VOTF by church leaders was primarily *identity*-based. Bishops issuing bans placed less emphasis on the objectives of the movement (e.g., supporting survivors of abuse and increased lay participation) and more on VOTF's right to raise these questions as Catholics acting collectively outside the existing structures of the church. Church leaders framed movement requests as illegitimate without subordination to institutional elites and extant institutional practices.

In November 2002, some nine months after the founding of the lay movement, Boston's Cardinal Law agreed to meet with VOTF leaders. Their conversation about the archdiocesan ban and refusal to accept Voice of Compassion funds pivoted around Law's questions regarding VOTF's Catholic identity and institutional standing in relation to the church. Law questioned the movement's respect for his authority as archbishop, and, as recollected in the *Boston Globe* by VOTF's president, told VOTF leaders that "this would all have been so much easier if you had come to me initially as your bishop and said you wanted to form this organization" (Paulson 2002b). The meeting did not persuade Law to lift the ban on new VOTF affiliates nor change his mind regarding archdiocesan refusal of the Voice of Compassion fund.

Within a couple weeks of VOTF's meeting with Law, however, Catholic Charities of Boston agreed to accept Voice of Compassion funds (more than $50,000). Independently, the board of trustees for Catholic Charities in Boston had discussed and researched the legality of receiving Voice of Compassion funds despite the archdiocesan announcement that no Catholic group could accept the money. Archdiocesan officials objected publicly to this decision by

Catholic Charities. Catholic Charities' acceptance of the funds further muddied lines of authority between church leaders and laity, both legitimizing and delegitimizing the VOTF movement as a meaningful actor in church activities and decision making.

Voice of the Faithful's membership formally petitioned the Vatican for Cardinal Law's resignation from his archbishop post in December 2002, in light of increasing disclosures revealing Law's role in reassigning priests known to be abusers. Theirs was not the only request for the cardinal's resignation; in an unprecedented move, fifty-eight priests from the archdiocese also signed a letter requesting that Law step down as archbishop. Earlier in its development, VOTF was unable to reach a consensus internally in calling for Law's resignation, resistant to engage in such a confrontational tactic. But by year's end, facing repeated refusals for collaboration and dialogue, VOTF saw the resignation petition as best for the well-being of the Boston Archdiocese.

The petition for the resignation of Archbishop Cardinal Law signaled a strategic shift in the VOTF: from optimism about working together with archdiocesan leaders to a somber recognition that dialogue and collaboration, at least under the current leadership, was unlikely. Requesting Law's resignation was the most aggressive strategy VOTF had taken to date; it was an especially bold move for Catholics who, just prior the scandal, would not have predicted their own stern opposition to a major leader in their church.

Conclusion

Establishing legitimacy and locating the authority to advance stated positions are common struggles for emergent social movements, especially poignant for IISMs. VOTF faced the challenge of pushing for change while authenticating members' legitimacy as insiders to the Catholic Church. Rejection by Catholic leaders—area priests' hesitancy to offer Mass at the VOTF convention, the Boston Archdiocese' refusal of VOTF-raised funds, numerous bishops' banning of affiliates from parish grounds, and limited success in dialogue with the Catholic hierarchy—shaped VOTF's movement identity and understanding of its position within the institution of the Catholic Church. While the movement had emerged on the premise of being faithful Catholics changing the church from within, the institutional context of the church forced its participants to first authenticate their own Catholic identity and right to demand reform internally. These identity negotiations—intensified within their religious context—centrally informed the shape and direction taken by the VOTF movement.

The next chapter details the ways in which Catholics from various regions of the country started VOTF affiliates to address the crisis and support survivors, while also having to negotiate their identity as Catholics seeking change from within the institution. Movement participants learned of indivisible boundaries surrounding appropriate Catholic behavior for managing church finances, interacting with local bishops, and partnering with other groups supporting victims of clergy abuse. VOTF would need to find ways to balance their desired internal positioning with their reform agenda in order to effect change from within.

3

Supporting Survivors

VOTF provided a name and identity for an organized lay response to the crisis of child sexual abuse in the U.S. Catholic Church. The movement mobilized a burgeoning nationwide momentum to say and do something about the abuse of children by clergy and irresponsiveness of the Catholic hierarchy. This chapter follows this momentum into local VOTF groups (called VOTF affiliates) in California, Virginia, Washington, D.C., and Maryland. Examining the organization and decision-making processes of these affiliates reveals how VOTF structured its relationship to the church, established boundaries around its collective identity, and negotiated tactics for supporting survivors that reflected the movement's intrainstitutional positioning. Affiliates' attempts to support survivors of clergy abuse elucidate the ways in which IISMs are limited in how they address movement goals.

Mobilization Beyond Boston

As the VOTF movement grew in Boston and garnered attention nationally, it resonated with Catholics throughout the country already searching for a way to connect with like-minded people and formalize a response to the scandal as committed lay Catholics. While many had been dealing with news of the crisis on an individual or interpersonal level and had seen the barrage of media coverage, they had found no forum to dialogue with others beyond post-Mass social gatherings or parking lot conversations. Starting a local VOTF affiliate (with instruction from the VOTF website) provided a way to organize a lay response.

Hundreds initiated or joined new VOTF affiliates in their parishes and local communities, filling a need for formal mobilization and assigning a label to countless conversations that were just beneath the surface, without the framework offered by a consolidated lay movement. In Santa Barbara, California, for example, after six months of incessant media coverage on abuse and indiscretion among Catholic clergy, four lay Catholics began discussing the possibility of bringing the VOTF movement to life in their own community. Though only casual acquaintances until then, they found unity in their common interest in addressing problems in the Catholic Church that they feared could not be solved without the input of the laity. Using existing church mailing lists and ads in local publications, the small group of academic, legal, and corporate professionals began to mobilize Santa Barbara Catholics in October 2002. A flyer announced the first gathering with the following in large, bold print: "Should we form a Voice of the Faithful group in Santa Barbara?" It was enough to catch the attention of longtime Catholics in the area.

Santa Barbara most notably dealt with child abuse by clergy ten years prior to the 2002 revelations that sparked the VOTF movement. An independent panel organized by the St. Barbara Province of the Franciscan Order revealed in 1993 that clergy members had sexually abused thirty-four boys between 1964 and 1987. The primary site of abuse, St. Anthony's Seminary, closed down because of financial troubles in 1987 after nine decades operating as a boarding high school for aspiring priests. In response to the 1993 panel's findings, Los Angeles Cardinal Mahony then stated, along with his sympathy, that the seminary, run by the Franciscans, was not under the jurisdiction of the archdiocese.

Revelations in 2002 that clergy abuse was more widespread resurrected the history of abuse in Santa Barbara in significant ways. Victims began to organize. A 2003 healing retreat for those abused at the seminary resulted in the creation of SafeNet, the Survivors Alliance and Franciscan Exchange Network. The group, led by survivors of abuse, aimed to support survivors in Santa Barbara and elsewhere by forging reconciliatory relationships with Franciscan clergy and brothers. It was unique in its attempt to "bridge the gap between survivors and the clergy and to promote peace, healing and reconciliation on both sides" (http://mysafenet.org).

Legal changes in California also accompanied the surge in attention on abuse. Modification to the statute of limitations created a one-year window for those abused to refile their claims. Significantly, the law also allowed institutions (including dioceses) to be sued, provided that the victim could submit evidence that the institution's actions failed to protect him or her against abuse. Diocesan lawyers attempted unsuccessfully to have the law overturned on the basis that it unfairly targeted the Catholic Church during a media frenzy on abuse (the *Los Angeles Times*, e.g., ran some 600 stories on church abuse related issues in 2002 alone).

Consequently, abuse victims could file civil suits against the St. Barbara Province of the Franciscan Order and the Archdiocese of Los Angeles a decade after the original panel released its findings on the prevalence of abuse. In 2006, twenty-five individuals alleging abuse by Franciscan priests and brothers at St. Anthony's Seminary and the proximate Old Mission Santa Barbara reached a $28 million settlement. Insurance covered a portion of the settlement money; another portion came from the $23 million sale of the seminary building in 2005. The Archdiocese of Los Angeles contributed just under $2 million.

It is not altogether surprising, then, that the initial founders for a Santa Barbara affiliate of VOTF included a handful of parishioners from the Old Mission, for whom stories of abuse on and near their parish's grounds were familiar and painful. On October 14, 2002, 120 people packed into a meeting room at the Old Mission, a few hundred feet from St. Anthony's Seminary, to discuss starting a VOTF affiliate. Emotions ran high; attendees spoke out about their frustration not only toward the church, but also toward those making abuse allegations. Said one attendee, "I haven't yet felt sorry for any victim." Said another, "Ask for therapy, not for money." The history of abuse at St. Anthony's Seminary held an invisible but noted presence. One woman recounted her experience of this history:

> In 1987 we had a local problem at St. Anthony's. Pastors didn't even respond, so attorneys were brought in. Had it been different, we wouldn't be here. Since then, it has been a legal—not pastoral— response. Now they are doing something. Why not then?!

Another woman present added that "If there had been a woman involved in 1987, this would not have happened this way!" A Franciscan priest in attendance defended the actions his order took to create an external advisory panel in response to the situation. "I'm proud of the way we handled it," he said. "We've been open to complaints from victims ever since."

The four organizers presented information on what they understood VOTF to represent and what it would take to organize locally. Smaller groups of attendees then debated whether and how to create a VOTF affiliate in Santa Barbara. Participants suggested that a Santa Barbara affiliate focus on the need for accountability and transparency, further implementation of Vatican II principles, and offering a local perspective that would differ from that of VOTF in Boston, all while retaining a basis in Catholic spirituality.

The response was overwhelmingly supportive: a nearly unanimous vote came at the meeting's end to establish a VOTF affiliate in Santa Barbara (VOTFSBA). Given the size of the area's population (fewer than 150,000, including surrounding towns) and its ten Catholic parishes, the affiliate would operate as a regional group rather than being parish-based, the predominant form in Boston. One woman in attendance described her motivation for volunteering to help in a leadership capacity after attending that first meeting:

> Personally, in our life, we were affected by the sexual abuse issue. Terribly affected, I mean, extreme mental anguish. And we were incredibly frustrated and hurt by our treatment at [our parish] . . . Our faith wasn't shaken, but our sense of betrayal and lack of empowerment was just overwhelming. So, when [VOTF] came out, I thought, yeah, this is where I can put my energy. Because that was part of my personal struggle at that time: I had nowhere to go. Nowhere to be empowered at all. Everything—from the sexual abuse case and the situation at [our parish]—was absolutely, it was just not going to improve. So, there came this opportunity.

She was one of eighty-nine who signed up to participate that evening, the first official members of VOTFSBA.

Grassroots momentum was also rising elsewhere. Some three hundred miles from its Boston epicenter, Catholics in the Diocese of Arlington, Virginia, were also dealing with revelations of abuse and nondisclosure. Among them was Bob (age fifty-eight), who likened the news of the crisis to discovering that a member of his own extended family was an abuser. He described feeling as though he "had some responsibility as an active, participating member of the Catholic faith to do something about this. I just couldn't sit still." But in Bob's efforts to converse with fellow parishioners at his parish, he found that they were not as interested in responding as he had expected. Bob describes his surprise:

> What I discovered was, even though these were people that were highly committed and highly service oriented and generous with time, money, whatever, very few people wanted to touch this. And I was really shocked! I couldn't believe that this didn't grab people.

The resistance Bob met reflected the hesitancy of many Catholics to engage in protest against an institution to which they held so much commitment. VOTF participation carried with it a level of risk, with an uncertain reward.

Unable to inspire a response from fellow parishioners, Bob sought out the local chapter of a victim support group called SNAP (the Survivors Network of Those Abused by Priests). It was the only way he could think of to support those who had been abused, to whom he felt indebted as an active member of the Catholic Church.

Others in the Diocese of Arlington were also grappling with the crisis independently. Upon hearing the news, believing herself to be an advocate for children, one woman found herself saying: "I just can't sit back any longer. I have to leave the Catholic Church, or do something." On the recommendation of a friend, Avery (age fifty-three) looked up the website for VOTF. Its stated goals and mission resonated with her own desire to address the crisis in the church. Avery contacted VOTF's national office and received a list of names of those in her area who had also expressed an interest in the movement.

Bob received an email from Avery just days after he first heard of VOTF and added his own contact information to the national list. At Avery's invitation, ten Northern Virginia Catholics—strangers before that day—gathered over dinner in July 2002 to discuss the idea of forming a VOTF affiliate in their area. It was a relief to each of them to discover that they were not alone in their feelings of outrage, anger, and urgency. Although unsure of how to focus these emotions, they agreed to start their own VOTF affiliate.

The newly christened VOTF-Northern Virginia (VOTF-NoVA) affiliate began gathering with some trepidation, knowing that Cardinal Law had banned new Boston affiliates from meeting on church property. They anticipated an unwelcome reception in parishes, especially given their diocese's reputation as one of the most conservative in the nation. As one measure of conservatism, the Arlington Diocese was one of only two at that time (the Diocese of Lincoln, Nebraska, being the other) to maintain a policy that denied girls' participation in the Mass as altar servers.[1] When one VOTF-NoVA founder's pastor refused her request to gather at the parish because he "didn't want to take a chance," the affiliate instead began meeting regularly at a public library.

In the neighboring Archdiocese of Washington, D.C., another Catholic interested in the movement encountered resistance in his own efforts to start an affiliate at his Prince George's County, Maryland, parish. Gary (age forty-four), himself a victim of abuse by clergy, attributed his primary motivation in forming an affiliate to his desire to stop abuse by adding numbers to the VOTF movement. He contended that "the more numbers we have, the more the church would have to listen." Gary's personal experience of abuse was also central to his response. When the priest that abused him went on trial in 1992, Gary thought that would finally bring closure. He trusted the bishop who told him in 1992 that there was no way this would happen again. Then when the issue again rose to the surface in 2002, in even greater magnitude, Gary began a personal letter-writing campaign to church leadership. He insisted that it was not about his own abuse: "I got over the abuse! It was when I found out in '92 that the guy who had abused me had been reported at least three times before he ever knew me! And that . . . that was devastating." Receiving no response from church leaders, Gary found VOTF online and decided to direct his efforts toward starting an affiliate in his Maryland parish.

Gary first approached his pastor, requesting permission to start a VOTF affiliate in the parish. After spending some time reading about the movement and hearing Gary's concerns, the pastor agreed to let the group meet on parish grounds and announce VOTF gatherings in the church bulletin. After the first announcement for VOTF ran in the parish bulletin, however, Gary encountered strong resistance from fellow parishioners who disagreed with his desire to start an affiliate in the parish. Even close friends vocalized anger toward Gary and his wife, including one who complained that VOTF "reeked of Protestantism," and another who accused Gary of not being Catholic. Complaints among parishioners reached the pastor, who consequently asked Gary to hold VOTF meetings in a location other than the parish. This was a huge disappointment; Gary felt undermined after having previously received the pastor's support. Despite the setback, he proceeded with starting an affiliate. Twenty people showed up at his own home for the first meeting of VOTF in Prince George's County.

Two other affiliates forming in the Archdiocese of Washington, D.C., felt a stronger sense of welcome in their parishes. It was a parish priest's own efforts that led a VOTF affiliate to form in Montgomery County, Maryland. After this pastor held listening sessions in response to the scandal that attracted more than 250 people, one attendee, Jane (age sixty-four), felt drawn to transform her anger into action by starting a VOTF affiliate there. Jane connected her own reasons for wanting to start an affiliate to her upbringing, which spanned the time of the Second Vatican Council. She also identified herself as a questioner by nature. Although Jane and her husband had been quite satisfied in their parish for nearly four decades, the scandal forced her to recognize issues in the church that went beyond her own "little island": "When it broke in Boston, I could no longer put my head in the sand. I had to say 'hey, you know, you're part of the problem, too, if you're not part of the solution.'" Jane's pastor agreed to let her hold an exploratory meeting on parish grounds. He also encouraged her to strive for a countywide rather than parish-based affiliate, casting a wider net and creating some separation from the work the pastor had already begun. She agreed, and the hundred or so that gathered in the fall of 2002 voted to start a Montgomery County affiliate of VOTF.

In a third parish in the Washington Archdiocese, this one at a historic District of Columbia parish, lay Catholics were also exploring the idea of starting VOTF, having heard about what was happening in Boston. Among them was Megan (age fifty-eight), whose motivations for starting an affiliate were similar to Jane's. Megan, too, linked her reasons for getting involved in VOTF to her experience with Vatican II during her formative years, saying, "I feel it's not only my privilege, but it's my responsibility as an adult Catholic to raise a voice when I think something's wrong." As with other affiliate founders, Megan found VOTF appealing because it provided her with a means to respond to the news of the abuse and institutional failings. She liked the professional and centrist approach that the movement appeared to be taking. Along with a dozen similarly oriented Catholics in her parish, she took steps to build the VOTF movement. The group was allowed to meet on church grounds and to announce gatherings in the parish bulletin and on its website.

Affiliate founders elsewhere came across VOTF online or in the media as its publicity increased. Others attended the VOTF convention in Boston and were inspired to bring the movement to their own communities. The movement grew in Northern California when founding VOTF President Jim Muller met with a couple in San Francisco to strategize ways to spawn participation on the West Coast. The couple phoned everyone in their extended network, and an affiliate was born. Although a small number of affiliates were started by survivors of abuse, most were initiated by nonvictims who nonetheless felt concern for those who were victimized and for the structural elements that facilitated the abuse. VOTF was emerging as the most recognized lay Catholic response to the scandal.

Two important themes surface in how VOTF affiliates began in communities outside of Boston. The first theme, reflecting the intrainstitutional positioning of the movement, is that each affiliate sought some form of permission (use of parish facilities, permission to gather as VOTF, etc.) from their local parish leadership. In the sample of affiliates presented here, most received permission to meet on parish grounds. Two affiliates met in a nonparish space, but only after first seeking (and being denied) permission to gather at a Catholic parish. This process contradicts the expected nature of a social movement: why ask the target of your reform for permission to mobilize? However, it aligns with the character of an IISM, holding a dual alliance to reform and institutional allegiance. It is also strategic to build bridges between the IISM and its targeted institution. Resulting partnerships help to explain why many in the VOTF movement would come to identify the target of their reform as higher levels of church hierarchy, not their local parish or pastor.

[handwritten margin note: history of permission]

A second theme is that the local context of each affiliate significantly shaped its emergence and formation. Histories of abuse locally framed affiliates' founding membership, motivation, and direction. The concentration and distribution of Catholics in the area mattered in how affiliates were structured. Affiliates often organized on a community or regional level rather than as individual parishes, the predominant model in Boston. Whereas Boston affiliates successfully mobilized large groups of people within individual parishes, other regions were more likely to have just a few VOTF participants in each parish. This reflected, in part, the lower density of Catholics in various parts of the country as well as the decreasing intensity of lay response as the movement grew in locations away from its Boston epicenter. It was pragmatic to form affiliates on a broader community basis, covering multiple parishes and increasing the membership in affiliates.

Differences in local context left the VOTF movement highly susceptible to the influence of localized surroundings, diocesan receptivity, and the subjectivity of an increasing proliferation of VOTF leaders. The movement's rapid growth revealed a lack of cohesiveness and organization at the national level. There was little sense of where affiliates were, who was leading them, or who could justifiably speak in a representative capacity for VOTF. One indication of the lack of connective thread among affiliates was the fact that a full year passed before the VOTF affiliate in Northern Virginia learned that there were three other affiliates in their immediate geographic area. Similarly, the Santa Barbara affiliate had no knowledge of another affiliate meeting just an hour south until they saw media reports quoting an unfamiliar woman identified as the "VOTF Southern California Coordinator."

Variation in affiliates' leadership structure also reflected the rudimentary national direction of VOTF. Local groups generated their own rules for designating leaders, organizing membership, and governing movement activities. Some operated on only a skeletal structure or with no leadership structure at all, particularly in the early stages of the affiliate's development. In Washington, D.C., for example, Megan's affiliate operated without a formal organizational structure for the entire first year. Megan, along with three other interested parishioners, simply planned events and built the membership list. After a year, their core group expanded to about fifteen, enough for a general steering committee and smaller subcommittees devoted to each goal. A separate communications committee helped to manage the email list and mobilize participants for larger events. This ad hoc, emergent model of leadership was common among affiliates.

The VOTFSBA affiliate, on the other hand, made it an early priority to elect a seven-member leadership team (including the four whose own initiative had established the affiliate). They chose seven because it constituted an odd number for decision making and provided enough people to manage the multiple tasks of their growing affiliate. Each new team member agreed to serve a six-month term, modeling the short initial terms imposed by the Boston group. They distributed power evenly among all seven members of the team rather than centralizing it within one or two main positions. VOTFSBA leaders were mindful from the beginning to avoid a hierarchical design, instead aiming "to consciously be as collaborative as possible, seeking consensus. And just sort of to prove that it can be done." Separate committees addressed membership, finance, meeting arrangements, parishes, public relations, prayer, education, sexual abuse, and synod. In this way, VOTFSBA's leadership structure was formulated as a direct response to that of the institution they were aiming to change.

As affiliates formalized leadership, they also encountered the challenge of asserting their legitimacy among area Catholics. Critiques of VOTF often related to the movement's rather ambiguous goals and scope of reform advocated. During one affiliate gathering in Washington, D.C., for example, a newcomer—Dan—asked a number of questions about VOTF's intentions so that he could determine whether or not to contribute time and money to the movement. Dan's primary question was if VOTF was entirely about the sex abuse issue, or if it instead encompassed a boarder scope of reform (including, for example, the ordination of women). Those in attendance recited for Dan the mission and three goals of VOTF, which avoided these more controversial topics. "Does VOTF ever discuss such topics?" Dan asked. Yes, others responded, but not within the formal context of VOTF. Most admitted that they personally supported more progressive measures for change, but these do not appear on VOTF's agenda. Dan retorted: "If everyone agrees on these issues and yet they aren't on the VOTF agenda, then obviously the process isn't working." It was Dan's first and only appearance at a VOTF function.

In responding to questions and critiques of their Catholic identity, VOTF affiliates further established their *collective identity* as a movement.[2] Collective identity in social movements refers to the shared characteristics of participants that solidify group cohesion, the sense of "we-ness" shared (see Gamson 1992; Mueller 1994; Snow 2001; Taylor 1989; Taylor and Raeburn 1995; Taylor and Whittier 1992; Whittier 1995).[3] The formulation of collective identity in IISMs differs from other types of movements in that for IISMs, a shared collective identity is a prerequisite to mobilization and ensuing action. Shared institutional identities are crucial to the very creation of an IISM; collective identity becomes a central space for collaboration as well as potential contestation with the institutional actors being targeted. As insiders to the institution, IISM participants start with the premise of a shared identity vis-à-vis the institution they are targeting for reform. In the process of building a movement, their collective identity expands from this starting point into a more bounded "we" that differentiates between movement participants and nonparticipants.

VOTF affiliates engaged in identity work through their interactions with local Catholics both in and out of the movement. Encounters with dissenting voices (establishing a "them" to contrast an emergent "us") allowed movement participants to solidify group coherence by resisting naysayers. Joy (age thirty), in Santa Rosa, California, described her affiliate's preemptive strategy for encountering critics, in which they clearly expressed at every gathering the specific limits of VOTF's reform intentions:

> Invariably, you get people in the meetings that either have
> preconceived ideas or have specific agendas, so we are very clear
> every time about what our goals are. What we do represent. What we
> don't represent. There are people in our meetings from other
> organizations, and that's just as well. But in terms of speaking about
> VOTF per se, this is what we represent.

Nonetheless, questions about the specific intentions of VOTF continued to plague affiliates. What did it mean to support survivors? Who constituted a priest of integrity? And the most ambiguous goal of all: what did the terms "structural change" imply?

Many affiliate leaders and participants admitted that they, too, were confused about the movement's exact goals. Interpretation was relegated to the subjective opinions of a diversity of disconnected leaders at the local level. Ambiguity surrounding the meaning and scope of movement goals also made it difficult for affiliates to determine which tactics to embrace at the local level.

For this reason, a number of affiliates adhered closely to goal number one: the support of survivors of abuse by clergy. To many VOTF participants, goal one was far less ambiguous and elusive than the other two. It was also at the heart of the movement, and why so many lay Catholics had mobilized to reform the church. In Northern Virginia, for example, VOTF participants reached consensus during early meetings to direct their energy primarily toward the support of survivors. To them, this goal seemed more explicit in its strategy and intentions. Avery described the group's process in making this strategic choice:

> Everyone had some ideas, "let's do this, let's . . . ," but there was
> nothing we could really get our hands on. So we decided the one
> thing that we could do and make a difference—and it would be all up
> to us—would be to support the survivors. And we decided okay, the

focus of our group, because it's a small group, would be to support the survivors.

Participants then began to strategize ways in which their newly formed affiliate could support—and locate—victims of clergy abuse in their area. They decided to form a supportive network for victims of abuse, whom they felt the church had largely ignored. Bob's prior knowledge of survivor support groups, including SNAP, enabled VOTF-NoVA to establish contact with persons living in the area who had been abused by clergy. The affiliate began hosting monthly meetings featuring panels of survivors and family members, along with representatives from survivor advocacy groups. A handful of attendees revealed their own history of abuse, often for the first time in a public setting. The sharing also helped nonvictims to understand more fully the experience of abuse.

Feeling as though these listening forums were an effective means to promote recovery for survivors, VOTF-NoVA members then collaborated with SNAP to form a separate monthly support group for those abused by priests, apart from the affiliate's VOTF meetings. The chosen meeting location for the survivor forums was a public library—a comfortable space for gathering, untainted by the negative feelings many survivors came to associate with a church building. When, at one point, the meetings were relocated to a Catholic parish, attendance dropped substantially. Consequently organizers returned the meetings to the library, which was less likely to evoke negative emotions surrounding survivors' abuse.

Other affiliates embraced similar strategies, contacting local survivors to hear their stories and offering to help where they could. Many affiliates sponsored Masses of Healing, hoping to create a welcoming place of reconciliation within the church. Jane explained her Montgomery County affiliate's decision to primarily pursue goal one during their first year, saying, "Well, the easiest focus was survivors. I mean, it's really kind of a no-brainer. We felt that we needed to commit ourselves to stand with them and find out what it was that we could do." They, too, collaborated with SNAP and other survivor groups.

While VOTF affiliates' cooperation with SNAP offered a direct way for lay Catholics to reach out to survivors, this collaboration came with a price. Although collaboration between VOTF and SNAP made practical sense, VOTF was also working to establish boundaries around their collective identity and institutional image as committed Catholics. VOTF and SNAP, both founded in direct response to abuse by clergy, had very different missions. VOTF was comprised of self-identifying Catholics interested in supporting survivors, priests, and structural change in the church. Central to the identity of the VOTF movement was its desire to remain *within* the church, as committed Catholics seeking increased collaboration between the laity and the hierarchy. As an IISM, committing to the church and being seen as legitimate and authentic lay Catholics was fundamental to the VOTF movement.

On the other hand, SNAP had a mission focused entirely around support and justice for survivors. Its members shared a common identity as victims (or victim advocates), but not necessarily as Catholics. Most, in fact, no longer identified with the Catholic Church and had no outwardly stated interest in preserving the Catholic Church as an institution. Rather than seeking dialogue with church leaders, SNAP mobilized to identify and punish abusers and those who sheltered them. Some VOTF participants consequently described SNAP's membership as more emotional, stemming from anger and desired vengeance for abusive behavior:

wordy)

> SNAP is so narrowly defined by people who are, I think, very angry.
> They want to picket and protest. And that seems to be the depth of
> what they're after. Every time something happens, they're right in the
> forefront. So much so that I don't think they're a very thoughtful
> group. They're kind of a knee-jerk reaction. I, personally, don't think
> that kind of argument has much of a chance of either changing
> things within the church or continuing in the long-term. On the
> other hand, I believe our [VOTF] approach is a more carefully
> thought-out approach.

The tactical repertoire of SNAP included demands for legal changes, punishment for offenders, and financial compensation for survivors through lawsuits. In the minds of many Catholic Church leaders, SNAP was a threat. The group was also a very vocal reminder of the reality and consequence of sexual abuse by clergy. Its members were adamant about justice for survivors, even if this brought negative consequences for the church (financially or otherwise).

Some outsiders to the movement interpreted VOTF's association with SNAP as meaning that VOTF, too, was vengeful, threatening to church structure, and even anti-Catholic, as noted by one VOTF participant:

> I think the general public, and even, apparently, a number of priests,
> just treat us interchangeably. SNAP and VOTF. "Oh yeah, that's a
> group about the sex abuse thing." But all they're hearing is this other.
> It just makes me mad! That's just like a total misrepresentation. I
> don't think, in some of their statements, that they're even very
> Christian, let alone Catholic! I mean, Christ's message was one of
> forgiveness! They're just vindictive. Vengeance seems to be the thing
> they want the most.

A handful of bishops conveyed unequivocally that so long as a VOTF affiliates associated with SNAP, their diocesan representatives would not engage in dialogue with VOTF representatives. Individual pastors, too, set boundaries around how much VOTF could collaborate with SNAP, as was the case in Megan's Washington, D.C., parish: "[Our pastor] will not let us mention SNAP, he will not let us have SNAP on the premises. You know, just a total blackballing of SNAP within the archdiocese. Completely, just, 'they don't exist,' as far as they're concerned." Affiliates' collaboration with SNAP threatened the movement's committed Catholic identity. As an IISM, VOTF's tactical choices were closely linked to the movement's intrainstitutional collective identity.

The Prince George's County VOTF affiliate felt the repercussions of an affiliation with SNAP when Gary invited a survivor of abuse—a SNAP member—to share his story of abuse at a VOTF meeting. Gary secured permission to hold the meeting at his parish during the affiliate's first year of operations. While speaking to a parish filled with Catholics, the survivor's anger with the church became evident. Gary and his wife Jill recount the experience:

GARY: Unfortunately, this was the first time he spoke in front of a group about this. And I didn't know that going in. He is a very angry guy. And not well-spoken.

JILL: Well, I think there were a lot of people who were not quite comfortable with his talk. But I still thought that he did a pretty good job presenting. But, I was still agreeing with everything that he was saying. And, I guess, being compassionate to it.

GARY: I think most people saw that, too. They were looking at a kid who was just angry. You know, a little boy—an angry little boy lashing out.

JILL: Who happens to be in a 42-year-old body now.

GARY: Correct.

JILL: And just, you know, showing pictures of teens or young adults who committed suicide because they haven't been able to handle their experience. And he threw it right out there, and right away. To a bunch of people who might not have ever really heard a story before, even though it happens. But then, he had an angry tone about him. And then he eventually wound up, he's from SNAP, so he was passing out envelopes to contribute to SNAP, saying that, you know, if you're angry with the church about this, then we have to do something. So instead of contributing at church, you can contribute here. And at that point, [Gary] was pulling out his hair. He was so nervous. And this was not planned, it wasn't . . .

GARY: I didn't know he was going to solicit funds. I didn't know he was going to do that.

JILL: We would not have given permission for that to take place. So, it was uncomfortable.

GARY: 'Cause it was on church property. It was kind of inappropriate.

Not long after the event, Gary received a copy of a letter that the local bishop had written to his pastor. It lambasted VOTF, but was centrally concerned with the solicitation of funds for SNAP within the parish. Gary wrote a letter of apology and explanation, but received no response. The damage to his affiliate's relationship with the archdiocese and with his own pastor had been done.

The encounter made it clear that there were indeed limits to the type of expression and protest allowed within the (literal) institutional space of the church. Although supporting survivors was acceptable, when the support converts into anger and direct solicitation of funds for punitive action against the church, then this is not acceptable, not a "Catholic" thing to do. If VOTF desired to present a Catholic identity committed to the church (required in order to dialogue with church leaders and ultimately participate in church decision making), they would need to choose tactics carefully.

Questions about a SNAP association were part of a larger series of questions about the "real intentions" or "hidden agenda" harbored by VOTF. To forge positive relationships with area pastors and diocesan officials, affiliates had to first clarify their purpose and scope of reform. In some instances, affiliates created opportunities to build legitimacy in the eyes of the church hierarchy through letter writing or face-to-face meetings. Joy's Santa Rosa affiliate, for example, set up a meeting with their local bishop to respond to his concerns about VOTF:

We had written a letter of introduction [to the bishop] asking for approval. Not really approval, but just sort of letting him know. Ultimately, we ended up getting a meeting with him. And he shared what his concerns were about the affiliation with SNAP, and asked what we meant by changing the structure. So, we wrote a letter addressing those things and what our goals are, including and versus what SNAP might be, and how we incorporate everybody that is working toward healing and improvement. And he wrote back a letter and basically said "Thank you for clarifying my concerns."

The affiliate subsequently had a subtly more amicable relationship with the bishop, said Joy: "I hear it through the grapevine, from other priests and stuff, that we had a nod, rather than a folded arms kind-of feeling."

The Santa Barbara affiliate endured a similar litmus test of the authenticity of its Catholic identity and commitment to the institutional church. VOTFSBA had in fact found early success in their communications with local Catholic hierarchy. Significantly, in late November 2002, the seven-member leadership team of the fledging affiliate met with the bishop serving as the Episcopal Vicar for the Santa Barbara Pastoral Region. Their conversation focused primarily on the implementation of an archdiocesan-wide effort to prevent abuse, entitled the "Safeguard Our Children Parish Committee Program." The bishop also gave them information on the procedure for removing a priest from the ministry against whom a credible accusation of abuse has been made, and discussed the scope and financial impact of the scandal on the archdiocese.

Meeting with a regional bishop gave the newly formed VOTFSBA an opportunity to legitimate themselves as active Catholics who loved the church and saw a need for reform within it. In what could be read as a sign of subtle support, VOTFSBA secured permission to hold leadership and committee meetings at the regional diocesan center in Santa Barbara. A February 2003 issue of *Christian Science* quoted their regional bishop as welcoming the efforts of VOTFSBA, saying, "They're very good and involved Catholics; they represent a fairly broad segment of people, and their primary interest is not so much in a particular platform but in involving the laity in figuring out how we should move ahead." The affirmation was formative in the VOTFSBA's development.

Affiliates' acceptance by church hierarchy was nonetheless tenuous, however, as VOTFSBA learned in planning a Healing Mass for victims of abuse. Their regional bishop agreed to preside over the Mass at a downtown Santa Barbara parish until, a few weeks prior to the scheduled event, the *National Catholic Reporter* newspaper ran an article that again enflamed VOTF's identity issues. In describing the Archdiocese of Los Angeles' refusal to disclose abuse-related documents, the article cited VOTF's Southern California coordinator (a person and title previously unknown to VOTFSBA leaders) as linking the goals and strategies of VOTF and SNAP (Jones 2003). Also problematic for the affiliate was a brochure distributed at a diocesan event featuring a quote by their regional bishop and again linking the agendas of VOTF and SNAP.

A member of the VOTFSBA leadership recalled the incident:

> It was a pretty innocuous quote. But it happened to be a quote that
> was interspersed with others from SNAP, and SNAP is a much
> different group. SNAP is a victim's support group, but it has no

affiliation with the Catholic Church. They're not trying to reform the church, and they're not trying to work within the system. So their approach is totally different. But the conjunction of VOTF and SNAP was disagreeable to the bishop.

Upon hearing that the bishop was disconcerted by the use of his name on a brochure linking VOTF and SNAP, VOTFSBA asked if he preferred to withdraw from presiding over the Healing Mass scheduled to take place just two weeks later. He agreed, withdrawing his offer to lead the Healing Mass.

Although the Healing Mass did take place—presided over by another willing local priest and relocated to another church in Santa Barbara—the fallout from its planning had significant influence over the future tactical choices of VOTFSBA. In its immediate aftermath, the affiliate composed a letter to VOTF National requesting that they clarify the relationship between VOTF and other groups such as SNAP. Santa Barbara's letter to VOTF National reflected the pivotal role of perceived Catholic identity for the movement. "Without this change," they wrote, "we fear our efforts for credibility will collapse. We will lose membership and some very good VOTF work promoting change will be lost." Their affiliate's letters, said one member, were meant to convey that their VOTFSBA found it "highly objectionable that we should be painted with the same brush" and that "we don't want that image to be placed on us."

In contrast to the approaches of other affiliates, VOTFSBA consequently disassociated itself as much as possible from SNAP. It worked extensively to establish a reputation that was entirely separate from that of SNAP, hoping that this would again open an avenue to meaningful dialogue with the church hierarchy. To establish a relationship with church leaders, VOTF needed to strip their organizational identity of association with a group whose mission did not uphold the interests of the church. The VOTFSBA affiliate consciously and frequently separated their self-described moderate and more "thoughtful" approach from what they considered to be an overly abrasive, "bomb-throwing" SNAP approach. As an IISM, VOTF discovered that it needed to practice caution in forming alliances with movements that did not share their IISM positioning.

Even the VOTF affiliates who choose to work with SNAP recognized the barrier they were building between themselves and church hierarchy who disapproved of SNAP. Leaders of VOTF-NoVA described their impression of diocesan resistance:

As long as VOTF is aligned with SNAP, they're not going to support us. They're not going to listen to us. And we really can't understand why. We haven't gotten to that point. We had met a couple of times in the Arlington Diocese with the initial director of child protection services, and we felt that they were on the same wavelength, they understood the issue. She had actually worked in the trenches and understood. But the bottom line was getting to, we could not get to the bishop. We couldn't, based on the affiliation with SNAP.

If you mention SNAP, if you indicate your alliance with SNAP, if you advocate SNAP, [diocesan leaders] won't have anything to do with you. And if you didn't, maybe they'll talk to you . . . Because SNAP has been viewed by the bishops as being so antagonistic and so confrontational, and so unyielding. Nothing they do is right. It's easy to say, "SNAP is in your camp, forget you." But who is kidding whom? Even if SNAP wasn't in our camp, do you really think they're going to do anything other than . . . ?

The response to survivors, then, became an extension of VOTF's identity negotiations. Affiliates had to balance the movement's first goal—supporting victims of abuse by clergy—with their intrainstitutional positioning. Some hypothesized that their lack of support from church leaders related to a general lack of empathy for survivors on the part of the church hierarchy:

Truthfully, I think in a way, they're afraid. Because our bishop certainly hasn't listened or met with any survivors. Hasn't been willing to. I think they look at it, and this is truly my guess, I feel like they look at these people suing the church, getting their money, and they look at it as some kind of rebelliousness: "Look what you've done to our church." Instead of the bishops looking within, they're saying "Look what *you've* done."

This cool reception fueled debates over what tactics were most appropriate for supporting survivors while keeping to VOTF's intrainstitutional movement identity. Affiliate leaders disagreed about collaboration with SNAP and received few guidelines from national VOTF leaders. Some felt strongly about the inclusion of victims of clergy abuse in VOTF efforts even when "they have a very bad taste in their mouth leftover from the church." Others countered that this "does not help in establishing a dialogue with the cardinal, nor will it bring more members to VOTF."

Given this contentiousness, VOTF participants admitted that supporting survivors was difficult. One participant critiqued his affiliate's efforts in this area:

On helping victims, I don't think our particular chapter has really accomplished very much. Not that we haven't tried. We've invited them. We'd love to see them be part of our organization. We'd love to have the opportunity to talk to them, but except for [. . .], he's the only one that has talked to us.

In Washington, D.C., Megan, too, felt disheartened at her local hierarchy's unwillingness to help survivors. She lamented her VOTF affiliate's inability to truly help victims, given the resistance leaders faced at the parish and diocesan level:

[Bishops] feel that the victims are their enemy because of all of the litigious activity. So they don't deal with them at all. So really, our most basic purpose of existence we've failed miserably at, to be really honest. Other than trying to reach out to several survivors. And we did have four at our healing service that came forward. And [our pastor] came and participated. But it's just such a little chink when you think about it that way. But, I try not to do that. I try to keep on just dogging along.

Certain tactics for supporting survivors seemed to position VOTF against the Catholic Church, antithetical to their desire to be perceived as committed Catholics.

Given the antichurch perception that accompanied supporting survivors, affiliates found themselves placed in the position of either pursing their goal of supporting victims of abuse or negotiating a place of respect and recognition within their parishes and dioceses. Supporting survivors and staying within the church were at some levels mutually exclusive: an affiliate could fully and successfully do one or the other, but not both. The movement's intrainstitutional positioning mandated compromises on survivor-support tactics.

Conclusion

Voice of the Faithful affiliates emerged in settings throughout the country, connecting with lay Catholics looking for a way to respond to the crisis of child sexual abuse and its institutional handling. In the speed and scattered dispersion of VOTF's growth, decisions regarding the form, leadership structure, and tactics of individual affiliates were relegated to grassroots participants. Many lay Catholics interested in VOTF turned to local parish leaders, asking for permission to mobilize. In this submission to church leadership and in affiliates' chosen nonhierarchical leadership, VOTF affiliates both accepted and sought to reform the institution within which the movement operated.

The collective identity of the movement—what VOTF was as well as what it was not—proved consequential in its selection of strategies to address the goal of supporting survivors. Collaborating with existing survivor-support groups such as SNAP carried with it the consequence of VOTF's public identity being construed as anti-Catholic and not supportive of the church. Accordingly, VOTF affiliates had to choose between fully addressing their first goal of supporting survivors or compromising the full range of survivor-supporting tactics in order to accommodate their desired positioning within the church. Some tactics were deemed less "Catholic" than others. VOTF could not forge a bridge between the church and angry survivors seeking vengeance; rather, affiliates could more comfortably balance a dual identity of committed Catholics and committed survivor advocates by engaging in institutionally accepted tactics such as Healing Masses.

In this way, the movement's collective identity served to both define and limit the mobilization possibilities of VOTF (see Taylor and Whittier 1992). The Catholic Church's own failures in fully supporting survivors were necessarily replicated in the VOTF movement. To retain their intrainstitutional position and collective identity as committed Catholics, VOTF would have to tread carefully in choosing (and framing) strategies to address their goals. The next chapter traces the impact of institutional positioning and collective identity negotiations on affiliates' attempts to address the VOTF goals of supporting priests of integrity and structural change within the church.

4

Moving Beyond Abuse

Boundaries posed by its institutional positioning centrally influenced VOTF's local mobilization and efforts to support survivors. Affiliates made decisions that strategically kept in mind their desire to retain a Catholic identity and garner acceptance within the church. In this chapter we see how institutional boundaries shaped the ways in which the movement addressed its two other primary goals of supporting priests and advocating for structural change in the church.

Evidence from local affiliates mobilizing within the Diocese of Arlington, Archdiocese of Los Angeles, and Archdiocese of Washington, D.C., reveals three distinctive paths for IISMs in response to their movement environment: institutional integration, parallelism, or independence. Different VOTF affiliates elected to pursue different paths in response to their reception by local Catholic leaders. The three IISM paths provide a useful theoretical framework for understanding how institutional boundaries impact social movements as they respond to institutional authorities.

Seeing Abuse as a Symptom

Especially in the early stages of mobilization, VOTF affiliates nationwide emphasized the need to develop a network of support for survivors of clergy abuse. The movement gained traction through its attention to individuals victimized by priests and the inadequacies in responsiveness to survivors on the part of church leadership. VOTF sought to establish an alternative face for the Catholic Church in responding to clergy abuse: one of committed Catholics who were deeply sorry for the failings of their own church, determined to make amends with survivors and prevent future abuse. Affiliates contacted and conversed with survivors, invited them to share their stories of abuse, sponsored Healing Masses and diocesan prevention measures, and pushed the issue of clergy pedophilia to the forefront of the media and internal church affairs.

In time, VOTF affiliates also began strategizing ways to translate what had mobilized them—the abuse of children by clergy and the ineffective response from the church hierarchy—into a more holistic reform aimed at empowering the laity, supporting the ordained, and changing the structures of the church that had facilitated repeated abuse. Although Boston founders had established a movement mission and goals with this in mind, local affiliates were empowered, and yet beleaguered, with the responsibility of navigating a tactical path to achieve structural change at the grassroots level.

Affiliate leaders in Northern Virginia, for example, met with increasing interest among members for pursuing goals two and three, going beyond the survivor support they had prioritized in the early stages of their affiliate. As membership grew, it also became more feasible to move in multiple directions and approach larger issues behind the scandal. Affiliate leaders Bob and Avery described this transition:

> Inevitably, as you would expect, people would say, "Well, what are we doing about these other goals?" . . . You could see the energy being pulled towards, "Yeah, but what are we gonna do about this church? These bishops? These leaders?" So we started to try and address those needs. (Bob)

> The first year, I felt that we accomplished so much. We really accomplished the goals we set out to do, which was to reach the survivors. We wound up going to different SNAP meetings. It was so meaningful. Now we're expanding . . . because I do realize that in order for this crisis not to happen again, there's got to be some financial accountability, there's got to be transparency. And so we're focusing on that. But we don't want to lose sight of the victims. (Avery)

While survivors remained foremost in the consciousness of affiliate leaders, the movement inevitably shifted from the immediate aftermath of revelations of abuse into contemplation of the larger contributing and preventative factors. Operating within the framework proposed by Boston founders in the early months of the movement, affiliates discussed strategic options for pursuing goals two and three (supporting priests of integrity and supporting structural change). As with the first goal, interactions with Catholic hierarchy in addressing these goals—particularly the goal of structural change—would test the authenticity of VOTF's religious identity and ability to implement reforms as insiders. Affiliates encountered a choice between further integrating into the existing authority structures of the church, creating a parallel structure that would allow them to address similar goals without merging into existing structures, or diverging independently as an extrainstitutional movement.

Supporting Priests

Voice of the Faithful's goal of supporting "priests of integrity" at times translated into a useful tactic for affiliates to communicate the movement's intended Catholic identity. The Prince George's County affiliate, for example, having already encountered resistance in its survivor-support efforts, embraced this goal as a safer means of building outsiders' confidence in (and lessoning suspicion of) VOTF. The affiliate's fifteen members hosted a reception after Mass one Sunday to recognize a well-liked visiting priest. It seemed the path of least resistance in the face of complaints surfacing among fellow parishioners against VOTF. Receiving no negative publicity from the event other than a few parishioners refusing to participate due to VOTF's sponsorship, affiliate leaders called it a success. Although atypical for a social movement strategy, the tactic worked well within the religious institutional context of VOTF.

Other affiliates took on similar peacemaking tactics, hosting potlucks and picnics in honor of favored priests. One affiliate pointed to their conscious effort to speak respectfully to priests as one strategy for supporting priests of integrity. VOTF-NoVA tried several different approaches to include and recognize area priests. The affiliate extended personal invitations to several priests to attend an informal discussion at one VOTF meeting. Three priests attended (including one whom Avery characterized as "a little nervous about doing it"). Avery described the evening:

> It was really a neat experience because [the priests] were so open and
> so apologetic. Their concern was supporting, you know, not getting
> all the priests caught up in this abuse crisis. That there are good
> priests out there, but there's a lot of people that are putting them all

in one basket. That experience, meeting those priests, was such an awakening because I thought, okay, these people are wonderful, they're saying, "What can we do to help you? How can we show our support for you?" They renewed my faith in the Catholic Church.

As a result of this encounter, two of the priests proposed the idea of hosting a Healing Mass in their parish. Although it would not be a VOTF event per se, area affiliates planned it and Arlington's bishop agreed. In both a literal and figurative sense, VOTF-NoVA—which at that time was still meeting outside the parish because none had welcomed their meetings—had finally moved into the church.

Affiliates' success in the VOTF goal of supporting priests served two important functions. First, it helped to communicate the movement's desired positioning within the church. By supporting priests, VOTF conveyed that it adhered to the existing structure of the church, including the authority and leadership of priests. Second, it introduced opportunities for laity to have open and meaningful discussions with priests regarding the scandal or other areas of concern. Through newly emerging lay roles, local Catholics were learning how to express their support and concerns to the leadership of their local parishes. For many in the movement, these seemingly minor interactions between the lay and ordained were a big shift in their lived identity as Catholics. They could support their priests and simultaneously have a voice in church decision making. Many in the movement expressed great affection for their own parish and pastor but frustration with failures in the larger church; addressing this VOTF goal allowed them to balance both of these sentiments.

Other affiliate efforts to support priests were less successful, however, as the movement again encountered questions of intent. One VOTF participant, Fred, thought it would be fairly easy to find priests willing to talk with laity about the needs of priests in the wake of the crisis. He extended multiple invitations on behalf of his affiliate for conversation over dinner in an informal, home setting, but no priests would accept. Fred spoke of the surprising challenges he encountered in these efforts:

> I tried to get at least ten priests to engage in dialogue. I had a pastor who would talk to me one-on-one about it, but he didn't want to come to my house and have dessert and talk amongst a group of people. Because he wanted to be below the radar screen. He said, "I don't need any of this to get out." He said, "I have confidence in you, but I don't have confidence in . . . what I say might get back to the bishop. And I've got enough problems." They don't want to speak their mind, where their mind may be in contradiction to what the

bishop's thinking . . . I thought, when I started it, that it would be easy! There have got to be priests that want to talk about this. And dialogue with the laity about it. I couldn't find 'em.

Fred's description demonstrates that even as Catholic laity began to articulate more forcefully their own voice in the church's decision making, some priests admitted difficulty in supporting these efforts for fear of reprimand by bishops (some of whom had banned VOTF from meeting). In conversations with his pastor, Fred learned that priests were talking some among themselves about the crisis, but most were not willing to risk going out on a limb to support VOTF. Moreover, none of Fred's fellow parishioners had approached the pastor to discuss the scandal.

In the Santa Barbara affiliate's effort to support area priests, participants again encountered requests to first defend their position as Catholics faithful to the church. As a citywide affiliate, the group wanted to rotate the location of monthly meetings from parish to parish. This required an initial conversation with each pastor, who could in turn grant or deny access to his parish. Conversations with some priests became battlegrounds for legitimacy. Two members described this resistance as it unfolded with local priests:

> Each priest was concerned that we were going to picket out in front of their church at Mass. That was their biggest fear. And once they realized that wasn't our direction and sat down and engaged in conversation, everything just sort of dissipated.

> The first thing we had to get out of the way is, what is it that we're trying to accomplish? What is it that we're doing? We're not an organization that's going to appear handing out leaflets after Sunday Mass. But we are an organization that's interested in change. And having had that discussion for about half an hour, [this pastor] opened up and was very supportive.

Not all pastors welcomed the group to use their facilities as a meeting space. Another VOTFSBA member said that her own parish priest refused to have a conversation with VOTF because "he hasn't realized that we're not bomb-throwers, we're not militants, and we're not volatile, just—we're extremely moderate." To move within the institution, VOTF had to first (and continually) authenticate their right to belong.

Some priests, as well as many VOTF members, lacked a clear understanding of what a "priest of integrity" meant, as it was phrased in the official VOTF goal written by Boston founders. This made it difficult to lend support in meaningful ways, as a few affiliate leaders described:

> We've tried to recognize priests in the community. That's an awkward one. Because I don't know what it really means to recognize priests of integrity.

> We don't really have a strong sense of what does that mean, what do you do? Other than what we have done—recognize certain priests who have helped us. We don't like the wording—priests of integrity.

> The priests of integrity [goal], we found that difficult to do. What does that mean? Who gets the integrity badge?

Others expressed reticence in mobilizing to support any priests, given that it was priests who had inflicted abuse or failed to report it. It seemed a betrayal to survivors to focus on supporting priests, as one VOTF participant in Northern California explained:

> A lot of the victims feel that it's a little too soon to do something in a real big way for clergy appreciation, and I think so, too. Because it could very easily be used by the bishops to say, "Everything's fine, our healing ceremonies worked. We said that we're sorry and now we just move on." So, that would be a problem.

Some priests were put off by the implicit judgment that accompanied the "priest of integrity" label. It could imply exclusivity rather than forgiveness and support for all priests, even those accused of abuse. One priest conveyed his discomfort with the title:

> On supporting priests of integrity, I think many priests didn't care for that term. Because who are the priests of integrity? And, you know, obviously the priests who abused children, there are problems there, but some of those priests also had thirty, forty years of actually very effective ministry. So, it's a complicated question. And we don't feel like, just because we haven't been accused, that we should be held up as priests of integrity. I mean, we try to be, but we have failings like everyone else. We would have preferred if they'd said to just "support our priests," or something like that. But again, they are coming out of the anger of the crisis. And I think that's why they chose that term. To distinguish from supporting priests who had done abuse.

Another priest agreed, saying that he "knew what they were trying to get at, but I thought it was poorly phrased. Because there was something about it that was divisive." The goal that was arguably most closely aligned with the existing authority structure of the church also created institutional debate and separation. Again, VOTF found itself meeting limitations in its attempt to reshape the church as committed Catholics.

Shifting to Structural Change

Many VOTF participants identified goal three—shaping structural change in the church—as being at the heart of the movement and their own reasons for participation. Not surprisingly, then, structural change did not take long to enter the forefront of affiliate discussions and movement tactics. This movement goal was no less ambiguous than the goal of supporting priests of integrity (on the contrary, it was critiqued as being the most unclear and open to interpretation). But this ambiguity also provided local VOTF participants the chance to discuss larger issues that had inspired lay Catholics to join the movement, and to envision a more perfect Catholic Church. It created a space within the institution of the Catholic Church where Catholics could openly talk about their desire to continue identifying and participating as Catholics but also critique the lack of a place for lay voices in the church.

The shift to goal three was especially noticeable in Santa Barbara, where VOTF participants had stalled in their efforts to support victims of abuse and priests of integrity. Outrage at clergy sexual abuse clearly inspired their mobilization, but those active in VOTFSBA began to explain the crisis in terms beyond its immediate circumstances. Other objectives related to lay participation, diocesan transparency, and accountability began to emerge as central foci for the affiliate. One VOTFSBA leader justified this shift:

> [The abuse crisis] is how it started, but then we're trying to put things in place of, where are we going from here? And that's to have more of a transparent organizational church, where laypeople participate more in what's going on, and there's not a lot of secret things going on that people don't know about . . . What kind of system do we have in place for Catholics in the pews, for instance, to express something? Express a concern they might have?

Another local participant echoed this broadening in focus:

The goals of transparency and collaboration and accountability, which are VOTF goals, are directly related to the sexual abuse . . . It seems like a sexual abuse issue, but really it's also this horrible secrecy. I mean, one of the things that emerged from finding out about how much abuse there was, was how secret it was all kept. Bishops kept it from priests and priests kept it from one another. Everyone was pretending like they didn't have to tell anybody. So, if there can be a climate of accountability, you're not going to have sexual abuse anymore, and you're not going to have a lot of other abuse either.

Participants described clergy pedophilia as "still one of those key objectives" and the issue that "brought us together and we never want to forget it." Nonetheless, the goal of structural change "really came into the forefront" and thus became for many the "most important" goal for the affiliate, as another participant noted. The Santa Barbara group came to centrally embrace goal three—structural change—in their affiliate's activities.

Not all local VOTF affiliate leaders embraced the shift to goal three, fearful that survivors of clergy abuse would again be relegated to silence. Although Bob in Northern Virginia supported structural change in direct relation to the prevention of sexual abuse, he grew frustrated with the diminishing attention participants gave to survivor issues:

I think the survivor issue in VOTF has waned considerably. People still say the right things, but I think it's more token than it is substantive. The interest has clearly shifted towards that third goal of shaping structural change.

As the movement moved into this potentially more contentious area of addressing the very structure of the church, some VOTF participants left the movement. Some elected to find alternatives where they could directly and primarily support survivors. But conversation among those who stayed highlighted abuse by clergy as more of a symptom than a root cause. A Santa Barbara member described how he saw the turn to structural issues as fundamental to success for the movement and, ultimately, for the longevity of the church:

I hate to put it in these terms, but once you blow all the excitement of the sexual abuse issue, then will people hang onto the *real* issue? Because sexual abuse is not the issue. It's a symptom of what the issue is. If it weren't a closed organization, from an organizational point of view, probably most of the sexual abuse would not have been a problem. It would have been squelched when it came up, because they would have been talking about it. But instead, it's a closed organization.

This realization opened an entirely new area of movement aims and tactics. If the abuse was indeed merely a symptom of the "real issue" of structural failings in the church, then VOTF had barely brushed the surface of the possible scope of internal reform.

Seeing the crisis in this light, VOTF affiliates began concentrating on how to open avenues for dialogue among the laity and with the church hierarchy, to increase lay participation in decision making, to create structures of participation and accountability, and to discern ways to avoid future abuses in the church.

With this daunting task ahead of them, many affiliates gravitated toward an educational component of structural change: learning what church writings had already established by way of lay participation, dialogue, and increased openness within church structures. Numerous speakers at VOTFSBA meetings, for example, piqued the interest of local Catholics who had long and quietly harbored desires to vocalize suggestions for change within the church. Speakers addressed church life under themes such as authority in the church, the formation of priests in seminary, and fostering meaningful dialogue between priests and laity. The educational component of affiliate meetings energized a community of Catholics with moderately progressive political leanings and notable educational and experiential backgrounds.   theological soph

Affiliates around the country took on similar strategies. A handful of theologians, professors, progressive priests, scholars of religion, and journalists took on near celebrity status within VOTF circles. Speakers introduced new energy for envisioning a different kind of church, sparking conversations in affiliates about the very meaning of a lay Catholic identity. Movement participants adopted the notion of structural change as a way to assert their own rightful place in the church as active, baptized, lay Catholics. One VOTF participant described her enthusiasm for discussing structural change in this way:

> That's where my heart is. Because that's where the work is. Which is to empower the laity to take their rightful place by virtue of their baptism in the guidance and governance of the church. I like that so much. Shaping structure. Structural change.

In this way, VOTF affiliates facilitated new conversations about how lay Catholics fit into the structure of the church and possessed the capacity to implement changes to it. The goal of structural change shifted movement discourse toward the meaning of living out one's Catholicism along with ways to preserve the church, reclaim the promises of Vatican II, and empower Catholics in the pews to take ownership of their church.

While affiliates' lectures and discussions sparked interest in changing the church, grounded activism to accompany this momentum came about more slowly. To address the nebulous area of structural change, most VOTF affiliates found it more manageable to embark upon action at the local level, in parishes and within their diocese. This was the structure of the church they knew best. In Montgomery County, Maryland, Jane explained her own affiliate's motivation to start with the familiar, creating genuine mechanisms for listening to lay concerns based on what was already there:

> Take the mechanisms that are already in existence. Parish councils, diocesan councils. Make them truly representative. That there's truly lines of communication so that concerns are listened to. You don't have to reinvent the wheel. Why not a synod? Where people truly make a serious attempt to listen to people's concerns. You don't know what people's concerns are if you spend all your time in the chancery and you only go out for ceremonial things where people kiss your ring and you say Mass. I mean, that's not listening to the people.

In Santa Rosa, California, Joy's VOTF affiliate forged a relationship with their area's Diocesan Pastoral Council (DPC), hoping to integrate the movement agenda of VOTF into that of the DPC. VOTF members spoke at DPC meetings, and DPC members spoke at VOTF meetings. At Megan's Washington, D.C., parish, a number of VOTF participants joined parish committees. The Northern Virginia and Santa Barbara affiliates both conducted surveys to determine which area parishes had pastoral and financial councils, and how members of these councils were selected.

By relying on previously established mechanisms for lay participation in the church, VOTF affiliates were able to introduce their own reform initiatives in a form recognizable to church leaders. In Santa Barbara, knowing that their struggle to find legitimacy and voice among the church leadership had limited their influence, leaders decided to bolster efforts already approved by the archdiocese. The archdiocesan-wide "Safeguard the Children Program" and synod,[1] for example, offered the affiliate avenues through which they could advocate VOTF reform goals on the local level without having to legitimate independently created strategies. Two leaders described this somewhat circuitous route to implementing change:

> When the synod came along, as we looked at the documents in that and we looked at the process, the laity were involved. Clergy and

religious worked together in sessions. We began to see whether the goals and the dreams that the VOTF had for structural change were right there in the synod documents. So, we bought into that. And one of our members is now going to be on the regional council.

VOTF wants to see parish councils be truly representative and truly functioning, not just rubber stamps. So really, the synod has more power to have that happen. We can't go to a pastor and say, "Look, you've got to get your parish council in order." We're limited in that way. It's been very fortunate that we have the synod, and we feel that we should work along as partners with the synod.

In accordance with this approach, two VOTFSBA members acted as representatives in the creation of a regional lay council to implement synod goals. A third was elected to serve on the council once it was created.

Even while the Santa Barbara affiliate welcomed the opportunity to pursue shared VOTF goals via this council, its members expressed caution in believing that the collective was truly representative:

The reason we're monitoring the process is to see if they are sort of handpicked to tow the company line. I would have to say that what we saw, for example, at the regional council, was very positive. Of course, the people who went to the regional council were asked by their pastors. But the attitudes that we saw expressed were, they didn't look company managed.

Another tactic affiliates used to promote structural change was the regulation of financial contributions to the church. Many stopped participating in diocesan-wide financial appeals. In hushed conversations at the sidelines of affiliate meetings, several learned that parish weekly contributions were "taxed," meaning that a certain percentage each week went to the diocese. When some in VOTF learned that certain fundraising efforts were exempt from this tax, they changed their giving pattern from offering weekly contributions to writing larger checks only for those collections that would benefit just their parish, not the diocese.

The legal arena presented an additional forum for VOTF affiliates to shape the way the church responded to clergy sexual abuse. To some VOTF participants, legal tactics seemed more likely to impart real change than unrequited requests to work with church leadership:

I think we have a better chance in the courts than we do with the cardinals. And, we're doing direct work for the survivors that way.

I don't see, I don't know what's going to happen in order to really communicate with the archdiocese.

Affiliates commonly lobbied for extensions on statutes of limitations for reporting abuse. Less common were tactics employed by other survivor-support groups to hold bishops (and even the pope) criminally liable for not disclosing priests' histories of abuse.

In Northern Virginia, leaders invited a state senator to discuss a proposed bill that would mandate that clergy report any abuse they become aware of in their parish (with a clause exception for confessions). VOTF-NoVAwrote letters in support of the bill and urged others to do the same. In lobbying for extensions to statutes of limitations, VOTF representatives were at times pitted directly against lobbyists representing Catholic dioceses. Jane from Montgomery County, Maryland, testified on multiple occasions, as she explained:

> For three years now, I've gone to testify at the legislative hearings.
> They've all had to do with child sexual abuse. Reporting laws for
> sexual abuse and neglect. Extending the statute of limitations to file
> civil suits, in cases of sexual abuse and neglect of a child. And this
> year, the Catholic Church was the only opponent to the bill.

In these instances, Catholics participating in VOTF publicly took a stand against official church representatives even while communicating their commitment to remaining in the church. To some, this was an intimidating and unfamiliar position. However, legal strategies provided VOTF with some recourse in addressing structural issues in the church that contributed to abuse. The movement's efforts were consequently bolstered by the external accountability proffered by the legal system.[2]

The tactic most common among affiliates for pursuing structural change was writing letters to leaders in the church. Unlike legal strategies that led VOTF to seek external accountability and collaboration, this strategy brought movement participants into closer (or at least attempts at closer) collaboration with the Catholic hierarchy. In contrast to other groups responding to the scandal, VOTF principally desired to work with church leaders and within the institution of the church, meaning that letters and requests to meet with the church hierarchy constituted logical tactics. Affiliates would write bishops suggesting changes in the church's approach to dealing with survivors or including the laity in decision making. Significantly, letter writing kept the conversation within the institution of the church, out of the view of the media and non-Catholic parties. Affiliates could target internal reform directly, conjuring a shared Catholic culture and discourse unfiltered through a more public movement.

Another advantage of letter writing as a tactic for promoting structural change came in the ability of affiliates to voice and control their side of the conversation with church leaders. Affiliates neither requested nor needed permission from Catholic hierarchy to write and deliver letters. Local affiliate leaders spoke of preferring this private reform approach offered by letter writing. Some saw a positive response from it. In Santa Barbara, for example, leaders took pride in seeing their archdiocese issue a report about the scandal after they had requested it in a letter to Los Angeles' Cardinal Roger Mahony:

> The cardinal came out with a report to the people about the sexual abuse issue, and VOTF had written a letter asking for such a report. We got a two-page response saying "someday we'll write that report." We wrote another letter saying "this diocese is doing it, this diocese is doing it. Los Angeles deserves, LA's people, they deserve . . ." And lo and behold, the report came. We didn't know whether there was a cause and effect there at all. But [a VOTF member] happened to go to a meeting at which the lawyer for the diocese happened to be speaking, and at that meeting she said that VOTFSBA was one of the groups that had influenced the cardinal to put out his report.

Although written requests allowed VOTF to manage their side of the conversation, the influence of the church over just how letters were written was nonetheless notable. The Santa Barbara group, for example, carefully tempered their language so as to be taken seriously by diocesan leaders. It was this moderate and faith-based orientation to which some participants credited the letters' success:

> We have really sought cooperation and goodwill with the archdiocese. In our writings to the cardinal, you know, the tone of our letters has been such that we ask the questions within the realm of charity and goodwill and all.

> The letters are very respectful, but they don't use grand titles like "Your Eminence" and stuff like that. But they're very respectful letters.

By maintaining a somewhat conciliatory tone, the Santa Barbara affiliate found legitimacy as lay Catholics to propose reform internally. A more tempered tone was, in the minds of many participants, consistent with VOTF's expressed desire to engage in respectful dialogue with the hierarchy.

Other affiliates found less success in letter writing to local church hierarchy. The Northern Virginia group, for example, wrote a number of letters to diocesan leaders sharing what they had learned from survivors. Among their suggestions were inviting survivors to come forward, welcoming them to meet on church property, and naming all of the priests in the diocese known to have abused. They, too, wrote the letters in a moderate tone to maximize their chances for continued dialogue. The affiliate received minimal response, however, as VOTF-NoVA participants described:

> [The letters] made a series of recommendations. "We'd like to meet with you, we'd like to sit down and discuss this," and it was giving very concrete kinds of things that you could do as bishop. All of which got either ignored, or got a form letter back.

> We took up a position of being nonadversarial with the bishop. We were being very nice: "Will you lead us, will you help us, will you . . . " as opposed to "This is what we're going to do." And we said, well, if we can get them in dialogue, support the survivors, then we can add the next two, we can add on the support priests of integrity, and structural change in the church. But [the bishop] never entered in dialogue. We sent him six or seven letters before he responded even once. And then when he responded, he said that it would be better if we did this as individual Catholics, and not as members of the VOTF. So, he's telling us to get out of the group. He said, "Oh, I love your recommendations, but I wish you would pursue them as individual members of the church."

This response emphasizing the need to advocate change as individual Catholics rather than as VOTF sent a very clear message of, in Bob's words: "We don't recognize you as a legitimate organization." Others interpreted it further to signal that the opinions of laypeople simply did not count in diocesan affairs.

Myriad responses or nonresponses from the (arch)dioceses engaged by VOTF affiliates reflected variation among diocesan cultures.[3] Though connected by Canon Law, the U.S. Conference of Catholic Bishops, and ultimately accountable to the pope, local bishops have great latitude and relative autonomy in their dealings with the Catholics living in their dioceses. The organizational culture of dioceses can vary considerably (Harper and Schulte-Murray 1998). Some diocesan cultures are more consultative, others more directive.[4] Just as VOTF affiliates felt the effects of being part of a national effort influenced by localized contexts, so too do dioceses. As such, affiliates received varying responses and degrees of welcome in their local dioceses.

Receiving minimal return on letters to their diocesan leaders, members of VOTF-NoVA began to realize that their strategy—perhaps even all conciliatory interactions with the church hierarchy—was ineffective for introducing structural change. The nonresponsiveness stifled the affiliate's desire to reach out to church leaders at all:

> We had written a number of letters to the bishop. I'm very good at writing letters, but [exasperated sigh]!! What does it accomplish?! You know?! You've got it in the hands of somebody else, you feel better about yourself, maybe. But *nothing* changed! We never got a meeting with the bishop, we never got . . . !!

> We're up against a big, huge, gigantic wall. I'm discouraged. We go to meetings and we talk about doing stuff, but there's nothing really positive we can do because if you write to the bishop, he doesn't answer! So you write a letter, so who cares? He's got a pile of thirteen, and he could care less. The church definitely is just stonewalling everything. They don't want our participation. They love their power! They want to "fix" this problem. And I keep thinking, "You're the ones who caused it!" . . . The more stonewalling we got, the more angry I got. Where's the humility here? You should be down on your knees, begging forgiveness!

The lack of response demonstrated the primary downfall of the private nature of letter writing. Without public accountability or reciprocal concern among the hierarchy, VOTF affiliates found limited success in advocating structural change from within the institution.

For this reason, VOTF-NoVA altered its discursive approach. Collaborating with other affiliates in the region, leaders wrote a letter to the (arch)bishops of Washington, Baltimore, and Arlington that took a far less conciliatory tone. They did not request a meeting with the bishops or make suggestions. Rather, they submitted a critical assessment of recent diocesan actions, writing as if they were independent evaluators of diocesan progress. The new approach was liberating for members, explained Bob:

> We wrote a letter that this time instead of saying, "Please meet with us" or "Please do these . . . ," it was written as, "this is our report on you." And to me, that changed the momentum, in my mind, of who we were and what we were doing.

Bob likened prior attempts to knocking at the door as the hierarchy turned off the lights, shut the door, and left them standing there. This new strategy, in Bob's mind, shifted the power back into the hands of the laity:

> It shifted, and said, "We are who we are. We're standing, we're holding you accountable, this is our report of how you're doing. We still have a series of things that you could do, but whether you do them . . ."—instead of saying, "If you would just do these things . . ."—"Whether you do them or not, we're holding you accountable to them." Let's stop knocking on the door. We'll send them whenever we want; we'll speak to whomever we want.

While still holding to their own identity as Catholics who cared about the church, participants in VOTF-NoVA built new ground upon which they could make their concerns known, apart from that for which they had been granted permission by church authorities. They had taken ownership of their right to assert meaningful critiques of the Catholic structures of which they were a part.

None of the three (arch)bishops in the region replied to the affiliates' letters. Rather than reading this as yet another defeat, VOTF-NoVA leaders instead interpreted the nonresponsiveness as a welcomed affirmation of their newly embraced independence. Their less aggressive letters had received only formulated responses thanking them for their suggestions and requesting that they pursue them as individuals rather than as VOTF. The new letters countered with the insistence that the group no longer needed recognition or permission to offer accountability. They had approached the VOTF reform agenda on their own terms.

permission .

Conclusion

Affiliates clearly differed in their approach to the shared mission of integrating laity into the governance of the church and addressing specific goals of supporting survivors, supporting priests of integrity, and shaping structural change. Local dynamics and personalities caused affiliates to use different tactical approaches; the lack of definitive direction from VOTF National produced a proliferation of movement paths. Inconsistency in the ways dioceses responded to VOTF affiliates' letter-writing and other strategic initiatives also stemmed, at least in part, from differences in diocesan cultures.

The divergent ways in which affiliates adapted to the boundaries of their institutional environments can be considered along the lines of *integration, parallelism*, and *independence*. Introduced previously by West and Blumberg (1990) within the context of gender in social movements,[5] I apply the framework here to explain how an IISM responds to boundaries posed by the targeted institution.

Institutional integration means that movement participants primarily appropriate existing institutional resources in order to achieve movement aims. Structural change is achieved by making these existing structures function better and toward the interests of movement goals. Taking the path of integration, participants are more likely to dialogue and collaborate with institutional authorities, join institutional committees, and work to change the institution using resources that are already available within the institution. The VOTF affiliate in Santa Barbara fits this model well: they met on parish property, supported diocesan efforts such as the synod and Safeguard the Children program, and disassociated with groups such as SNAP that would create divisiveness between themselves and church leaders.

Institutional parallelism reflects the path of a movement that, rather than integrating into existing institutional structures, creates its own structures for accountability and change meant to parallel those of the institution. As an alternative to joining extant institutional groups (if they do exist), the movement works toward institutionally committed goals, but it does this primarily within separate groups or means that they create themselves. The VOTF affiliate of Northern Virginia most closely followed this path, as they invited priests to discuss the scandal outside of church-sanctioned settings, collaborated with SNAP, lobbied for legislative changes, and wrote letters evaluating diocesan progress. Like VOTFSBA, they sought to remain Catholic and true to the church, but they chose to work through less conciliatory avenues in order to effect this change. Parallelism is not necessarily the preferred movement path; it might be merely a reaction to activists' inability to integrate their reform goals using existing institutional resources.

Although none of the VOTF affiliates explored in this study exemplify *institutional independence*, this, too, constitutes an additional path for IISMs. This path is characterized by the creation of separate, movement-generated structures that foster goals not necessarily in line with sustaining the institution. This type of IISM forms within the institution but might ultimately exist separate from it. An example would be a movement that forms to change the doctrinal stance of a religious denomination but ultimately decides to create an entirely new denomination. Participants may conclude that IISM movement goals simply cannot be met within the original institution and thus separate their movement from the institution (even if a shared identity is sustained). There is a long history of this among Protestant congregations and denominations. Given that

VOTF has in its mission statement the desire to remain faithful to the Catholic Church, this path is not evident among formal VOTF affiliates (although some participants did leave VOTF to engage in more independent tactics for holding the church accountable). Closer to this path would be a Catholic IISM such as Call to Action, which originally emerged out of a bishops' conference but ultimately promoted extrainstitutional and counterinstitutional reform measures such as the unsanctioned ordination of women priests.

The decisions VOTF affiliates made in responding to institutional authorities depended largely on their success in merging movement aims with institutional ones: How well could they use existing church resources to accomplishment movement goals? What diocesan organizational culture did they encounter and how successful were they in dialoging with the church hierarchy? What was the response of church authorities to their collaboration with groups not received well by the church, such as SNAP? Affiliates tested their own perceived legitimacy within their diocese. Each embraced a Catholic identity, evoking rights as lay Catholics to participate in decision making in the church. However, many bishops as well as some priests and diocesan-approved councils and boards granted varying degrees of recognition to local VOTF affiliates. While church authorities welcomed the participation of lay Catholics in organizing a response to clergy abuse, others were reticent to recognize the movement as authentically Catholic or acting in the best interest of the church.

Those affiliates that found success in this quest for legitimacy moved closer to the path of integration. Those that met greater resistance moved farther from church authorities and toward a parallel path where they could voice their opinions as lay Catholics from movement-generated structures for reform. Consistent across affiliates was the struggle to be recognized within the institutional sphere of the Catholic Church as an authentic Catholic voice for internal reform. Contestation surrounding VOTF's Catholic identity was the central barrier to the movement's full participation in responding to the crisis of sexual abuse within the church and in finding a place among the core structures of decision making and accountability.

The next chapter considers additional identity consequences for the movement stemming from similarities in participants' age, gender, race, and class. VOTF's demographic brought to the movement formative cultural perspectives, particularly those shaped by a lived experience of the Second Vatican Council.

5

Collective Memories

Who were the participants in VOTF, and whose voice did they represent? What were the sources and consequences of the Catholic identity they employed? VOTF's demographic composition characterized the shape and path the movement took in mobilizing to change the church. This chapter explores the social, cultural, and demographic contexts of the movement and the ways in which these identity markers shaped VOTF's positioning within the church. Notably, participants' lived memories of the Second Vatican Council, experienced within the context of 1960s social change, played a key role in how movement participants envisioned their place as Catholics and constructed their attitudes toward the church.

Voice of the Faithful members, rather than being a random cross section of the United States' 68 million Catholics, instead shared fairly high levels of similarity. Their demographic viewpoint can be likened to what the social theorist Pierre Bourdieu (1977) called *habitus*, or the cognitive structures individuals use to understand the social world. Habitus reflects distinctions based in social divisions such as generation, class, race, and gender. Shared habitus can emerge out of collective experiences, histories, and memories. Although this lens through which an individual views the world does not necessarily operate at a conscious level, it nonetheless manifests itself in the ways people engage in the activities of everyday life.

The habitus reflected by VOTF's membership was predominantly older, white, highly educated, and middle- to upper-class. A national survey of VOTF members conducted in 2004 (D'Antonio and Pogorelc 2007) revealed that 59 percent were women, fewer than 3 percent identified as people of color, and 87 percent had at least a college degree.[1] Eighty percent reported a household income of $75,000 or more. Members were also overwhelming older, comprised primarily of baby boomers (born between 1946 and 1964) and the World War II generation (born before 1946). Eighty-nine percent were born before 1960. This demographic pattern was similarly evident in the interview sample for this book. Interviewees consisted of 58 percent women and 2 percent people of color. Their average age was 58, and a quarter were retired. Ninety-six percent had at least a college degree. Overall, the VOTF movement was older, whiter, wealthier, and more educated than the average American citizen and average American Catholic.[2]

Commonalities among VOTF participants mattered because they both strengthened and limited the movement's collective identity along with its priorities, inclusiveness, and espoused brand of Catholicism. Shared habitus can operate as a cultural resource for a social movement (Edwards and McCarthy 2004). Within VOTF, it offered common knowledge of tools enabling mobilization, including access to institutional resources, leadership and public communication skills, and a background in the culture of Catholicism. Demographic and cultural commonalities also mattered because they limited the VOTF movement in the kind of Catholic identity it represented and the type of church it envisioned. Many perspectives were excluded—though not necessarily intentionally—from VOTF's efforts to change the Catholic Church. While the movement's name might have implied representation of all lay Catholics, the demographic composition of the movement did not. Subsequent sections outline the consequences of this along the lines of generation, gender, race, and class.

Generation

Generation was arguably the most salient demographic after religious affiliation that united VOTF participants. Given that most in VOTF were born prior to 1960, memories of the Second Vatican Council in the Roman Catholic Church (1962–1965) held a profound influence over the Catholic identity of movement participants. For many, their formative years as young Catholics spanned the time of the council meetings. Church leaders implemented substantial changes in the liturgy, ecumenism, and experience of the sacraments at the parishes and schools of VOTF participants in their youth. Participants' collective memories included attending Latin Masses as children and memorizing the Baltimore Catechism before witnessing the church open and change in response to Vatican II's relatively progressive outcomes.[3]

The *aggiornamento* ("updating") resulting from Vatican II has been classi- fied by scholars as itself a social movement (Ebaugh 1991; Seidler and Meyer 1989). While the convening of the council by Pope John XXIII surprised many, it was in fact deeply embedded within struggles stretching back centuries (Cogley 1973).[4] These included contested relations with Protestant Christians since the Protestant Reformation, debates between official church policy and local practice, and a contentious relationship with the modern world (a tension particularly salient for Roman Catholics in the United States). The council responded to increasingly permeable boundaries between religion and moder- nity. Sixteen documents produced by the council brought extensive change in the church and new views toward religious freedom, ecumenism, social mis- sion, collegiality, and local diversity.

One VOTF participant described how her Catholic schoolteachers memo- rably introduced some of the changes Vatican II brought:

> It was my first experience at Catholic education, and Vatican II
> happened at that time. And [the nuns] took us into a gym and closed
> the doors and said, "We're going to teach you to sing Mass in
> English, but don't tell your parents, because they would be really
> mad." What a way to win kids. We sang the Mass in English for the
> baccalaureate. So, we took ownership immediately.

Many VOTF participants described themselves as products of the Second Vatican Council, having come of age during this monumental time of change in the modern Catholic Church.

While the Second Vatican Council targeted the entire international church, its intersection with the cultural context of the 1960s magnified its resonance in the United States. The 1960s brought changes not only throughout the Catholic Church, but through civil rights, the women's movement, immigration, war protests, and civil disobedience. The Second Vatican Council was thus one piece of the coming-of-age story for many VOTF participants, as two describe here:

> Vatican II was when I was in Catholic college. For me, it was a
> fabulous time. I've always been Catholic because of social justice.
> When I came of age as a Catholic, I also came of age politically. And I
> was in the streets. It made perfect sense.

> My friends, the baby boomers, who started this movement, we grew up
> at [that] age—it was Vietnam we protested, it was the environment, it

was women's rights, it was civil rights. We were always cutting the
grass for something. Our generation grew up a generation of
protesters. And over time, most of my friends . . . have been involved
from time to time, in some form of political mayhem. I think we were
grounded in the secular world with an idea of justice. And Vatican II
comes along in the '60s and supports that liberating call: a different
way to be church. So, absolutely—that fueled much of [the VOTF
movement].

Several members drew a connection between their socialization in the 1960s
and their continued commitment to mobilizing for a cause, including that of
VOTF. Their generation, as Nancy T. Ammerman noted in her reflection on the
movement, has "been formed by the revolutions they were a part of, and
distinctively formed by experiencing those revolutions in a deeply Catholic
environment" (Ammerman 2008).

Although the theological and pragmatic influences of Vatican II were substantive, two were especially relevant to the formation of the VOTF Catholic
identity. First, the very notion of *aggiornamento* as proposed by Vatican II was a
testament to the possibility of institutional change in a church that had been
previously seen as immutable. A transformation this extensive had not occurred since the Council of Trent 400 years prior, in response to the Protestant
Reformation. The comprehensive reevaluation of beliefs and practices during
Vatican II opened the Catholic Church to competing models of accommodation and change from within. This had a significant impact on the thinking of
an entire generation of Catholics, as one VOTF organizer describes:

[VOTF participants] lived through the promise of Vatican II, and sort
of the collapse of Vatican II. That's clearly something that shaped
their thinking, and shaped their spiritual development. So, I think
that they have a much stronger bond to the church, and they also
have a much stronger bond to the notion that the church can change.
Because they witnessed it themselves.

For this generation of Catholics, the church became an arena for questioning
and change. One VOTF participant shared how her view of the church directly
related to the council:

My philosophy and my spiritual journey has always involved
questioning the church. I think it was because, I was growing up, I
was in high school during Vatican II. And we were encouraged to do
that. It's never occurred to me that I would leave. But I feel it's not

only my privilege, but it's my responsibility as an adult Catholic to
raise a voice when I think something's wrong.

Grounded in this experience, religion became a window through which to view
the world and a tool with which to enact change.

The second key influence from Vatican II was a reconceptualization of
authority in the church. Authority, rather than allocated only to the ordained, was
newly envisioned as belonging to the entire "People of God" (*Lumen Gentium*
no. 9): ordained, lay, and religious.[5] The laity was defined in council documents as follows:

> The term laity is here understood to mean all the faithful except those
> in holy orders and those in the state of religious life specially
> approved by the Church. These faithful are by baptism made one
> body with Christ and are constituted among the People of God; they
> are in their own way made sharers in the priestly, prophetical, and
> kingly functions of Christ; and they carry out for their own part the
> mission of the whole Christian people in the Church and in the
> world. (*Lumen Gentium* no. 31, November 21, 1964)

Vatican II documents called the laity to actively participate in the mission
and governance of the church, "either as individuals or together as members
of various groups or associations" (*Apostolicam Actuositatem* no. 15, November
18, 1965).

This reformulation of authority affirmed a religious identity that "derived
from a more egalitarian, communal sense of church ownership rather than
from the church hierarchy's universal definitions alone" (Dillon 1999:48).
While a bishop still has primary leadership over the "flock" of Catholics in his
diocese, Vatican II introduced the idea of a more collaborative and consultative
leadership model. Foremost in the minds of VOTF participants was the conclusion that the laity, too, share in the governance of the church.

While few VOTF members would reference specific Vatican II passages in
articulating the reasoning behind movement action, many alluded to the spirit
of the council changes that had intimately shaped their understanding of
church. Vatican II documents offered a powerful justification for VOTF's mission of increasing lay participation in decision making. The comments of two
VOTF members reflect this justification:

> According to Vatican II, the church is the people of God. It's not the
> hierarchy. It's us. And I think that VOTF has the right idea, in that,
> it's—we're all baptized into the priesthood of Christ. And they're

really trying to take seriously their baptismal commitment. I really respect that. Because the leadership has just failed. Horribly.

[VOTF] has everything to do with Vatican II . . . It was the first time in the history of the church that the church defined itself first as the people of God, and not as the pope, the bishops, the priests, the deacons, the laity. It turned it upside down . . . I think that all of us who felt that surge of hope and knew this—here we are today, because that's the church we want, we're looking for. We can connect back to it, because we were there at the beginning.

Council documentation, experience, and ideas thus had considerable influence in the mobilization of the Vatican II generation of lay Catholics in the aftermath of the child abuse scandal.

The 2002 crisis of abuse triggered a realization for many who joined VOTF that the Vatican II promises of shared responsibility had not come to fruition. News of abuse had a particular poignancy for a generation of Catholics whose memories included the introduction and implementation of the Second Vatican Council. One member articulated this generational effect:

There really is a big generational difference here. I mean, how many people of [the younger] generation really understand the importance of Vatican II? If you didn't know what the church was like before and what it is now, how can you get upset about what appears like the retrenchment? Where, you know, Mass was in Latin, the priest's back was turned to you, and it was hell and brimstone and all of that kind of stuff.

In its most pronounced form, VOTF's response to the crisis could be interpreted as the Vatican II generation's opportunity to impart a legacy of participation and accountability in the Catholic Church, to salvage the contributions of Vatican II before its promises fade into history. Some expressed this generational call aloud, connecting it with the past as well as with a commitment to children and grandchildren:

It's like we had this dream back in the '60s, and we haven't lost that dream. Here's a moment in time when that dream needs to be revitalized. Which, you know, just isn't a dream that young people have. They never had the before and after. So, we can't expect them to be in the same place that we're in. So, in many respects, it bothers me that we're a predominantly older group. But in another respect, I totally understand it. And if we achieve something that leaves young people a more vibrant, responsive church, then we won't have wasted our time.

We're sort of saying, you know, we are the Vatican II generation. And maybe before we leave this earth, you know, we can do something for our church! For our grandchildren!

I think that we feel that we are empowered by Vatican II. We realize that what has been revealed is intolerable. I mean, I never would have thought that I am speaking the way I am five years ago. But this is so wrong. And we have a responsibility, because if we don't do it, who is going to do it? I certainly got involved because I did not want to leave the church as it was for my children or grandchildren.

Many participants lamented their own children having already left the church. Involvement in VOTF felt like a way to leave behind a positive legacy in the church.

Voice of the Faithful became a vessel through which a generation of Catholics could recall, preserve, and implement a model of the church that had revitalized them as youth: one that revealed a degree of openness to change and lay involvement. The notion that a more perfect church could once again revitalize and retain youth gave them hope for sustaining a committed Catholic identity in the face of the crisis of abuse. The culture of Vatican II Catholicism pervaded the culture of the VOTF movement.

Gender

Generation was not the only salient identity marker among VOTF participants. Gender, race, and class were likewise operative in shaping the movement. Women outnumbered men in VOTF three to two. Women's somewhat disproportionate participation in VOTF can be traced, at least in part, to their over-representation in religious practice and underrepresentation in traditional structures of church leadership. Even while U.S. women attend and volunteer in Catholic churches at higher rates than men, they occupy just 27 percent of top diocesan positions (e.g., chiefs of pastoral services, finance, personnel, education, and community services) (USCCB 2004).[6] Ex-Catholic women are disproportionately represented among Protestant leadership, particularly within the Episcopal denomination (Perl 2005). Vatican II led to a proliferation of feminist groups in the church and the questioning of patriarchal practices

(Katzenstein 1998). Feminist, womanist, and mujerista movements have mobilized to increase women's roles and discuss women's issues, working for church reform internally in the absence of legal recourse (Bonavoglia 2005; Katzenstein 1998; Weaver 1999).

Although VOTF did not explicitly convey a gendered message, gender nonetheless played a role in the movement's mobilization and collective identity.[7] The first media coverage VOTF received in the *Boston Globe* alluded to the "women in red" who spoke out at the Cardinal's Convocation. The absence of women in decision-making structures of the church was constant fodder for side conversations, including hypotheses that the inclusion of women could have prevented the crisis from occurring. Two VOTF participants conveyed their own interpretation of women's marginalization as Catholics:

> I think [church leaders] don't want their hierarchy being influenced—not only by laypeople, but specifically by women. In any way, shape, or form. So, as long as women are in some sort of marginal place, baking the cookies, having bake sales, cleaning the alter—that's okay. But they can't ever be in a place where they are allowed to have an opinion, think, participate, or anything else. Not in any real way. Just as little helpers.

> For pure moral integrity of the church, the sex abuse crisis matters most. For pure transformational power, the role of women in the church, the full role of women in the church is the issue that matters most.

The issue was clearly central to some VOTF members, but was slow to emerge publicly as an issue for the movement.

Members did not agree on how (or if) to address women's issues within the movement. Participants held divergent views on appropriate roles for women in the church and the legitimacy of a feminist agenda within the VOTF movement. Many disassociated the VOTF agenda from feminist efforts, even if they supported both. As one member put it, "I personally think that there should be women priests, but I wouldn't want to do that through VOTF," and another, "We're doing ourselves a major disservice by not having married priests. And women priests. But I am very careful that when I speak for Voice of the Faithful, that I don't go there."

For these and other reasons, a movement agenda explicitly connected to the rights of women in the church was, by and large, stifled. One leader spoke of her great difficulty convincing other VOTF leaders to broach the topic of women during sessions at a VOTF convocation:

It took me six weeks of talking to the, what I think of as progressive Catholics on this committee, to get them to go along with using the word "women" in one of the [convocation sessions]! We always said we wouldn't have "hot button" issues, and I said, "Listen! If women make a hot button issue, then we can't talk about men, either. And what are we going to do, talk about trees when we get there?!" . . . I think we have to support the point that half the church is female, half of this organization is female. If we can't use the word "women" now, who's gonna use it? It's as if it was appropriated by Call to Action or something.

She explained that it was not about advocating for women's ordination (despite her own seminary degree), but rather advocating for open and real dialogue around gender issues, particularly in light of VOTF's stated desire for authentic lay participation:

The idea is to push the envelope a bit . . . not call for women's ordination (I don't know the woman with a brain who'd want to be part of this church), but to push the dialogue about women's place in the church. You know, the pope said—the dead pope—that we can't talk about that. That's bull****! You know! We need to—I would like to see an initiative that Voice of the Faithful would adopt, to force the issue.

Based on this woman's advocacy, convocation organizers did agree to add a session to the program on how to "ensure that women's gifts, and those of all marginalized persons, effect a more truly 'catholic' Church." Consequently, a resolution emerged that suggested VOTF engage in a discussion of "the issues affecting women and other marginalized people within the Church."

Months later, a proposal was circulated to VOTF members requesting dialogue about "the formation of a Church that proclaims and lives the reality that both men and women share equal status in the eyes of God." Accordingly, it suggested that VOTF initiate "Church-wide discussion on advancing equal access for women to all positions of leadership and ministry within the Catholic Church." Emailed responses to the proposal highlighted cautious support for the idea but hesitation to take on its agenda under the umbrella of VOTF. One respondent, whose sentiments were echoed by others, wrote the following:

I do not support your resolution. I belong to three organizations which work towards justice for women in our church. I joined VOTF because its primary goal was to support the survivors of abuse by clergy and also to "change the church" so that laity (men and women) participate in its governance so as to keep the scandal of covering up abuse by clergy from happening again. I prefer that VOTF remain focused on the clergy abuse issue, as difficult and often frustrating as that may be, because no other reform group serves that purpose. I pray that VOTF will remain faithful to its original mission, rather than be tempted to latch on to another more popular issue.

In the face of these and numerous other requests that VOTF not meddle with the issue of gender, the proposal was formally withdrawn soon thereafter. The initiators provided no explanation for its removal to the general VOTF membership. Individual affiliates did, however, begin to more openly theme their gatherings around women's issues and questions of women's access to leadership positions in the church.

Action (and its limits) in the area of gender signaled another way that VOTF participants constructed boundaries around their collective identity, treading carefully to represent themselves as faithful to the church. Operating within an institution with an entirely male ordained leadership structure, even the very topic of women became a "hot button" issue, along with the likes of abortion, celibacy, and married priests, that VOTF ought not "latch on to." Thus, even while six in ten VOTF members were women, conversations about gender were stilted and approached with reticence so as to avoid an overly progressive movement label that ran counter to church teachings.

Race and Class

Also intersecting the generational and gendered dynamics of VOTF were the movement's racial and class demographics. Although not explicitly discussed among movement participants as much as the dynamics of age or gender, the habitus offered by similarities in race and class nonetheless added dimension to VOTF's collective identity and nuance to the group's proposed mainstream Catholic representation.

Voice of the Faithful participants and leaders were overwhelmingly non-Hispanic whites. Nearly two-thirds (63 percent) claimed Irish descent (D'Antonio and Pogorelc 2007). Just 2 percent in the interview sample for this book identified as people of color. Some participants were more cognizant of this homogeneity than others; some described it as being more problematic than others. Participants frequently rationalized the lack of a multiracial demographic with assertions that the movement was still quite diverse, if not in its racial or ethnic composition. Many used cultural and class-based arguments to

explain why the movement had not been successful in attracting the participation of Latinos/Latinas in particular, approximately 70 percent of whom
are Catholic (Perl, Greely, and Gray 2006). Affiliates' attempts to recruit more
Latino/Latina participation waned early in the movement's development, seeing little return. Two affiliate leaders explained their group's efforts and lack
of success in encouraging the participation of Catholic Latinos/Latinas in
their area:

> At the very beginning, all of our flyers were translated into Spanish.
> We were trying to get the Latino population out. And we just gave up
> on that. They have other concerns. The structure of the church and
> even the sexual abuse crisis is just not top for them. Wages, family
> problems, housing—those are the big things for them.

> Well, first of all, we're probably fairly comfortable, and educated, and
> white, so we don't have the problems of poverty. We did a lot to bring,
> or I should say, we really spent time trying to invite the Latino
> community, and we did have one person that we just thought would be
> excellent, and we were working on that, and it slipped through our
> fingers. Because really, that is not their concern. Their issues are
> poverty and jobs and housing and all the rest.

Participants described the agenda of VOTF as simply not a "burning issue" for
those whose primary concerns were more economic in nature.

Others identified cultural explanations for the absence of Latinos/Latinas
in VOTF. In particular, some participants perceived Latinos/Latinas as
approaching their relationships with priests with more reverence and sanctity.
Questioning the authority of a bishop or priest was not a part of the Latino/
Latina Catholic experience. One VOTF participant explained:

> As far as the other cultures, like Latinos and stuff, I think part of it is
> a cultural thing. That you never question the priest. Never question
> the church. The priest is always right.

This same reasoning also led some to speculate that VOTF's vote for Cardinal
Law's resignation in Boston early in the movement had in essence precluded
any chance for Latino/Latina participation in the VOTF movement.

Voice of the Faithful participants also hesitated to assert themselves as representatives of a Latino/Latina response to the crisis, as one member explained:

> To define ourselves and then to think that we could—we would need
> to find a couple of really strong Hispanics. And give them the

encouragement to move in that direction, but then you risk being the white guy telling somebody how to work within their community. It's one thing for somebody to criticize us about that, and it's another thing for that cultural group, that ethnic group to stand up and want to know, too.

Voice of the Faithful was therefore caught between its desire to embody ethnic diversity and its hesitancy to force the movement's mission upon others, contrasting the grassroots nature of the VOTF movement. One member even suggested that there should be a separate VOTF for Hispanic Catholics because VOTF "can't be everything to everybody."

The demographics of the VOTF movement were also highly educated and middle- to upper-class, characteristics that again intersect with attributes of age and race. Baby boomers are among the most upwardly mobile generation of Catholics to ever come of age in the United States. With the passage of the GI Bill in 1944, Catholics rose in socioeconomic status in the United States throughout the latter half of the twentieth century. Some VOTF participants were cognizant of these socioeconomic changes among the Catholic population in the United States and attribute the very emergence of the movement in part to these factors:

> Now, Catholics are educated and some of them are even theologically well educated. And economically, Catholics are now above average in terms of the demographics of this country. At one time, we were the poor Irish, the lowest of the low. In that sense, it's not surprising, given that demographic change, that this kind of movement would spring up in the face of a crisis like we've just experienced, whereas a hundred years ago the crisis probably could have been swept under the rug without ever having revealed the flaw that needed careful consideration and inspection.

Indeed, Catholics today fall above the national average for educational achievement, occupational status, and family income (D'Antonio et al. 2001).

Voice of the Faithful participants recognized that the educational backgrounds and professional achievements of its participants provided the movement with an ample supply of skill sets. One founder explained this dynamic within the movement:

> One of the things about this movement within the church is that it started with and has been fueled by a lot of very well-educated, professionally accomplished Catholics. It's a very distinctive part about this movement. These are people who, they have a lot of savvy.

They know how to do things. They've been doing things in their professional careers. We had doctors, social workers, lawyers, and business people. And you put the skill set together and you say, whew, this is, this is a very impressive group of folks.

Taking this a step further, a few even speculated that the movement agenda of VOTF was, in a way, the fated task of the social elite: a suitable undertaking for those Catholics who now had the time, money, and resources to address the structural shortcomings of their church. One member spoke to this sensibility:

It's very much middle class, upper-middle class. We're educated. We have the luxury and the privilege of living in suburbs and having the time . . . So it's our task. It's our task. I'd would like to see it be more widespread than that, but it's a beginning. *burden · cross.*

Participants interpreted the movement as a way to bring the intelligence and professionalism Catholics had gained in other arenas into the arena of the church: no longer did they need to act like, or be treated like, children in their faith lives. It was inevitable that their awareness and ability as professionals would transfer into the church, where Catholics too often subscribed to what many in VOTF called the "pray-pay-and-obey" model of being a Catholic. This introduced new questions and expectations into the meaning and experience of a religious identity.

Demographic Consequences

Far from a random or representative movement of Catholics, VOTF drew especially from among older, white, U.S. Catholics with a lived experience of Vatican II and a socioeconomic status granting them the flexibility to participate in a change-oriented movement within the church. This bounded identity created a powerful recruitment tool for similarly situated and like-minded Catholics. Many who joined VOTF expressed that their activity within the movement allowed them to fully experience and openly discuss their faith among Catholics—a first, for many.

Demographic similarities were strategic in that the movement gave voice not to all Catholics, but, in a powerful way, to a specific group of U.S. Catholics whose personal, social, and cultural identities were tied intimately to that of the institutional Vatican II church. One VOTF leader spoke of how the movement aligned so well with this collective identity:

There are an awful lot of our members who are really reformed
Catholics. They desperately want the reforms of Vatican II to be
given, to come to pass in their lifetime. I think for a lot of the
members, who are in their sixties and seventies, and maybe even in
their eighties, but certainly in their sixties and seventies, there's a
sense that this is the last best chance that they have to see the church
become what they had always wanted it to be. And that is a church
that is, you know, as [Pope] John XXIII said, open the windows, let
the wind blow through. And the sunlight come in. So, you know,
someone like [a specific VOTF member], he's retired, he was a priest
at one time, he's got grandchildren. He has so wanted the church to
be what the promise was in the 1960s, with Vatican II. So wanted it.
Wanted it with every bone in his body, every cell in his being. And
maybe this is the last hurrah, you know, for this Vatican II
generation.

In this light, VOTF provided one last opportunity to preserve and advocate for
a church that was both traditional and open in its authority structure—a model
movement participants saw as necessary to the survival of the Catholic Church
for generations to come.

Even while shared identity markers built bonds among movement participants, some were nonetheless aware that homogeneity could be problematic
for the movement, not only in its exclusion of other lay voices in the church,
but also in projecting an uncertain future. One participant expressed her awareness and concern in this regard:

I think [the movement] is white. I think it's upper-class,
predominately. Educated. Catholics who came of age in the post–
Vatican II era. That's primarily who it is. And I think it's a really big
concern all of the groups that are left out of that demographic. And
what is the future of this movement, if it doesn't find a way to break
into other communities?

Another agreed that VOTF's future might be in question unless the movement
(and the church as a whole) could expand their membership base:

I don't think anyone's terribly different in VOTF than I am. And one
of the major things that concerns me is that the next generation is
gone. If it's not gone, it's going. And that's a huge void.

In this sense, the movement captured a particular cross section of the Catholic
Church, giving voice to a group of Catholics whose message was beginning to

age and whose urgency stemmed from fears of absorption into the church's fading institutional history. The demographic composition of the movement trapped it largely in a singular social context, meaning that as the VOTF message faded, so, too, would that of a generation of Catholics (and vice versa). The VOTF ethos, then, could face a future similar to that of the Second Vatican Council in inspiring institutional change.

Conclusion

Voice of the Faithful's collective identity, bound by its demographic barriers, helped reach many Catholics whose shared memories of the Second Vatican Council informed their perspectives on the church. Similarities in generation, race, and class, along with a semisilencing of gender distinctions, allowed VOTF to capture the message of a cohort of Catholics with the means and desire to shape their faith in new ways. Simultaneously the movement excluded potential participants whose own identities did not fit within the habitus erected by VOTF. Even while the movement emerged in a multitude of U.S. regions and parishes, the internal composition of the movement led to a more specific, bounded collective identity that could not envelop a truly representative voice for lay Catholics.

Despite these limitations, VOTF participants embraced fully their shared identity as Catholics. Moreover, the movement challenged the definition of "Catholic" and the ways in which Catholicism is lived out through the church. It is this identity exploration that is discussed in the next chapter.

6

On Being Catholic

Although the movement's demographics may have limited their representation of all Catholics, VOTF nonetheless ordered its very existence around being Catholic. Its members founded and expanded the movement from a starting premise of its Catholic identity, firmly committed to remaining within the Catholic Church. But in mobilizing to confront the structural underpinnings of abuse by clergy, including the perceived complicity of bishops, VOTF participants repeatedly encountered challenges to authenticate their Catholic identity. Even while promulgating a public identity of "faithful Catholics in communion with the universal Catholic Church," the movement was banned from meeting on church grounds, restricted from advertising their gatherings in Catholic publications, and denied attempts to dialogue with bishops. In the eyes of some church leaders and lay Catholics, the brand of faith VOTF espoused was neither acceptable nor welcome under the umbrella of Catholicism. What began as an attempt to protect the church from future abuse was reframed as threatening to the very structure of it; a mainstream Catholic label was not enough to legitimize VOTF as faithful Catholics.

While sociologists have discussed examples of institutional attempts to silence internal dissent in movement settings such as the field of science (Moore 2008), public schools (Binder 2002), and political parties (Rogers and Lott 1997), the arena of religion poses a notable variation. Whereas contention in other fields is often framed by differing views of the institution in the eyes of activists and institutional leaders, contention within religious arenas is also *identity* driven. Legitimate insider status does not accompany the "Catholic" label in the same way that it might accompany the label of "parent" for mobilization within a school setting or "scientist" within the field of science. Church leaders and other Catholics critiqued not only the goals of the VOTF movement, but also the very identity of the movement and its participants as being legitimately Catholic. The argument stretched beyond "we don't like your ideas," to "you are not one of us." Essence, rather than action alone, is contested in the oppositional situations of a religious IISM.[1]

This chapter explores the ways in which VOTF constructed a Catholic identity in the face of such challenges from the institution. Their identity labor exemplifies the way that collective identity and religion—as culture—are instrumental and highly contested in IISMs.

Asserting a Mainstream Religious Authenticity

Being Catholic was the most integral marker of collective identity in the VOTF movement. To those who had long served the church in capacities such as Eucharistic ministers, religious education teachers, or financial contributors, the notion that they, in criticizing the administrative functions of their church, were not truly Catholic was foreign to them. Members described their movement as one filled with "extremely committed Catholics who put their faith into action," "people who are really committed to walk a Catholic walk," and "the heart of a parish." As one member described, VOTF members were

> people who have been attending church for a long time; they've given money to the church; who volunteered; who've helped put on parish festivals; who've supported Catholic schools; who've helped to rebuild the building funds; who've had their priests over for dinner; that's who I think they are. People who believe in the Trinity and believe in the sacraments and appreciate their Catholic heritage and don't want to toss it out the window.

From their own perspective, at least, members were as Catholic as they come.

A national survey of VOTF membership (D'Antonio and Pogorelc 2007) confirmed high levels of Catholic identity and parish participation among movement members. Those in VOTF were more likely to be registered in a parish, attended church more often, and were more involved in parish life than the average, self-identifying Catholic nationally. Nearly all (93 percent) were born into the church and baptized Catholic. Seventy percent had attended Catholic grade schools, significantly outpacing the average Catholic (about half of whom attended a Catholic grade school).

Given this movement base, the collective identity of VOTF was wedded to a definition of Catholicism that included parish participation, respect for the role of the ordained, and a belief system that affirmed the Nicene Creed. For movement participants, Catholicism played an "ethnic" or "quasi-ethnic" role, to use the words of sociologist Andrew Greeley (1972) in describing how churches offer individuals a sense of self and niche in the social order. A common Catholic identity among movement participants provided a shared cultural toolkit (Robnett 2002; Swidler 1986) from which members could draw to achieve unity around movement goals.[2]

Voice of the Faithful participants were careful to situate their identity in relation to the institutional church. Characteristic of an IISM, VOTF defined itself with close ties to the institution it was targeting for reform. An early iteration of the movement's "Statement of Who We Are," published on the VOTF website, clearly indicated participants' perception that their own authority as lay Catholics was contingent on a firm commitment to Catholic beliefs and an internal positioning that accepts traditional church structures. The document described the Catholic identity of the movement as follows:

- We are faithful Catholics in communion with the universal Catholic Church.
- We love and support our church and believe what it professes.
- We accept the teaching authority of our church, including the traditional role of the bishops and the pope.
- We will work with our bishops, clergy, and other members to strengthen unity and human moral integrity in our church.

Thus, even while the movement ignited renewed lay empowerment among Catholics, VOTF participants nonetheless understood their Catholic identity as existing in close relation to the traditional structures and leadership of the institutional church.

Also promulgating an institutionally aligned identity, VOTF participants and leaders readily described VOTF using modifiers such as "mainstream" or "centrist":

We're mainstream, in the sense that we want to stay within the church and we want to cause the church to grow in a loving, sincere, spiritual way with the blueprint of Vatican II. We're not extremists, I don't think, in either direction.

We're centrist. And we're committed to that. Even though from time to time, each of us has extreme opinions about any given issue—we still want to express it in a centrist way. Because it's not about you coming around to my point of view. It's, can you see it from this perspective, and appreciate that something needs to be changed because of this. You can't do that if you're coming from either extreme.

Our purpose really is centrist. It's to effect change so that we can get involvement of the laity in a meaningful and constructive way.

Voice of the Faithful participants did not necessarily equate mainstream Catholic with a moderate theological perspective, nor full acceptance of church teachings. Many instead attributed the mainstream approach itself to one of questioning and critical thinking, done in faith. If the majority of Catholics are not in line with all of the church's teachings, some participants reasoned, then VOTF must be mainstream:

I don't know what [mainstream] means, but I think that people I know that are involved, they're truly Catholics, they're not just people that have some Catholic identity, but basically they believe the Catholic faith, although certain elements of it may not be important to them, and they may wonder about them. But it doesn't necessarily mean that they accept all the teachings.

It has something to do with this fundamental question of what it means to be a faith-filled person. There is a vocal group of people within the church who say no, if you're gonna call yourself Catholic, the primary responsibility you have is to follow every order that the bishop says. That's not the way I conceive of Catholicism. To me, that's not Catholicism.

Some members drew specific lines around which Catholic teachings they viewed as acceptable and which should change:

I don't think most mainstream Catholics are in agreement with all of the church teachings. I guess maybe I'd like to call myself an informed Catholic. Or a conscience-driven Catholic. Somebody who's—I reflect a lot on these issues. And where the church is, from my perspective, where the teachings are correct and just, like on the death penalty, I totally support that. The area of sexuality, I'm sorry, they're screwed up. They really are. And I think it comes out of their own being out of touch with sexuality. Because they're not, you know, none of them are allowed legal sex!

This flexible definition of the meaning of Catholic identity is largely consistent with the ways that average Catholics view religious commitment, particularly Catholics in the United States. A 2005 poll, for example, found that two-thirds or more of self-identifying Catholics agreed that you could still be a good Catholic without going to church every Sunday or obeying church teachings on divorce or birth control (Hoge 2005). Indeed, denominations that permit ideological slack may be better able to absorb dissent (Sutton and Chaves 2004).

A malleable Catholic identity, however, made it difficult for movement outsiders and those in the church leadership to situate VOTF within more traditionalist views of Catholic teachings, which identify clear stances on many of these moral issues. If faithfulness equates to orthodoxy, then VOTF did not, at least through its membership, consistently portray a voice of the faithful.[3] The collective Catholic identity VOTF espoused invited a more natural alliance with progressively minded, pro-change Catholics.

Especially problematic in forging a mainstream Catholic identity was ambiguity surrounding the VOTF goal of advocating for "structural change" within the church. Inconsistency and uncertainty in defining this goal contributed to resistance on the part of more conservative Catholics to participate in VOTF functions. Critics balked at the notion of a mainstream or centrist Catholic identity that could reconcile criticism of church structure, particularly the role of the hierarchy. One conservative Catholic group suggested that

> As for VOTF, if it is the mainstream group it says it is, they should stop attacking the hierarchical structure of the church. They should at least invite speakers that reflect the teachings of the church.[4]

This notion was also reflected in Newark Archbishop John Myers' open letter banning VOTF, in which he accused the group of having an underlying mission to "openly attack the Catholic hierarchy."

Cognizant of the need to reach out to Catholics across the spectrum, VOTF leaders extended invitations on multiple occasions to host speakers who were known for advocating traditionalist approaches to Catholicism. Organizers of the first VOTF Convention in July 2002, for example, attempted, with little success, to recruit known conservative keynote speakers. The primary recruiter for the convention recalled his experience in trying to secure the participation of conservatives:

> I was in charge of the program for the July conference in 2002. I called a bunch of people who were known to be conservatives. None

wanted to get near it! They had all sorts of excuses. Yeah, we only had two months, but this was going to be an event! [One] said, "Oh, I know all about VOTF." I had to bite my tongue and say, "You don't know a darn thing about VOTF! We hardly know about ourselves! We just know that we see injustice, and we want it fixed." But, to this day, it's hard to get the conservatives, the traditionalists—call them what you will—to get interested in any reform of the church.

A few national VOTF leaders acknowledged early mistakes in this realm, one admitting that the organization had done "a horrifically poor job of reaching out to conservatives." Some came to realize that the movement, by its very reform nature, would never attract conservative Catholics:

> The conservatives, as much as we try, are always going to be in a minority. Because what we are calling for is in itself progressive. Even if we steer clear of all the doctrinal, theological issues, the fact that the laity can and should have a voice, that's progressive in and of itself. And you cut out a whole segment of the population when you assert that.

Desiring to project a middle ground for Catholicism, VOTF mounted a defense on the idea that administrative or structural functions of the church could be separated from doctrinal ones. The movement aimed not to alter church teachings, but church operations; faith, in effect, could be separated from form. The practice mirrored American Catholics' documented tendency to "compartmentalize the teaching of the church hierarchy from participation in the doctrinal and communal tradition" (Dillon 1999). By rationalizing the separation of their Catholic faith from the structure of their church, VOTF participants could be faithful, practicing Catholics while simultaneously working to change the church's operational failings.

This dichotomous view of Catholicism was evident in members' descriptions:

> VOTF, laypeople are not questioning whether Jesus was the son of God. We're not questioning salvation and the gift of faith. We are simply saying that the church, that the *structure* of the church doesn't serve its people well!

> I think when it comes to real church doctrine, I'm a fairly orthodox person. I really am. But you gotta separate church doctrine from church behavior and church governance and church this and church

> that . . . When it comes to doctrine, read the creed. I go with that. I
> think all that's very important.
>
> Democratic terminology isn't necessarily wrong, in terms of the
> vision around guidance, governance, or temporal issues that involve
> the church. Very different from doctrinal issues, no matter how
> they—the bishops—try to pretend that they're inseparable. Oh yes,
> they are separable. Plenty of churches separate doctrine from
> governance, and have no problem doing it, and have laypeople very
> active.
>
> We're not interested in changing the doctrine. We don't want to get
> into that morass. What we want to do is open up the church to
> greater lay participation, and eventually get at the decision making.
> Not to take over the church. Where it's an administrative thing, there
> should be room for laity with administrative expertise. It's not magic.

In this way, members made conscious efforts to identify separate spheres within the church: the sphere of doctrine or faith and the sphere of structure or administration.[5]

Voice of the Faithful made numerous intentional and public attempts to separate its movement goals from "doctrinal" issues. Leaders stated publicly that the realm of their intended reform did not reach doctrine; they were Catholics who were faithful to church teachings. The movement's "Statement of Who We Are" included a stated belief in what the church professed, union with the universal Catholic Church, and acceptance of the teaching authority of the church and traditional roles of the bishops and pope. VOTF affiliate brochures described movement participants as "faith-filled Catholics who for years have served and are still serving as the heart of our parishes," who "serve as Eucharistic Ministers at Mass" or "sing in the choir."

Despite these efforts, several bishops banned VOTF on the premise that the movement was not authentically Catholic nor justified in its collective mobilization for change. Pope John Paul II's 1993 papal encyclical "Veritatis Spendor" (The Splendor of Truth) empowered bishops to make such claims on the authenticity of Catholic organizations:

> A particular responsibility is incumbent upon Bishops with regard to
> *Catholic institutions*. Whether these are agencies for the pastoral care
> of the family or for social work, or institutions dedicated to teaching
> or health care, Bishops can canonically erect and recognize these
> structures and delegate certain responsibilities to them. Nevertheless,

Bishops are never relieved of their own personal obligations. It falls
to them, in communion with the Holy See, both to grant the title
"Catholic" to Church-related schools, universities, health-care
facilities and counseling services, and, in cases of a serious failure to
live up to that title, to take it away. (no. 116)

As such, bishops are charged with the power to singularly classify and regulate
that which is legitimately "Catholic."

The banning of VOTF from meeting on church property in several dioceses
led participants to further emphasize the legitimacy of their Catholic identity
and right to gather as laity. Responding to the ban, three Catholic theologians
drafted a petition entitled "Voice of the Faithful has the Right to Exist." For
justification, the petition drew upon excerpts from church documents approved
at the Second Vatican Council that spoke to the role of the laity. The petition
concluded with the following:

Thus, we fully support the right and responsibility of Voice of the
Faithful to meet in prayerful discernment of the signs of the times,
and to present to the hierarchy for confirmation and implementation
what their sense of faith requires them to voice.

Sixty theologians signed the petition, which was subsequently posted online
to accompany VOTF's "Statement of Who We Are." Individual members
presented these materials as justification to their local priests and bishops,
leading in one instance to the reversal of a diocesan ban on VOTF. Often,
though, as one VOTF leader put it,

the reaction in general was a certain openness to talking to them
about it, but a real healthy skepticism or concern that this wasn't a
group of well-meaning Catholics. And frankly, you know, many
members of VOTF, we've shot ourselves in the foot, by things we've
said or done.

Other moments in the movement's development also introduced public
conversations about how Catholic—or what brand of Catholic—VOTF really
was. The inclusion of a speaker with prochoice ties at the first VOTF convention in July 2002, for example, did not evoke contention until news of the woman's opposition to Catholic teaching on abortion sparked public attention in the
days after the convention. A VOTF conference organizer recalled the event:

One of the people who was chosen to speak at the conference . . . she
was the expert on child abuse. But she also had worked on sex
education programs in the schools or other things. And boy, Voice

was just excoriated for having invited her. Even though we had instructed her, "Don't go near some of those issues." And she gave an excellent presentation. On what she'd been asked to do. And she was hung out to dry! And so was Voice, for having invited her! So, we weren't careful enough. And yet, it was a very professional thing.

Voice of the Faithful challengers pointed to this event as further evidence that VOTF did not have an authentically "Catholic" agenda. The conservative Catholic *Crisis Magazine* subsequently referred to the group as "a wolf in sheep's clothing" (e-letter 8.8.02).

These and other moments gave fodder to challengers of the movement, many of whom were themselves Catholic and did not want VOTF speaking on their behalf. A website entitled "Faithful Voice" existed to counter the efforts and legitimacy of VOTF in its representation of all lay Catholics. The site's stated purpose was "to expose the underpinnings of VOTF" and, as such, it encouraged visitors to print out the Web page explaining this to show their pastors as well as friends who had joined VOTF.

Public communications surrounding VOTF's Catholic identity reinforced the notion that achieving collective identity is not only an internal negotiation, but also a very public endeavor (see Gamson 1997). VOTF encountered public opposition in the form of critiques from church hierarchy and questions regarding the authenticity of the movement's religiosity. Public identity work created boundaries around an acceptable Catholic identity for the movement.

This identity work also played out in VOTF's decisions regarding whether or not to affiliate with other existing Catholic organizations. Cognizant of the risk in public perception surrounding VOTF's identity, the movement took lengths to avoid close association with existing movements of progressive or liberal Catholics, as seen in some affiliates' distancing from organizations such as SNAP. Any movement's public communication surrounding "who we are" will also include negotiations around who the movement is *not*. Although many VOTF members had at one time or another belonged to other Catholic reform groups, leaders made a conscious decision to distance VOTF from other groups, avoiding collaboration and the risk of jeopardizing their intended mainstream identification. One member described this identity negotiation and risk calculation as follows:

> One of the practical issues we've struggled with is, as a voice, do we form coalitions with other Catholic groups? Call to Action, Future Church, Opus Dei, whatever. Across the political spectrum. And I think the wisdom has been that they've all been in existence for a long period of time. Their identity is clearer. We're still working to try

to be clear about who *we* are and what we stand for. And so, it's more important for us to keep working on, everyday, on being a clear and reasoned voice. Will we form coalitions somewhere in the future? Maybe. I think that there will come a time when the leadership in this organization will say the time is right to do that. But, I think this is not the time to do that.

Some VOTF members critiqued groups like Call to Action for being too broad in focus and thereby diluting their agenda. Despite its 1976 inception as a combined bishop/lay response to Pope Paul VI's plea to create a more just world, Call to Action's image had developed into the poster of Catholic liberalism, its efforts largely marginalized with time. Even some in VOTF who supported the Call to Action movement admitted that avoiding collaboration might stave off a similar fate for VOTF, at least in its formative stages.[6]

Not all members agreed with this approach, however; a few voiced their distress over VOTF's hesitancy to even consult with other groups more experienced in targeting the church, including Call to Action:

There was this idea that we don't need Call to Action. We're bigger and more important than they are. Well, guess what? Call to Action has about as many members as we do. They have a budget that's twice as large as ours. And they have a convention that's nationally known every year that attracts thousands and thousands of visitors . . . My philosophy, my perspective, was learn from others. They're our friends. We're reforming the Catholic Church with them. We shouldn't be competing with them. We're of the same church.

That has become an issue, as to who you go to bed with. Do you want to go to bed with Call to Action? Or Future Church? Because they've got those "hot button" issues. But really, all of those organizations are concerned about the life of the church. It's how you solve the problems. Somehow, there could be collaboration.

These boundary debates also resonated on the affiliate level, where VOTF affiliates came to different conclusions regarding their association with SNAP, as described previously. Even within the VOTF movement, then, members constructed classification schemes for who might be categorized as authentically Catholic and what identities were unfit for mobilization within the intrainstitutional context of the Catholic Church.

Despite VOTF's public efforts to establish space for change in structure that did not touch the sphere of doctrine or faith, the movement encountered cultural and historical resistance to this separation of faith and form. Indeed, defining distinct spheres for doctrine and administration contradicted a Catholic history that has long embodied a marriage of the two. The intersection of faith and form had inflamed even the Protestant Reformation of 1545.

Catholic teaching conveys a reliance on scripture as well as tradition, which includes the authority of the bishops. The *Catechism of the Catholic Church* describes the compulsory union as follows:

> Sacred Tradition and Sacred Scripture, then, are bound closely
> together and communicate one with the other. For both of them,
> flowing out from the same divine well-spring, come together in some
> fashion to form one thing and move towards the same goal. (no. 80)

In VOTF's attempt to change one sphere without touching the other, the movement confronted an entanglement of both. Their challenge of one was interpreted as an affront on the other.

One participant shared his frustration with the resistance he faced convincing others that VOTF did not intend to change doctrine:

> We're not trying to change doctrine, we're just trying to change the
> way the church operates. Man, that just causes such an uproar! "Oh,
> you can't change the church! The church hasn't changed for 1500
> years! Yada yada yada." And it's hard to make 'em believe that.

Given the very nature of the Catholic religion and culture, separating doctrine and structure was difficult to achieve within the movement context. Theological justification accompanied the administrative operations of the church.

The Complexity of Catholic Identity

Struggles surrounding collective identity within VOTF raise significant implications for the very meaning of being Catholic. In contrast to an emphasis on individualism within Protestantism, the Catholic Church has preserved more authority over the authenticity of religious identity through its emphasis on community, structure, and tradition. The church has the power to baptize and to excommunicate; its leaders are in the position to make public assertions regarding the legitimacy of Catholic expression and access to spiritual goods. Even though individual religiosity among Catholics varies substantially, the organized, institutionalized patterns of Catholicism retain a considerable role in constructing the meaning of being Catholic. Structure matters, especially when forging collective identities tied to the very structure one is trying to change.

By attempting to separate their faith (belief, doctrine) from its form (the structure of the church), VOTF participants were accused of not being truly Catholic. They could not seek change in one arena without the perception of a threat to the other. VOTF's chosen intrainstitutional positioning meant that they could not separate the two spheres and remain legitimately Catholic. In a sense, their decision to act from within the church undermined their very efforts at change; they struggled to find a middle ground where they could be both Catholic and critical of the church. The movement emerged as a voice for lay Catholics in the midst of a crisis in the church. To subsequently establish a message that the problem was in structure—not in lived Catholicism or belief—conveyed that their identity as lay Catholics might in fact be irrelevant. And if their identity (and authority) as lay Catholics was irrelevant, then so, too, was their message regarding church structure.

Contention over religious identity among adherents is not a uniquely Catholic phenomenon. Muslim American women have used clothing (especially the hijab) to project an authentic and autonomous religious identity (see, e.g., Williams and Vashi 2007). Within Judaism, identity boundaries are fuzzy for those who claim either a Jewish religious identity or a Jewish ethnic identity, but not both.[7] Examining Jews and Buddhists in the United States, Cadge and Davidman (2006) concluded that religious identities were a product of both ascription and achievement. Central to their study, participants' religious self-identities were "individuals' own senses of personal membership, rather than external recognition of membership by others" (p. 36).

Here, though, is a key difference in conceptualizing religious identity among adherents who are *also* acting to change their religion. For VOTF, their own self-identification as Catholic mattered just as much as how others defined them. In order to enact change, VOTF participants had to (on the basis on their own intrainstitutional positioning) be seen as authentically Catholic. Movement outcomes, visualized as structural changes within the church leading to greater participation among laypeople in decision making, were tied to a shared acceptance of who is Catholic and who is allowed to participate. Participating in a religious IISM involved extensive identity work for movement participants. Through interactions within the institution, VOTF participants had to "do" their religion in a way that convinced others that they were indeed authentically Catholic. Religion, therefore, is an ongoing performance accomplished by movement actors, in much the same way that gender and other identities are performed.[8]

This was, in a sense, a catch-22 for VOTF. They had to be Catholic in order to move from within, but as soon as they moved for change, they were accused of no longer being legitimately Catholic or acting in the best interest of the church. The movement was therefore pushed from independence to isomorphism.[9] As the next chapter details, replicating the existing institutional structure through a shared cultural meaning system consequently became the only conceivable "Catholic" pathway to advocate for change.

Conclusion

Beyond the demographic consequences of VOTF's membership, the movement's collective identity was deeply embedded in participants' Catholic commitment. This religious meaning system, so engrained in the culture of the movement, substantially shaped the discourse, structure, and tactics of VOTF. Moreover, by claiming both a Catholic and change-oriented identity, the movement carved out a powerful space within which lay Catholics could reenvision the very meaning of being faithful to and active in the church.

Exemplifying this, one VOTF participant recounted a conversation with his pastor regarding his affiliate's lobbying efforts to change the statute of limitations for abuse accusations. The pastor's reaction made it clear that this was a new and unusual way of expressing one's Catholic commitment:

> It was quite easy to refute every one of [the pastor's] reasons. He seemed a little surprised that I was even "reasoning" against the bishop. It was almost as if he never thought to question any of the reasons given to him—he just accepted them. When I showed him there was a different way to look at it, he seemed surprised. Not surprised at what I said, but more at the mere fact that I was doing it.

And another, in summarizing the efforts of the movement, "We're trying to be Catholic without being sheep."

Through VOTF, participants embraced a Catholic identity that could accommodate both faithful commitment and simultaneous critique, or what Leming (2006) has called "religious agency." It challenged the "pray-pay-obey" model so many VOTF activists described as having been a part of their faith. In so doing, VOTF intensified the question of who and what constitutes an authentic or mainstream Catholic identity. In their effort to assert their legitimacy as concerned and faithful lay Catholics who had rights and ownership within the church, VOTF participants were delegitimized and forced to prove their authority as well as their authenticity within the Catholic Church. Movement outsiders subjected participants' religious values to litmus tests and questions of orthodoxy. The movement's collective identity was constructed and deconstructed as the group encountered challenges and dominant authority structures (see Gamson 1997; Taylor and Whittier 1992).[10] As Robnett (2002) describes:

> External events and institutions directly affect how participants see their position, the possibilities and limits of change, and the dilemmas they face. Internal attempts to confront such events shape changing collective identities. (p. 268)

Participants negotiated VOTF's collective identity in light of external challenges to it.

Consequently, Catholics active in VOTF had to "do" religion consciously and publically. Even when trying to separate faith from form, they encountered resistance from others less willing to accept a Catholic identity that drew this line. The driving motivation of VOTF to be seen as Catholics faithful to the church would substantially inform organizational structure, discourse, and tactics in the movement. The next chapter traces the ways in which VOTF's intrainstitutional positioning, closely shaping movement culture, influenced the form that the movement took along with the language it used to convey its message of change.

7

The Salience of Culture

The culture of VOTF, closely shaped by the culture of the Catholic Church, mattered substantially for the discourse, form, and tactics that the movement employed. While scholars of social movements have emphasized the important role of structure in shaping movement action, IISMs (and especially religious ones) require that we be more attuned to the important role that *culture* plays in shaping a movement and its outcomes. Seen in this way, religion emerges as not only a source of resources, including potential members, finances, and leadership, but also, significantly, as a *cultural code* for movement behavior. It is within the intrainstitutional context of the church that "distinctions made by individual social actors are translated into social boundaries" and "where classification systems are anchored and infused with material consequences" (Armstrong and Bernstein 2008:83). The meaning system of the institution, so integral to the identity of movement participants, becomes embedded in the movement itself. VOTF's Catholic culture, in tandem with its desire to manifest a Catholic identity, was consequential for the shape of the movement as a whole.

The cultural code of Catholicism provided a map for VOTF participants with which to navigate as they sought to make changes within the institution of the Catholic Church. In drawing from the "cultural toolkit" (Swidler 1986) of the Catholic Church, VOTF shared tools with the very authority figures they contested. Behavioral norms were internalized, at times emerging as nearly invisible to movement actors. The culture of Catholicism embraced by VOTF participants provided both shape and boundaries to the movement's discourse, form, and tactics. Consequently the movement would both replicate and rescind the very institution it was trying to change, as evidenced by the discussion of movement discourse, form, and tactics in this chapter and the next.

An Adopted Movement Discourse

The institutional context within which VOTF operated offered the movement a preexisting set of Catholic norms, language, and symbols upon which participants could draw to legitimate their position in known terms. Essential in forming a movement discourse was convincing the church hierarchy that participants were faithful Catholics committed to the church, not harboring secret agendas or promoting doctrinal dissent. Using a familiar meaning system, including phrasing, references, and symbols, would make the movement's aims understandable to church leaders and other Catholics. Religious movements frequently mobilize cultural resources such as these to frame the movement agenda in terms that both outsiders and insiders to the movement can understand (Williams 1995; Williams and Kubal 1999).

Among the resources offered by the Catholic institutional context were religious texts (such as the Code of Canon Law, the documents of the Second Vatican Council, and writings by popes and bishops) and theological terminology (in which the "Holy Spirit" is understandable as an inspiration for action). Such material and discursive resources lent intelligibility, legitimacy, and moral authority to the movement. Although VOTF participants varied in their ability to strategically use the more theological language proffered by Catholicism, the institutional context of the church supplied the movement with a plethora of discursive resources that VOTF appropriated for its movement goals. One VOTF leader shared that although he "didn't have the church-speak that I needed," others in the movement were very familiar with a theologically based lexicon and therefore "able to speak in ways that have the potential to be less easily dismissed" by church leaders.

For example, the life of Jesus and character of the early church were frequently cited by movement participants as authenticating forces for renewal: the premise upon which the Catholic Church was built had been subsumed by an unaccountable power system. Accordingly VOTF participants presented the full participation of the laity as a reclamation of Jesus' original intent for his church. Comments made by VOTF participants displayed the intensity of this connection to Jesus and early Christianity, even claiming Jesus himself to be among the laity of the church:

> If you go back to early Christianity and you start thinking about, "Exactly what did Jesus intend, teaching his followers the Way?" Jesus used to lash out at the religious establishment of his time. So, where would Jesus be in all this if he came back? I feel almost certain that Jesus would identify himself as a layperson. I don't think he would identify himself as a priest. I really don't.

> Well, in Jesus' time, it was a very equal society. This feudal system that we've got is never what we, is not what Christ established. It was man-made. And it's harmful. It's harmful to people.

> [The church] has to be changed. We remember Jesus started this; can we do what Jesus said? I think we got away from that. There were only supposed to be two rules: love God, and love your neighbor.

The Gospel story of Jesus' own admonishment of church structures also offered validation for VOTF's reform demands.

Drawing from the cultural meaning system of Catholicism and the early church, the movement described its own authority in religiously grounded terms. A founding member of VOTF, whose degree in divinity led her to a career in spiritual counseling, equated the original authority of VOTF to a "spiritual authority." She described how this legitimacy based in spirituality was fundamental to VOTF's early development:

> That [first gathering] was our original sense of legitimacy. And authority. Because it was a highly charged spiritual movement. There was a palpable presence of what we would call the Holy Spirit . . . I, as a professional, saw [those present] gaining legitimacy and authority from their personal religious experience.

By acting out of faith-based motives, VOTF members found both reason and courage to claim authority within their religious institutional space. The initial gathering of laity in the basement of St. John the Evangelist mobilized around a sense of empowerment to save their church through their stated commitment to it.

In this way, the widely publicized scandal of abuse and its cover-up was itself among the cultural resources contributing to the emergence of the VOTF movement. Public accounts of abuse created a window of opportunity for change within the church; lay Catholics consequently carved out a space to mobilize around already-brewing critiques of church structure. Public questioning of church leaders by those both in and out of the movement invited a recalculation of authority and legitimacy: attention shifted from a power-centralized, hierarchical structure to an increasingly vocal group of lay Catholics emerging from the pews who were outraged at the behavior of authority figures in the church. Movement discourse tapped into an authority based in spirituality and the quest for a more perfect church. The scandal itself, therefore, was an essential source of legitimacy for VOTF.

Voice of the Faithful intentionally made efforts to increase its receptivity by deploying a movement discourse both understandable and acceptable to church leaders and the institutional context within which it operated. Participants recognized the need to moderate their message so that they would be perceived as representing a reasoned lay voice committed to the church. One member described this approach:

> Whenever we speak, we speak with a very moderate, respectful voice
> that, every once in a while, will have an influence. As long as we
> continue to do that, we're not going to be perceived as a radical group
> or a fringe group or anything like that.

Language, particularly a lexicon familiar among Catholic laity and leaders, was an important tool for the movement to convey movement goals.

The close discursive connections between VOTF and the culture of the Catholic Church became particularly evident when VOTF leaders in Boston hired a non-Catholic to train affiliate leaders for direct action initiatives. Jenna was both an outsider to the movement and an outsider to the Catholic faith, not identifying as Catholic herself. Although most VOTF members Jenna encountered did not perceive this to be a problem, her non-Catholic identity nonetheless did not go unnoticed, as one participant noted:

> [Jenna's] not Catholic, which is in many ways irrelevant. But it's
> relevant in that she's not in the movement. She's not a Voice of the
> Faithful person, really.

Movement participants clearly drew lines between insiders and outsiders to Catholic culture. Jenna herself reflected on moments in which her non-Catholic identification limited her acceptance by movement participants:

> There have been a few instances where people have refused to work
> with me or have refused to join the movement because I have owned
> the fact that I am not Catholic. That was a choice on my part, to
> practice transparency. I wouldn't want it to come out later from

somebody else that I had come and pretended to be a Catholic when I wasn't. And so, that's a choice I've made. For the most part, it's been fine. But there definitely are specific people I can point to that it has affected them negatively.

The Catholic collective identity of the movement created boundaries between "us" and "them"; Jenna is here defined as not being a part of "us," given her non-Catholic identity. Despite being labeled "not a Voice of the Faithful person," leaders deemphasized Jenna's religious identity, instead accentuating her skills in organizing.

Where Jenna's non-Catholic identity emerged more noticeably was in the discursive accommodations she made in order to work within a Catholic institutional setting. As affiliates had already been learning, compromises and adjustments accompanied VOTF's desire to remain within the church and to be seen as legitimate, faithful Catholics. Part of this adjustment involved translating movement aims into the lexicon of the institutional church. One leader in VOTF's national office described the initial difficulty Jenna encountered when beginning to articulate the goals of her grassroots organizing initiative for VOTF:

> I remember when [Jenna] first came into the office. The early language of the training program read, "The purpose of this is to change the power dynamic in the church." I said, "That is the worst possible language we could use!" For two reasons. It's not in the lexicon, or it's not part of the language of the church. It's not part of Vatican II. And number two, why don't we just put a bulls-eye on our back? And let all the bishops take shots? It's gonna inflame every concern about hidden agenda. And I said, ultimately, that may be a result. But why not say, "The purpose of our training is to teach people how to take responsibility for the church."

Essential to Jenna's ability to work with the movement and within the church was adapting her language of organizing to the boundaries of her new cultural and institutional context.

Accordingly, Jenna found ways to adapt her own set of professional tools to fit with the cultural toolkit familiar to the movement. She spoke of how this was a central component to her work with VOTF:

> That's been a real fun challenge for me to translate all of these secular concepts of organizing into a faith-based context. And not only to change verbiage, which is one thing, but taking a very secular definition of organizing and making it a VOTF definition of

organizing. How to integrate prayer. So, making sure to integrate in our training book, in the training itself, and in what we're recommending for people—periods of prayer and discernment to figure out exactly what strategy is in alignment with the values we want to be practicing.

Jenna shifted her language and very definition of social change to accommodate the religious institutional context of VOTF. The definition of VOTF's grassroots organizing she developed as a result, reflecting the culture of the church, read as follows:

The process of bringing laity together through building relationships and developing leaders, to use our unified power to advance the Gospel mission of Christ's Church by altering the power differential among members of the hierarchy, clergy, and laity.

While the component of a power differential remained, it was now also embedded within a clearly religious framework.

An embedded Catholic culture clearly infused the discourse of VOTF as a social movement. A shared set of language and movement tools, at times recognized and at times nearly invisible, allowed movement participants to translate their message into one easily understood by church leaders. Culture reverberated both strategically and powerfully, absorbed into the movement such that institutional affiliation was both apparent and authenticated.

An Adopted Movement Form

In addition to the discursive adaptations that the movement made as a result of its intrainstitutional positioning within the Catholic Church, VOTF also took on an organizational form that both reflected and rejected that of the church. Again, given the overlap in meaning systems, identity, and the cultural toolkit available to movement participants, VOTF in time began to mirror the governance, leadership, and structural elements of the very target of its reform.

Given the grassroots nature of the movement, a nationally cohesive governance system emerged slowly for VOTF. Fueled by media attention on the abuse crisis, membership in the movement increased in 2002 and 2003. By mid-2003, VOTF leaders reported 181 affiliates in forty-one states. VOTF itself ranked fifth in frequency among religion news stories in 2002[1] and was often mentioned within the context of scandal-related stories that continued to dominate religion news in subsequent years. Amid its rapid growth, VOTF had been slow to implement an effective and agreed-upon system to manage the influx of movement participants and affiliates. A comprehensive organizational structure had not been foremost in the minds of national leaders while in the whirlwind of the nascent movement, as one Boston leader describes: "In the early days, the pure emotional response and need to support survivors and address the underlying issues of secrecy and authoritarianism and arrogance was so strong that I don't think anything could have broken us up." Although power was "generated from the grassroots," described another leader, this did not "serve the organization well, in many respects, because no one knows where the buck stops."

It had also been difficult for early activists based in Boston to excise themselves from the movement's definitively Boston focus. One VOTF leader described Boston, with its 362 Catholic parishes and two million plus Catholics in 2002, as "the crucible of the Catholic Church in the U.S.A." The city had emerged as the epicenter of the crisis, and the most logical place to initiate a lay response. Some 13,000 of the 25,000 members VOTF claimed in late 2002 (52 percent) lived in Massachusetts. VOTF's board, officers, and staff consisted entirely of individuals living in close proximity to Boston. The myopia was also understandable given the cascade of news and events related to the scandal that emerged out of their community. An eventful 2002 had concluded with the resignation of Boston's Cardinal Bernard Law. National VOTF leaders were wary to take their focus off the countless fires flaming in their immediate surroundings.

Moreover, to many Boston VOTF supporters, the movement continued the city's tradition of advocating for representation in the face of authority. The proposal for the 2002 convention had even likened the VOTF mission to that of the Boston Tea Party, suggesting that Boston's solution for taxation without representation now be applied to the church. This sense of ownership was especially tangible for St. John the Evangelist founders; others hypothesized that the use of consensus in the early stages was a means to ensure the founders' influence over decision making. Although the ultimate goal was to impart far-reaching reform, the crux of power was clearly in the hands of Boston's lay Catholics.

The recognition that local efforts had indeed spawned a national movement necessitated a more systematic approach to leadership in the movement, along with meaningful engagement with regional Catholic cultures beyond Boston. VOTF had assigned a name and mission to an emergent national lay response to the crisis of abuse and leadership in the church; the movement could no longer be contained to or explained by the concerns of Bostonians alone. The movement faced the dubious task of institutionalizing, which O'Dea

(1961) characterizes as "the symbolic and organizational embodiments of the experience of the ultimate in less-than-ultimate forms and the concomitant embodiment of the sacred in profane structures," carrying with it the potential for "severe functional problems for religious institutions" (p. 31). In this task, VOTF's decisions regarding governance and organizational form were again embedded in the Catholic culture of the movement.

Efforts to structure VOTF's leadership were closely linked to the movement's Catholic identity, the cultural code of Catholicism, and VOTF's desired positioning within the institutional setting of the church. The heart of the VOTF mission ("to provide a prayerful voice, attentive to the Spirit, through which the Faithful can actively participate in the governance and guidance of the Catholic Church") tied directly to structures of leadership already in place within the church. Consequently the movement struggled to model open, accountable, and participatory leadership while remaining true to their intrainstitutional positioning. Intentionally critiquing the top-down, hierarchal, and nontransparent model they were protesting against in the church, VOTF sought to create more of an open, inverted triangle that could mobilize the substantial grassroots power of the movement.

For this reason, in its earliest days as a fledging movement meeting at St. John the Evangelist parish, VOTF founders operated under a model of 100 percent consensus. Everyone had veto power. Although consensus allowed the group to circumvent issues of hierarchy and representation, it was not a feasible model for a national movement. It had even fallen apart on the local level, when several hundred participants who gathered in April 2002 failed to come to unanimous agreement in requesting the resignation of Cardinal Law. One leader describes how this event shifted their leadership approach:

> Early on, there was an attempt to call for Cardinal Law's resignation, and it was out of almost a mob mentality at the meeting. People got just, you know, "This is a disaster and he's the leader, let's just throw, we should throw him out! Let's call for his resignation!" And when they took a vote on that at the meeting, there must have been several hundred people in the room. The vote was a couple of hundred to less than ten. We didn't reach consensus. Our first president tried to help us get to consensus and work with the ten or so people that weren't supportive of it, but could not achieve that consensus. So that was shelved. Out of that experience came an understanding that you're never going to have absolute consensus.

The stress of this meeting led the founding VOTF group to move to a consensus model requiring just two-thirds majority rather than unanimous agreement.

Nonetheless, beginning with unanimity was important in that it conveyed to lay Catholics that it was not necessary to, in the words of another leader, "conduct themselves in an autocratic, imperial fashion." Everyone's voice was heard. They were rescinding the leadership order of the targeted institution.

The election of officers, hiring of an executive director, and selection of a board of trustees reflected a similar avoidance of the hierarchical model evidenced in the larger church, along with a clear desire to assert VOTF's insider position. Officers were elected for short terms (not more than one year). An established board of trustees, originally called a steering committee, drew heavily from among members of the founding parish. Many trustees brought experience as insiders in the church hierarchy, having attended seminaries, served on diocesan committees and seminary boards, and held leadership positions in numerous Catholic nonprofit settings. One man explained his reasons for accepting the offer to serve as a trustee for VOTF:

> Part of the reason I got hooked is I had served briefly [in] the
> Archdiocese of Boston. I was hired and fired by Cardinal Law. And so
> I knew something about the inner workings of the Catholic Church
> from that experience in the archdiocese. Given my love for the
> church, my lifelong interest in the church—church has always been
> an important part of my life—and my interest in doing things of
> service at this stage of my career, VOTF fit in very nicely with what I
> was thinking about.

His preestablished relationships with Boston's church hierarchy were strategic in the movement's commitment to working within the church. Activists' familiarity with the tools of the institutional church could in turn be translated into tools to meet movement goals.

Another important appointment in VOTF leadership was given to a man with a history of working among pastoral and archdiocesan councils in Boston, whose experience had familiarized him with the inner workings of the institution. An outsider to the founding group at St. John's parish,[2] the new leader was described by one member as "classically management style" rather than a "rabble-rouser" who "wanted to go down that path of really challenging the authority of the hierarchy." Some expressed disappointment that VOTF did not establish a leadership more welcoming to confrontational protest strategies. Insider positioning mandated greater moderation in leadership choices.

Wanting to avoid replication of the inaccessible and unaccountable leadership in the church, the movement encountered difficulty in securing an effective alternative leadership model. Some grew frustrated having to channel energy into starting just another organization rather than making headway toward the goals of the growing movement. One leader spoke of the difficulty she faced in formalizing bylaws for VOTF during the early stages:

> We ran into a brick wall, in that [the founding chairperson] simply did not permit the bylaws to come to the agenda of the board. He is not bureaucratic. He didn't want to get bogged in. He was a visionary leader, as opposed to a nuts-and-bolts, create-an-infrastructure leader. Anyway, we ended up, because we had to have them to incorporate, we ended up just getting boilerplate, very skeletal bylaws from your average nonprofit in Massachusetts.

The process again reflected VOTF's commitment to an inverted triangle of grassroots empowerment, along with their opposition to an overly bureaucratized leadership structure in the church.

Because of a lack of leadership structure, the movement was also stifled in its ability to make progress nationally. It was difficult to even gain a sense of just how many people had joined VOTF or participated in VOTF events. A minimally staffed "National Parish Voice Office" managed information from an influx of existing and emerging affiliates. The Newton, Massachusetts-based staff approximated a count of VOTF members based on the number of individuals who signed onto a national e-mail list (regardless of their actual level of participation). This number quickly grew to 19,000 in mid-2002 and 25,000 in late 2002 before reaching a seemingly intractable plateau of 30,000 in mid-2003. Not all affiliate membership lists were shared or added to the national list, however, and a large constituency supported the cause or attended events without officially "joining." It was also not uncommon for married couples to provide a single, shared e-mail address. Multiple attempts to input contact information for members throughout the country resulted in several unconsolidated databases. Thus hundreds—likely even thousands—of individuals may have been active in local VOTF affiliates or independently supportive of the movement but were not included in national membership counts.

Further preventing cohesive leadership for VOTF nationally was a "representative council" comprised of nonelected VOTF participants from affiliates throughout the country. VOTF's 2002–2003 annual report named 167 representative council members; its 2004 report named 292. The council, which was neither representative nor influential in movement decision making, also carried a Boston (or at least northeastern) focus, with little meaningful connection to affiliates nationally. The lack of clarity regarding who could and should legitimately represent VOTF led to situations such as that in Santa Barbara, where the local affiliate learned only through media reports that their area had a regional representative. Any suggestions introduced by the council lost their salience once passed through other independently governed structures of VOTF's leadership structure. The movement faced O'Dea's (1961) dilemma of administrative order in producing "an unwieldy organization with blocks and breakdowns in communication, overlapping of spheres of competence, and ambiguous definitions of authority and related functions" (p. 35). Although the diffusion of leadership did reflect the inverted triangle model originally envisioned, it also highlighted the elusiveness of a unified movement vision.

The rudimentary structure of governance approved in the earliest days by VOTF trustees and officers created tension and uncertainty at the top levels that reverberated subtly throughout the organization. A small national-level staff dealt with hundreds of inquiries from affiliates during every stage of development. As VOTF affiliates emerged throughout the country, local leaders clamored for stronger direction and agendas for action from the national office operating out of Massachusetts. Local leaders felt ignored; national leaders felt overwhelmed. One local affiliate member suggested that there had been "a failure at the national level to facilitate our existence as chapters."

Boston-based leaders had also anticipated that affiliates would develop at the parish level. This was not the case in most areas throughout the country, as many affiliates organized on a city or regional level. Diverse approaches among local affiliates highlighted differences in a so-called national agenda. According to VOTF National, any group would qualify as an affiliate "if its membership agrees by a two-thirds majority with the mission statement and goals of Voice of the Faithful." This statement opened up the possibility that a full third of any given affiliate might disagree with the VOTF mission statement and goals, the core of the movement's purpose.

Diffused and minimally defined governance produced uncertainty surrounding the degree to which the national leadership should direct individual affiliates. Given that VOTF had been founded to work toward ideals of greater democratic and participatory structures, a heavy-handed leadership within the movement could undermine the participatory aims they had for their church. It was also infeasible for national leaders, whose efforts were already spread thin, to take on the direct leadership of affiliates. Many leaders at the national level had envisioned lay Catholics everywhere being empowered—on their own—to locate arenas in which they could offer support and advocate change. The approach echoed the principle of subsidiarity infused within the culture of Catholicism that guides such organizations as Catholic Charities. This Catholic social teaching emphasizes the importance of addressing problems at the smallest, most localized level possible, thereby avoiding overcentralization and bureaucracy.

One Boston leader described her disbelief when affiliates began asking for direction:

> You know, people are like children. I've gone to give a talk in an
> affiliate meeting, and the first question after my talk would be, "Well,
> what can we do? We meet every week and we don't know what to do."
> In my life, I have never had that problem! What to do? Look around!
> If something doesn't exist, create it! So, we do all the work for people.
> That's the reality. People feel that they need directions. I think that's
> one of the things we can do: promote tried and true things that other
> affiliates have done, and the know-how to do it. And maybe from
> that, they'll get a little jumpstart and their own creativity will become
> evident later. With some people, I think we're just going to have to
> carry them.

Another leader from the National Parish Voice Office shared a similar sentiment, wanting affiliates to empower themselves while also acknowledging the need for shared direction and support:

> As a young organization, some of the officers . . . were resolute that
> the affiliates had to do things on their own. My belief is, that's where
> we want affiliates to be, but you need to build the infrastructure.
> People need to learn to crawl before they can walk. I can't tell you
> how many calls we would get from affiliates: "Can we do this? Is it
> okay for us to do this? We got called from the paper; what should
> we say?" You can't go back to that group and say, "Listen, you're on
> your own."

This leader's preferred response to affiliates was "You need to do the shoveling, most of it, yourself. But we're gonna give you a shovel. We're gonna show you how to shovel. And if you get tired, we can help you out a little bit."

The laissez-faire attitude of many in the national office ran counter to the cultural code of Catholicism most familiar to movement participants. Being active in the church meant following the leadership of the ordained, committing to traditions with centuries of practice. VOTF participants in local affiliates frequently felt as though they were on their own, without the direction they were so accustomed to. One member described the phenomenon as "typically Catholic": "As much as people want to have a collaborative environment, they also want to be led." The central mission of the VOTF movement to increase lay participation in the church found resistance in a Catholic culture of obedience.

It was in some ways paralyzing to the young movement: in VOTF National's desire to empower affiliates to do things on their own, using the ideas and abilities of their own members, less effort went toward building an infrastructure of support for implementing real reform on the local level. Serious governance issues caused internal rifts among movement leaders, with no firm standard for who was entrusted with final veto power. An external consultant hired in fall 2004 to assess the movement's organizational dynamics cited three main areas of strife within VOTF: 1) there was no agreed-upon, functioning governance structure; 2) there was disagreement over the strategic focus of the organization; and 3) there were growing tensions between the national office and the elected officers. Organizational choices intended to rescind the hierarchical model of the Catholic Church were accompanied by failures in movement leadership and national direction. Voice of the Faithful had, in many ways, replicated the very cultural characteristics of the institution whose leadership and accountability they were so dedicated to changing.

A Constraining Culture

Sociologists recognize that one of the powerful characteristics of culture is its ability to constrain behavior. Once individuals learn a certain mode of behavior, it becomes more difficult to imagine alternatives to that behavior (see, e.g., Gramsci 1990). Scholars of religion have identified this as one reason why an individual's parents' religious affiliation is a strong predictor of his or her own affiliation. Culture, embedded in the language and practice of everyday life, fosters enduring identities and commitments, and consequently an inertia toward the familiar.

The Catholic culture and collective identity of the movement clearly (while also implicitly) informed how VOTF constructed its discourse and form. It also constrained the movement, particularly given the boundaries presented by VOTF's intrainstitutional positioning. Participants shared most familiarity with the organizational form of the church, thus they looked to this institution in shaping the governance and behavior of their own intrainstitutional grassroots movement. While cultural constraints are especially evident in the movement's chosen tactical repertoire, discussed in more detail in the next chapter, they were also very much at play in the movement's discourse and form.

This constraining character of culture in IISMs leading to institutional replication was especially evident in the restructuring of the VOTF Representative Council. Given the governance problems that continued to plague VOTF, leaders decided to restructure the council to be more representative of affiliates. In the movement's first few years of operation, the council had developed in a rather unstructured manner, convened at first from only affiliates in the

Boston area. Although it grew to include more leaders throughout the country, the council's disorder and lack of definition in governing the movement decreased its ability to impact any real decision making. When its loosely defined membership peaked at nearly 300 members in 2004, participants at both local and national levels raised concerns about its ability to truly operate in a representative capacity.

Several members decried the lack of a representative voice for affiliates, especially ironic given the driving motivation of the VOTF movement to secure adequate lay representation. One leader described VOTF's insufficient governance structure as a major weakness in the movement:

> A real Achilles' heel of this movement is that we have no functional government structure. Because it grew up so quickly, and wanted to be very democratic and everyone represented, the organizational chart it is unlike anything you've ever seen. I mean, there are so many different committees and groups . . . it's not clear how they're linked. It's not clear who makes decisions, who has the final say, who has input. None of that is determined. And so, it's very difficult to create a national agenda. To move forward in any unified fashion.

Failings in governance were, as this member put it, the "gaping wound" of the movement. Another participant expressed similar sentiments, saying that the lack of an agreed-upon governance was causing great internal strife:

> VOTF itself is in a tremendous crisis. Set aside all of the external issues. Now look at it from the fishbowl, inside. Well, they've got the same conflicts! There is this tremendous reluctance to concede that anyone else has any authority . . . How do you run a 30,000 member organization without somebody being in charge?!

Rescinding, yet echoing the very culture of the church the movement sought to reinvent, VOTF had itself established a structure that was neither authoritative nor representative. It simultaneously reacted against a hierarchical structure while also failing to establish a voice for all. In one participant's mind, there persisted "such a taint of hierarchical model that the voices here just can't concede." The institutional positioning of the movement led in part to leaders' inability to find effective alternatives for managing membership.

Countering this, VOTF leaders decided to restructure the movement's regional structure to parallel that of the U.S. Catholic Church. The movement's fourteen regions would mirror the fourteen diocesan regions designated by the U.S. Conference of Catholic Bishops. This was designed to proportionately represent the distribution of the U.S. Catholic population as well as create direct action platforms to collaborate with and contest church leadership in every region. The restructured representative council consisted of an elected body of affiliate members from every U.S. region, going beyond the heavily Boston-focused original council. VOTF's president expressed enthusiasm for the change and optimism for the future:

> The creation of this national council was a very important milestone, substantively and symbolically. The felt need was to create something that was truly nationally representative. A true national voice . . . Symbolically, to make it clear that we have a council, we have nationally elected officers, and we're no longer the Boston–New England group that we once were.

The restructuring was pivotal in the movement's institutionalization, a shift from its disordered Boston center to a broader and more systematic movement for change.

The decision to mirror the diocesan structure of the church was strategic in that it signaled VOTF's continued desire to work within and alongside official church structures. One Boston leader spoke to the motivation behind this decision:

> A lot of our interactions—trying to work with the church—will take place on the local level, with the diocese. Therefore we need to organize ourselves to deal with the church as it exists locally. We can have a national voice, but a lot of things will happen on a local level, because [every diocese] is independent of the other . . . No one can tell a bishop what to do, other than the pope. And when the pope has 3,000 bishops reporting directly to him, that doesn't leave much room.

The number of representatives elected for each region depended upon the number of VOTF affiliates and members in that region. The region that included Massachusetts (as well as Maine, Vermont, New Hampshire, and Rhode Island) had the most representatives (five). A total of twenty-six positions opened for nominations. Representatives were to be active in a VOTF affiliate, make a good faith effort to represent members' interests, be committed to the VOTF mission, and facilitate communication among the regions and with VOTF National. Individuals would be elected for a two-year term.

Replicating the spatial arrangement of the church serves as a prime example of how the institution within which VOTF operated shaped the boundaries of the movement itself. In attempting to be aligned with the familiar structure of the church, VOTF had in essence again replicated the very institution it sought to change. The movement's desire to remain within and be recognized by the church consequently shaped the form the movement took.

In mirroring the governance structure of the church, some VOTF participants' comments echoed a similar critique to those leveled at governance in the Catholic Church as a whole. One woman expressed her reservations about the process:

> There was this vision of representation, which is wonderful. But it was representation without function. The functional part of it wasn't worked out in advance of these people getting elected. So, they got elected to something, and they're not even sure what they're doing! We have this sort of vague idea of they're going to be policymakers. Well, what does that mean? And how does that connect with the role of the officers? The board of trustees? These are very complicated questions that need to be answered before that group has any prayer of being a functional entity.

Questions also surfaced regarding the ability of the representative council to be truly representative. Movement governance included no mechanisms through which elected representatives could get input from members in their (often quite large) regions. Most were familiar with only the work of their own affiliate, in their own local area. Lost in the process was the "voice" element so central to the change orientation of VOTF.

Attempts to clarify lines of authority in the movement reflected a clear distancing from the hierarchical model of the church. Out of a desire to prioritize consensus, no governing body relinquished any power to another, as one leader explained:

> They've got it set up in such a way that neither group wants to concede that the other group has power. Has authority. They're proposing that each group—I can veto what you decide, and you can veto what I decide. So, it forces me now to have to work with you now to find a solution, and vice versa. Who's accountable to whom? . . . Can you imagine any entity operating like this?

Protesting the cultural code of authority modeled by the church, the movement struggled to envision or activate a representative, functioning alternative.

Conclusion

Embedded in the movement through shared collective identity and experience, the cultural code of Catholicism reverberated in VOTF participants' discursive practices and governance decisions. Culture provided a preexisting set of tools that internal activists could appropriate for movement goals. A shared institutional language and structure made change efforts more accessible and acceptable to church leaders. Culture operated as a common meaning system able to bridge extant authorities and movement aims.

In this way, culture is especially powerful in shaping IISMs. IISMs are positioned with a preexisting familiarity and access to the institution. They know the ropes, the rules of the game. They know the players, the lines of authority, the language, and the consequences for speaking out. This provides great advantage to IISM actors. Culture can soften differences and translate grievances. It helps activists skip many steps in learning the inner workings of the institution they are targeting for change.

Even while culture offers these many advantages to IISMs, it is also constraining. Participants feel most comfortable with the existing rules and tools of the institution; change efforts are therefore forced (perhaps imperceptibly) into extant institutional boundaries. An embedded cultural code can ultimately lead a movement to replicate the very shape of the institution it is seeking to change. The familiar guides movement discourse and form; alternatives are difficult to envision or enact. We see this in VOTF, as the movement ultimately took on a structural form that mimicked that of the church: strategic, yet also conjuring questions of how authority and representation can effectively operate simultaneously.

The next chapter follows the salience of culture into its most telling and constrained ground: movement tactics. VOTF, committed to the church and acting from within, ultimately made a number of tactical accommodations in order to be seen as Catholics and accepted among church leaders. These bounded decisions carried both strategic successes and, as with discourse and form, the risk of replicating the very institution they sought to change.

8

A Bounded Repertoire

Culture binds social movements.[1] For IISMs, tactical options for reaching movement goals are bound by the culture of the targeted institution. This can happen in myriad ways: the influence of the cultural code of institutional behavior (the "tools" available in the cultural toolkit), the limits presented by how authority traditionally operates in the institution, or the intense negotiations and identity politics dictating who qualifies as an authentic insider. Power operates differently in different institutional contexts; learning and knowing (perhaps intimately) how power operates in the targeted institution gives movement activists the ability to choose tactics that match and challenge the current power structure of the targeted institution. Participants already know the rules of the game, therefore they know better how to play the game or alter it to reach movement goals.

The institution will also provide institutionally specific expectations for what tactics are most and least acceptable. As Armstrong and Bernstein (2008) point out in describing a multi-institutional politics approach to social movements, "What counts as disruptive will thus depend on the rules of 'doing business' in any given institution" (p. 92). This is especially evident in religious institutions, where an IISM may embrace tactics less common or seemingly less aggressive that those chosen by other types of social movements. Moving within the institution changes the rules of the game; IISMs must adapt their tactical repertoire to match their institutional setting. Katzenstein (1998) found this in researching feminist activism within the Catholic Church, in which conferences, writings, and speeches were dominant movement tactics. Said Katzenstein (1998) of women's discursive activism within the church, "much of the work women activists do when they come together is discursive: rewriting through texts and symbolic acts their own understanding of themselves in relationship to both church and society" (p. 120). This, within the given institutional context, is a powerful and strategic repertoire of contention.

Voice of the Faithful, acting within the Catholic Church, provides copious illustrations of the ways in which IISMs are tactically bound by their institutional positioning. The cultural code of Catholicism, activists' internal positioning, and implicit rules of the game pushed the movement into creative and adopted tactical decisions. With some protest strategies out of the realm of possibility within their institutional context, VOTF tempered its tactical approach, appropriated extant strategic options to meet movement goals, and, in many ways, replicated the internal functioning of the Catholic Church.

Framing a Repertoire of Contention

Tactical decisions for the VOTF movement emerged out of the movement's three goals of supporting survivors of abuse, supporting priests of integrity, and advocating for structural change in the church. The exact meanings of these goals, particularly goal three, remained unclear to participants even two years into the movement, reflected here in one participant's comment:

> What are you going to do to support victims? The terms aren't
> defined. And the priests of integrity, well what's a priest of integrity?
> Define. I think it would be helpful for—certainly the church, for
> SNAP, for the laity, for the hierarchy, for everybody—if the terms
> were more clearly defined. I think maybe when VOTF got started,
> maybe they didn't know. Maybe they just knew that those were the
> things that needed to happen. And maybe they didn't know how to
> define it.

Ambiguous movement intentions had pivotal consequences for the movement's efforts to be seen as legitimate by church leaders; moreover, the ambiguity had provided church leaders with a reason to refuse dialogue with VOTF representatives and dismiss the movement as a legitimate participant in church decision making.

The persistent struggle highlights the intertwining of identity and tactical choices for IISMs. Formulating and actualizing goals engaged identity negotiations at every stage. The ways that the movement described what it did mattered nearly as much as its actions. Requests came in from participants nationwide for national leaders to offer a more forcefully stated definition of goals. Without strong national direction and leadership, individual leaders were left to apply their own interpretation to the broadly introduced goals, leading to significant variation in the movement's reputation and strategy.

This variation in interpretation mirrored the cultural characteristics of the church. In the minds of some VOTF participants, the subjective interpretation of goals by individual affiliates replicated the very behavior the movement was trying to counteract. Affiliates were, in a sense, mimicking diocesan leaders in their lack of openness and accountability, as one member suggested:

> [I]f you've got different chapters of VOTF defining the terms
> differently, then you're gonna have the same problem you've got in
> the church, with the different dioceses. Each bishop interprets things
> to his own . . . I mean, he's not supposed to, but he does. There has
> to be some kind of uniformity.

This frustration on the part of members revealed another cultural influence of the church on the movement: regional variation and localized decision making. Historical roots of Catholicism in the United States have long interacted with the literal and figurative topography of the nation's diverse regions.[2] Just as different bishops foster largely independent organizational cultures within their dioceses, so too did VOTF affiliate leaders create differing affiliate cultures of their own in response to diverse diocesan contexts.

Consequently some VOTF participants felt the urgency for a unified movement message, as one member articulated:

> We have to first of all agree that that is the message that all of us are
> together on. If we all decide that that is the message, then how do we
> positively get that out? Without it saying it means this agenda and
> that agenda? Because, what if somebody else wants to have another
> voice?

Connected to lingering governance issues, participants argued for greater consolidation and exercise of power within the movement such that tactical priorities would be clear and actionable.

Framing goal three, "to shape structural change within the Church," proved most challenging to align with VOTF's desired intrainstitutional positioning and authenticated Catholic identity. Participants stumbled over what might constitute the boundaries of this kind of reform:

> We were getting beat up by that . . . by, you know, the church leadership was saying, "Well, what do they mean by that?" So we had to say what we meant. And at the same time, we had to get an idea of the whole organization—what is the consensus? Which was very difficult. Because people were very angry. And they didn't want to listen to each other.

Goal three stifled the movement's efforts to consolidate its voice, gain legitimacy among church leaders, and move toward fruitful outcomes. Both insiders and outsiders to the movement wanted to know the limits to what VOTF was advocating. While the movement had been formed in response to the crisis of priests abusing children and the church's failed response, the goals of the movement clearly expanded beyond the support of survivors and of non-abusive priests. If the mission was to address underlying causes, how far could this go? Was abuse related to the celibacy of priests? The lack of ordained women? Sexual orientation? One participant describes the floundering reputation of VOTF resulting from a lack of clarity around goal three:

> VOTF gets accused of favoring ordination of women, favoring the abolition of celibacy, favoring, you know, this kind of stuff. Favoring homosexuality. They get accused of all kinds of things. And where individual members might have their own preferences one way or another on those topics, that's not what the organization is about. People, like in any organization, are gonna have their personal opinions on anything. But VOTF only has the three goals.

Another suggested that the movement "really opened itself up to critics because goal three was not defined." Numerous critiques of VOTF, from both within and beyond the movement, were founded in this uncertainty regarding what structural change would mean.

Leaders attempted to counter the risk of an overly broad scope for reform by emphasizing a focus that stemmed directly from the scandal of sexual abuse. On multiple occasions, VOTF's president publicly stated that the movement's focus rested on only the stated goals and mission, stemming from the revelations of abuse. He corrected any assumptions that VOTF would take a stance on areas that emerged in movement lexicon as "hot button" issues, including women in the priesthood, married priests, and the like. Straying into these areas would, in his view, water down the central aim of increasing dialogue and accountability. Leaders also avoided revealing their own views on these topics, desiring to project a moderate image of VOTF. One explained this "laser beam focus" as follows:

> As an organization, we have to be laser beam focused on our mission and goals. That's kept us from some of the problems that groups like [other Catholic reform groups] have had. So we've stayed away from those issues. And I never answer the question of where I am personally on those things. I simply keep saying that VOTF—this is where we are, and this is what we are.

Not all members, however, could reconcile the invitation to voice one's opinions as a lay Catholic while silencing other issues that were so ripe for discussion. One member described her own difficulty with this "laser" focus and its limits on dialogue and change:

> I'm having a hard time doing the laser focus on the sex abuse thing. Because it's, I mean, the sex abuse issue is what brought VOTF, but that's still not VOTF's main thing. It wants to be the voice. But then when you start saying that you want to be the voice, then people think it's just a voice of dissent. We really want to be a voice of dialogue.

Within the movement, dialogue came with clear boundaries. This was a necessary compromise to remain within the church as a moderate Catholic voice for reform. While the movement was invested in increasing the participation of lay-people in the life of the church and its decision making, it was also constrained by the recognition that getting into certain areas of dialogue could undermine VOTF's desire to be seen as Catholics attempting to enact reform from within the church.

Concerns that the movement would be perceived as un-Catholic or not part of the institution, combined with the underlying, shared institutional culture of the movement, drove VOTF to establish a repertoire of contention that was more amenable to its institutional setting. Participants' desire to promote reform from within the church informed its selection of strategies to achieve movement goals. Even while the movement's goals promoted structural change, participants' desire to remain within the church created a psychological and tactical barrier against refuting entirely the hierarchical system upon which the Catholic Church was based. In this way, the movement's chosen positioning within the church introduced limits to its goals for structural change (see Tilly 1978, 1995).

Consequently, fairly conservative approaches to what constituted "protest" were a side effect of the movement's desire to stay within and maintain traditional definitions of the church. One founder's own definition of "protest" placed a clear boundary around what tactics a religious movement committed to its faith ought to embrace:

> Protesting, I see as signs. And you're marching and you're yelling.
> And you're going, "Bernie Law is a pimp!" And I'm thinking, "No,
> no!" That's awful! That's awful. Don't get to their level, you know,
> don't go there. Don't go there . . . What's our model all about?
> Jesus . . . the only people that he went up to were the high priests.
> But he just walked his walk, and people were drawn to him because it
> was right and good. He said "come see, come follow." Nothing less,
> nothing more. He didn't protest. He just stood up and spoke. So that
> might be, you know, playing with words, nuances about what protest
> means.

This founder was not alone in her attribution of "protest" to picketing, chanting, and more militant tactics. Another recalled that a conscious decision had been made early on that "we're not gonna be the protest group. We're gonna be the group that changes from within." Tactical negotiations, then, were again tied to negotiations around identity.

The conciliatory repertoire of contention related back to the movement's desire for legitimacy, and fears that other tactics would take away from the movement's desire to be seen as faithful and committed Catholics. One VOTF leader shared her assessment of participants' hesitancy to embrace more aggressive strategies for reform:

> I think there's fear about what [certain tactics] will make us look like
> in terms of our reputation. Does this radicalize us or liberalize us
> beyond the point that we want to be?

Another participant added that standard models of protest, such as picketing, may serve to "alienate more people than it would impress."

The movement operated under a heightened awareness of boundaries surrounding its tactical and discursive decisions. Action initiatives were bound by participants' perceptions of what strategies and tactics were appropriate for working within the church. Tactics had to be consistent with the movement's perceived Catholic identity. One leader spoke of reworking strategies to satisfy these imposed boundaries:

> I've never been this concerned with practicing what we preach, so to
> speak. If we want the hierarchy to be transparent, so too must we be
> transparent. And in organizing, a lot of times that's not what a lot of
> organizers or activists would say. It's in your strategic advantage

sometimes to take your target by surprise. Well, in this context? Not
sure that really makes sense. We're asking them to be transparent, so
too must we . . . I believe, and the leaders I've worked with have
believed that's the only way we can really move forward in organizing
within the VOTF context.

The institutional context within which the VOTF movement operated was
significant in determining its tactical approach to implementing reform.

Moreover, participants' own identity as Catholics also shaped the movement's repertoire of contention.[3] VOTF activists interpreted their own authority as necessarily understood in relation to the authority of church leaders.
This strategic approach necessitated some level of affirmation for existing
church structures—VOTF sought to work with and within them, even while
promoting structural change.

Participants were relatively open about this somewhat paradoxical desire to
work from within, as two explained:

> I believe in a hierarchical church where there is a leader who has the
> power. I don't want to be able to unvote a bishop out of office
> or unvote a pope out of office. I want to see strong leadership
> in a hierarchical model. And therefore I have, I believe in the
> magisterium, the teaching authority of the church, and the role of
> bishops as teachers and leaders in that magisterium and in our
> church.

> We're not about to tear down the structure of the church. We're not
> against all authority, because we recognize that there needs to be the
> authority of the bishop and the pastor. We're just saying to open the
> doors. No secrecy, but accountability. Let us do what we're gifted at,
> which would be a myriad of things.

Similarly, another participant referenced the Vatican II document on the laity
as not only empowering the laity with a rightful authority, but also solidifying
the authority of the church hierarchy. The commitment to staying within the
bounds of the church as a social movement is evidenced by his words:

> Lumen Gentium, actually, should be our marching orders. That gives
> us the authority. And it also gives the bishops their authority, too. I
> don't think we can—you can't touch that. The bishops are going to be
> the spiritual leaders of the church, if it's going to stay anywhere near
> where it is.

In this way, VOTF activists expressed comfort with balancing a somewhat traditional Catholic identity, which included support for the priests and even for a hierarchical church, with a more progressive reform agenda. VOTF presented itself as acting not to overturn entirely the structure of religious hierarchy, but rather as acting to rid this structure of elements (including secrecy and a lack of accountability) that had contributed to abuse in the church.

Voice of the Faithful's acceptance—both implicit and explicit—of the church's hierarchical structure, even while attempting to reform its distribution of power, was heavily influential in the movement's tactical negotiations. Even in its nascent form as a post-Mass, basement gathering, the influence of the setting over movement behavior was evident. Parishioners at St. John the Evangelist, for example, asked permission of their parish priest to meet and discuss the abuse issue. A similar dynamic characterized affiliates' emergence in settings throughout the country. The gesture was symbolic of the very problem the group would seek to rectify, and characteristic of the paradoxical role of social movements operating within institutions. Participants were not entirely unaware of this early irony, as one founder observes:

> Even at the beginning, we needed father's permission to grow. And
> therein lies the defining issue. We have been dealing with that issue
> ever since. As an internal, formative thing.

This also hinted at an essential struggle within the movement: the desire to affirm the voice and participation of the laity while also facilitating dialogue and collaboration with members of the hierarchy. When VOTF asked for permission, it relinquished its insistence on having authority in decision making. But when it did not, it risked compromising its ability to work together with church leaders.

Tactical negotiations within VOTF were also complicated by trepidation on the part of many movement participants to embrace strategies that went against their church's leaders. For a membership consisting predominantly of active Catholics born and raised in the church, a vocal critique of the Catholic Church felt unfamiliar and somewhat uncomfortable. Particularly when protest turns to the religious sphere, raising one's voice can cause discomfort, as three organizers described happening in VOTF:

> I think people have difficulty, Catholics in particular, have difficulty
> sort of standing up to authority and questioning authority because
> it's sort of outside of what we know and do. So the fact that VOTF is
> doing that I'm sure scares some people.

Many times, it's a parent–child relationship. So, it's training people in how to overcome this fear, really, of confronting an "authority" figure.

One of the drawbacks for the VOTF people is that they have been so trained to listen to their priests that they're still waiting for some priest to come up and say, "It's okay to believe this way." To make change. To throw Law out of Boston.

The cautiousness with which VOTF participants approached their reform agenda reflected this unfamiliarity; more conservative and familiar strategies had wider appeal within the movement.

Voice of the Faithful's vote to formally request Cardinal Law's resignation nearly crossed this tactical barrier, a bold step for a group of lay Catholics unaccustomed to denouncing their own church's leaders. One VOTF leader described the internal change among participants that accompanied the request for Law's resignation:

There's a psychological barrier that has to be crossed. And that is, for people who have largely been influenced by church authority to suddenly stand up, speak up, and criticize a cardinal. The cardinal archbishop, one of the most powerful, probably the most powerful cardinal church leader in the United States and one of the most powerful in the world. That's no small undertaking for people. Two kinds of people struggle with that: people who are not accustomed to using their voice, and people who are accustomed to using their voice but are not accustomed to using it in that way in the church.

Justifications such as the separation of faith and form helped Catholics to navigate this uncomfortable tactical terrain, but standing up to (and against) church leaders nonetheless really challenged committed Catholics who loved their church and would never have imagined questioning its leaders in this way.

Some early participants in the movement expressed their wish that VOTF had been more aggressive in its tactical choices, less concerned with its image among the hierarchy. One supporter voiced his preference for taking a bolder approach:

If I were elected to head up Voice, I would call all Catholics in Boston: this Sunday, let's gather at the cathedral to show our displeasure, our anger over this. And demand a different style of approach. You could get thousands and thousands of people. And then it would get them strength. Because they would feel, "Oh my gosh, there's a lot of people." But they're not gonna do it. Or at least, I haven't seen it. And I would have seen it by now. I think they miss those kinds of opportunities.

This tactical approach, however, simply did not fit within the culture of the church and the movement, thus stifling the participation of those who preferred more aggressive strategies. To some, these strategic compromises made by VOTF to remain within the church undercut the movement's ability to aggressively pursue real change.

Differences in approach were, in fact, divisive within the movement. Tactical choices and compromises led to the departure of some individuals for whom more aggressive strategies were preferable. Two participants who helped to found the movement later conveyed their frustration with the conservative path VOTF took:

> For me, VOTF was a lot more about action-oriented things with results. I think in a lot of other people, though, it's been, it's something different. It's a place to have an intellectual conversation about some of the changing dynamics in the church.

> At one point, I said, well why not move for parish-wide meetings? So that you get out of this, you know, parish council crap? Because I'm just not that kind of joining Catholic. I just hate that stuff. You have all of these people who feel that they're special because they get to go have dinner at the priest's house. It's all kind of goal two baloney, married with a very conservative view of goal three. I felt that goal one might have been able to radicalize all that, but it wasn't possible to keep it all up in the air.

For these and other participants in the movement, identity incongruence with the predominant approach of VOTF ultimately led them to sever ties and form other avenues of protest:

> Honestly, looking back on it, it was just a dream. Because you weren't gonna get, you know, there just aren't a lot of people like me in VOTF. And so I think that it was kind of, probably a misguided wish on my part that VOTF be different from what it was. You could argue that taking a more reserved and measured approach was more consistent with the clientele.

Maintaining a movement identity of Catholics who felt deeply the desire to be accepted within the church mandated the exclusion of some whose own approach did not fit the strategic approach of VOTF.

The more conservative and culturally bound selection of strategies represented a compromise between an intense desire for reform and an equally intense desire to be seen as Catholic, within the Catholic Church. Voice of the Faithful's institutional environment and Catholic identity was consequential, rather than passive, in controlling its operations.

An Adopted Tactical Repertoire

With more radical interpretations of "protest" out of consideration, VOTF turned to tactical options made available by the existing church structure. Movement scholarship has revealed that activism within institutions often relies upon the use of previously established institutional channels for effecting change.[4] As with any movement drawing upon an organizational base, that organizational base "fundamentally shapes the kinds and amounts of resources that activists are able to mobilize, the issues that come to dominate and identify their cause, and the strategies they adopt in interaction with authorities and opponents" (Minkoff 2002:261). In adapting and accommodating a tactical repertoire from and to the cultural toolkit of the church, VOTF also reaffirmed the very institutional structures that the movement sought to reform.

The movement's tactical repertoire developed in two primary directions. One, VOTF embraced very public national efforts to claim voice and authority as Catholics in the church. Given that the scandal had tarnished the public face of Catholicism, VOTF capitalized on the opportunity to showcase their authentic faith while also critiquing the structure of the church. Second, the movement embarked on a series of more localized efforts to appropriate existing parish and diocesan resources for movement aims. The national public and smaller localized action initiatives both situated the movement clearly in relation to the institution of the church, recognizing its authority structures and adopting its cultural resources.

Claiming a Public Voice for Catholicism

On Friday, February 29, 2004, VOTF ran an ad in the *New York Times* that stated in bold, capital letters:

OUR TRUST HAS BEEN VIOLATED. BUT NOT OUR FAITH.

The ad elaborated with a discussion of rebuilding the church, and provided a description of the history, activity, and justification for VOTF. It then listed the following three petitions for reform, requesting that readers sign on:

> I believe that the bishops of the Catholic Church who knowingly allowed children to be sexually abused by clergy must be held responsible for their roles in these crimes over the past 50 years. For this reason I call on:

> I. Pope John Paul II: To meet with an international delegation of victims/ survivors of clergy sexual abuse to begin reconciliation on behalf of the entire community of the Catholic Church.
> II. Pope John Paul II: To hold those bishops responsible who knowingly transferred sexually abusive clergy; to accept resignations offered; and to call for resignations where appropriate.
> III. Each U.S. bishop: To disclose details of their oversight in transferring abusive clergy and clergy who have credible allegations against them.

The ad concluded with "Add your voice to Voice of the Faithful. It's time to return responsibility to Catholicism." An identical ad also ran in the *National Catholic Reporter*.

The ad molded to the existing structure of the church in its stated allegiance to the faith and recognition of the pope and bishops in their positions of authority in the church. However, it also asserted a more forceful claim to the right of lay Catholics to participate in church decision making, conjuring the legacy of the Second Vatican Council in its assertion of shared lay responsibility. The ad clearly conveyed that VOTF members and supporters had trusted the church, trusted its leaders, and now wished to reconcile and correct that broken trust in light of the scandal.

This very public claim to a representative voice for the church, the most costly effort the movement had undertaken, did garner attention. The timing of its publication intentionally coincided with the 2004 release of a study commissioned by the bishops and conducted by the John Jay College of Criminal Justice on "The Nature and Scope of the Problem of Sexual Abuse of Minors by Catholic Priests and Deacons in the United States." In the mind of one major VOTF proponent of the ad, this study's release represented "the last big tsunami wave of news within the clergy sexual abuse crisis," so VOTF needed to capitalize on the opportunity to make a public statement on behalf of committed yet critical lay Catholics.

Within about two weeks, the petitions boasted some 10,000 signatures. Tim Russert of NBC's *Meet the Press* held up the ad when interviewing Washington's Archbishop Cardinal Theodore McCarrick. Wanting to maximize the number of signers, VOTF followed up with a direct mailing to all registered VOTF members as well as to the subscription list for the *National Catholic Reporter*, a progressive-leaning Catholic paper.

The idea for the ad originally emerged from one VOTF leader's conversation with the leader of another Catholic reform group, Call to Action. Call to Action ran their own *New York Times* ad on Ash Wednesday, 1990. The publicity succeeded in increasing their group's membership and presence nationally. Their success resonated with VOTF's desire to increase its own numbers and affirm its place in the public discourse surrounding Catholicism and the scandal. A full-page ad in the *Times* presented a way to connect with a larger population of American Catholics. The VOTF leader initiating the idea described his motivation:

> I was looking for the Rosetta stone. Which to me is: what is the code that helps Catholics in the pews say, "You can't rape children"? What is it that says to Catholics, "You need to treat me like an adult"? How do we get Catholics to say, "You know what, before I give you a dime, I want to know how you're gonna spend my money. And then I want you to tell me how you spent it"? How do we get there?

Prior to running the ad, VOTF held a series of focus groups in order to identify better ways to connect with those who had not yet joined the movement. One leader described what they learned from these discussions:

> A number of Catholics who were there would not join VOTF because they had concerns. Which I think we've all come to understand. I mean, how can a Catholic stand up against the church? Isn't there some other agenda that you have? The hidden agenda continues to plague VOTF. But what we also learned was, we said, "Okay, you won't join VOTF. But if we gave you a petition that said 'We believe bishops who knowingly transferred pedophile priests should be held accountable,' would you sign it?" They said "Absolutely." And so, we said, huh. If we distinguish between a message and a message giver, in this case, through a petition, we can take the petition and use it as leverage, use it as a news event, use it for public relations, use it for communication, and also build our database. And that way we can begin to establish a relationship with these people.

The conversations revealed the tension of moving within an institution, as Catholics voiced frustration with the church but hesitation to criticize in their capacity as committed followers. Joining the VOTF movement seemed an affront to their Catholic loyalty, despite agreeing with the principles of the movement.

The petitions remained open just over three months, until the June 2004 meeting of the U.S. Conference of Catholic Bishops. Slightly more than 30,000 Catholics signed the three petitions, which were mailed to the Vatican and hand delivered to the U.S. bishops at their June conference by VOTF's executive director and vice president. In delivering the petitions at the bishops' conference, which had been designated as "closed" to outsiders, VOTF representatives were asked to leave. VOTF's executive director described the encounter in a subsequent e-mail to VOTF members:

> While in the gift shop, a bishop I know and have met with entered. I approached him and shook his hand. In the midst of a productive conversation on unity in the church, we were approached by a sheriff, and I was informed, by name, that the management of the hotel had asked the sheriff to remove [VOTF's vice president] and me from the property. The bishop could have stopped the ejection—he did not. It was a brief dialogue.

Thus representatives from VOTF were excluded in a literal way from conversations and decision making related to church leadership and its response to abuse.

Reactions to the strategy were mixed, even among VOTF's own leadership. While some called the ad a success, others viewed the entire initiative as an expensive failure. The publication and subsequent mailings cost the organization upwards of a $100,000, which was, according to one leader, "money we didn't have." With only 30,000 names to show for the petitions, VOTF had in essence paid more than $3 per name. Several criticized the idea and its limited return as a serious tactical error; blame was aimed primarily at VOTF's executive director. Movement leaders' later requested the executive director's resignation (to which he admitted being "stunned"), highlighting persistent internal governance issues within the movement.

Publishing the *New York Times* ad helped to establish VOTF as a national player in conversations related to the church and the scandal. It presented a very public face for the movement and its demands for reform, and put Catholic leaders on notice. The tactic affirmed a commitment to the Catholic Church ("Our Trust Has Been Violated. But Not Our Faith"), while separating this commitment from the institutional failings of the church. Though seen by many and signed by some, participants active in affiliates throughout the country tended to gravitate toward what they perceived to be a more promising tactical avenue: a more localized focus on the grassroots level and in members' own parishes, where the movement could hear and act upon the concerns of lay Catholics as they lived out their everyday faith.

Claiming a Localized Institutional Space

More common than national, public strategies were those that affiliates addressed at the local level, among their own parishes and dioceses. It was what VOTF participants knew best: their own parishes and already-existing structures designed to facilitate lay participation. Many felt that working closer to home was more manageable and often more meaningful to the ways that they lived out their everyday religious lives. Although not acknowledged explicitly by movement participants, a more localized approach also echoed the cultural influence of Vatican II in its emphasis on localization over centralization. An important legacy of the council, pointed out by Catholic historian Michael J. McNally (2000), is its emphasis on the "need for indigenization" and on the parish as "the concrete, the practical, the local, the particular, the Incarnational" (p. 8).

Starting with the familiar offered movement participants a more tangible means of addressing VOTF's still ambiguous goal of structural change, as one member explained:

> We felt that we had to come up with something that we actually *could* do. I mean, sure, we can hold our breath until we turn blue and demand things, but we're in a position where the church leadership clearly has . . . the bishop has all executive, legislative, and judicial authority within the diocese. By Canon Law. So what can you do? What we said that we could do is start at the parish level. Only because it was possible. Because at that level, we're dealing individually, we're dealing with your pastor. Who may or may not agree with you, but you can meet face to face. And talk to him. And it was also necessary, because it was within the context of the parish that the abuse had happened.

The realm of structural change, then, at least in its early iteration, was relegated to the local level—improving one's own parish and modeling an accountable church. It was a response to the hierarchical structure of the church that left activists unable to directly counter church authorities at higher levels. A local parish focus also allowed the movement to avoid more abrasive tactics and traditional protest strategies, instead relying upon the existing repertoire offered by the institution. In this way, VOTF could adopt their tactical repertoire from among the cultural toolkit already shared with the institution.

One specific strategy emphasized was to examine the role of pastoral and finance councils at the parish level. VOTF members critiqued councils that were merely "rubber stamps" of the pastor's decisions and applauded those that were truly representative, consultative bodies. A member explained this approach:

> We need to enhance lay involvement in the life of the church. And how do you do that? Well, you can start with existing structures that are already there. Like pastoral councils and finance councils. And try to figure out, well, number one, do they actually exist?

Influenced by VOTF's desire to remain within the church, the movement most often opted to mobilize around enhancing already established mechanisms for voice within churches rather than creating external, independent bodies for accountability. It was also a response to church leaders' hesitancy to welcome an internal reform group (in the most severe instance, by banning VOTF) while encouraging individual parishioners to use existing platforms for voicing discontent and managing change.

In addition, localized action alleviated some of the pressure on the VOTF national office to direct all movement activity, as one leader in the national office shared:

> It shifted pressure off of the national office to do everything. That became beyond a point of no return for us. We couldn't keep up with that sort of stuff. If we have a bishop in Peoria who was outlandish, why should the National start attacking them? Let the Peoria affiliate deal with the bishop! We're not going to send somebody from the National office to Peoria to talk to that bishop! We want it to be local. Let's let the National provide some overall, big-issue stuff. So that whole shift in paradigm—from National does everything, knows everything, guides everything—to the affiliate having the authority and the encouragement to do things that are germane in its level, has made a world of difference.

Leaders were optimistic that the summer 2004 hiring of a professional organizer would help to empower local affiliates, while avoiding an overly centralized organizational structure mirroring too closely the targeted institution.

Under this directive, VOTF embarked on an extensive initiative to create successful movement outcomes. One affiliate leader described the impetus for VOTF to move in this direction:

> It comes back to the same question: What are you achieving? That's the question that VOTF at large is struggling with now. What has *changed?* This solution, this grassroots initiative, is to be able to say, "Look, this is what we have achieved."

Launched in 2005, the "Many Hands, Many Hearts" campaign[5] was designed to identify, train, and encourage grassroots leaders who could also contribute to VOTF leadership nationally, to identify issues members wished to address collectively, and, perhaps most importantly, to generate and implement action strategies that could be shared with other affiliates. This latter goal responded to increasing external and internal pressure on the movement to prove that they had made a difference, had done something to change the church from within.

Intensive training took place at a number of affiliates. The approach, echoing a Saul Alinsky model of organizing, solicited individual participants' reform ideas to construct a movement agenda. VOTF members conducted one-on-one conversations with other lay Catholics (both members and nonmembers of VOTF), asking them to identify their primary areas of concern in the church. The conversations also presented opportunities to invite newcomers to join the movement and to identify individuals willing to volunteer in given areas. Members also got to know one another better, and some spoke of being reinvigorated and mobilized to act. One-on-one conversations also generated a list of the most pressing concerns individuals had regarding the church and issues for which they were most likely to mobilize.

Participants in the Montgomery County, Maryland, affiliate conducted 106 one-on-one conversations, 21 of which were with Catholics who had not been previously involved with the VOTF movement. Out of these conversations emerged 217 issues relating to structural change, 64 relating to supporting survivors, and none relating to supporting priests. The most commonly raised specific issue fell within the area of hierarchy accountability, transparency, openness, and consultation with the laity. Other affiliates, though most conducted fewer one-on-one conversations, emerged with a similar sense that the most pressing issues among Catholics they interviewed related to increasing lay participation and making governance within the church more transparent. Some VOTF participants, however, questioned the strategy of one-on-one conversations, unclear on how the opinions of hundreds could provide better direction to the movement than strong national leadership.

The next step in the Many Hands, Many Hearts campaign involved identifying a collective action that each affiliate could reasonably undertake to address an area of great concern to its members. Affiliate leaders worked with participants to select a problem that would be widely supported, deeply felt, consistent with VOTF's goals, and that would avoid overly controversial issues. Once a specific problem was identified, they narrowed it down to a single issue that would have a clear target, bring others in, develop leadership, and present urgency. Finally, affiliates selected a concrete goal or target that could serve as a possible solution to the issue.

Action initiatives (and their success) varied among affiliates. In Rockford, Illinois, the VOTF affiliate identified as their primary issue the lack of recognition and acceptance diocesan leaders had extended to them. The bishop refused to meet with VOTF and had barred the affiliate from meeting on church property. Rockford leaders therefore decided to hold an affiliate meeting at their local cathedral, despite not having the approval of the bishop. The action was preceded by a series of requests and letters to the bishop, notifying him of their intentions to stage a sit-in if he did not agree to meet with them. Diocesan representatives responded, saying that VOTF could not meet on church property because it was not a sanctioned group (and, furthermore, could not be sanctioned). Consequently the affiliate attended Mass at the cathedral together, after which they remained in place to conduct a brief VOTF meeting despite having been prohibited by the diocese from doing so. Seventy-five VOTF members attended, praying in the parking lot beforehand and meeting at a coffee shop afterward to plan a secondary action (a phone call campaign to the bishop's office).

For participants in the Rockford affiliate, the cathedral sit-in created a visible moment in which they had asserted their rights as lay Catholics to gather on church property. They also received some media attention from the activity. The action merged a long-practiced movement strategy—the sit-in—with an institutionally deferential strategy of first notifying and asking permission of authorities prior to acting. VOTF participants also first attended Mass and prayed prior to conducting a meeting in the cathedral. The approach was a distant cry from more aggressive tactics that might have involved loud chanting, marching, or harsh public criticism of the institution. In contrast, the affiliate actually affirmed both their Catholic identity and the legitimate authority of the church by acting within in its parameters and, literally, within its walls.

The Rockford affiliate was the first to reach an action climax in the Many Hands, Many Hearts campaign. Other events resulting from VOTF's direct action campaign included parish-wide forums, surveys, support for legislation, responses to parish closings, and attempts to create mechanisms for dialogue with bishops. The smattering of small but notable initiatives garnered some public attention and raised awareness for an upcoming VOTF national convocation. Newly recruited leaders got involved in training others and running for positions on the new representative council.

Despite the locally oriented efforts, tempered strategies, respect for the extant authority structure of the church, and the common practice of building upon preexisting church structures for change, some VOTF members nonetheless critiqued some affiliates' tactics. To some, affiliates had gone too far; to others, the action initiatives did not go far enough. One participant commented on his lack of enthusiasm to support the Rockford affiliate's cathedral sit-in, while also recognizing that total agreement need not be the goal:

> Our goal is to be inclusive. What one or more affiliates do (within the three stated goals of VOTF) does not have to be what all do. If some of us support the Rockford effort, it is not our expectation that all need to walk in lockstep.

Another affiliate leader admitted his own reservations with attributing successful outcomes to the action-oriented strategies that affiliates such as Rockford had undertaken:

> I think it's all in the mind of the assessor, as to whether something has been achieved. The thing in Rockford—I guess for that group of people, who had been saying "Please, please, please, give us a place to meet in the church," okay, they sit in at the end of a Mass and have a meeting. It's a symbolic gesture. It's not exactly the Boston Tea Party, where now things have changed. He basically ignored them. So, so how is that . . . ? I look at that and I say, well, how is that any change?

His comment also hints at the challenge of change within a religious institution. As much as VOTF is influenced by the culture of the church, it is also targeting that same culture, desiring a shift in how authority is perceived and who participates in decision making. Measuring changes in perception and meaning systems is difficult and, as members themselves recognized, often subjectively calculated.

Limits on Moving from Within

Based upon their cautious selection of strategies, institutionally familiar form, and deployment of a shared cultural discourse, VOTF participants had mobilized with initial optimism that U.S. Catholic bishops would embrace their lay movement and be open to forming a working relationship that would rejuvenate Catholicism in the wake of the scandal. One Boston leader articulated the message that she wished the bishops would hear and believe about VOTF:

> We are the ones who are still in the church. Droves have left. We love our church. We want to be part of it. We want to work with [the bishops]. If we can just convince them that it's okay, that we're not about tearing them down. We're not about bashing them, or we're not about bashing anything to do with doctrine or dogma. We are really about bringing about the church as Jesus intended. And we're just saying that a lot of the things that have happened have really, really . . . We have felt very betrayed.

Participants truly saw themselves as part of the church, whose voices ought to be respected and heard.

However, church leaders from the beginning questioned the movement's position within the church and right to participate in decision making. It stemmed in part from the desire of those already in positions of authority in the church to manage any organizing and lay activity within the institution. When VOTF representatives met with Boston's then Cardinal Bernard Law in November 2002, subsequent to the movement's ban from church property and prior to Law's own resignation, the archbishop's primary critique was that VOTF had not first come to him for permission to mobilize. VOTF's president described the encounter to the *Boston Globe* as being primarily about the struggle for authority: "[Law] kind of laughed, but I think that's the mindset, and it's an issue" (Paulson 2002b).

Voice of the Faithful participants were continually faced with the realization that it might not be enough for their movement to state its willingness to accept and respect the church's hierarchical roles, to actively request collaboration, to engage in the cultural discourse of Catholicism, or to select more conservative tactics based upon their desire to stay within the church. The very mobilization of lay Catholics without explicit consent from bishops had from the start—in the minds of those who held power in the church—negated the group's chances for real and continued dialogue. It represented a clear struggle for ownership of the Catholic Church.

Some in the movement were deeply discouraged by this recognition. One expressed his sense that it was the shady and threatening movement goal to introduce structural change in the church that made VOTF's aims almost impossible to advance within the institution:

> Certainly in my mind, there was a chance there where you could see a VOTF group in every parish. At least in every diocese. To do that, it had to be pretty benevolent. Keep kids safe. Support priests of integrity. Well, all priests are of integrity, so you can get by that one. Support victims, who can disagree with that? And then build later on change, if you want to do it.

But in promoting reform under the umbrella of "structural change," the movement suffered the consequences of an unwelcome institutional presence and a less-than-Catholic reputation. This same member continued:

> Because of that, it didn't get the conservatives. It opened itself up to critics. It got wrong people in different parts of leadership that were pushing different agendas. So that certainly was a cost of, perhaps not moderation, but perhaps lack of clarity in the beginning and unwillingness to deal with it.

Voice of the Faithful found itself in a catch-22: it moderated and tempered its tactical repertoire, borrowing heavily from extant church resources and highlighting its allegiance to Catholic identity and church authorities, but ultimately continued to meet resistance on the part of church leaders who would not welcome dialogue with a lay Catholic group that had emerged apart from sanctioned church activity.

Conclusion

Intrainstitutional positioning allows extant resources to be strategically reappropriated by movement actors. Borrowing from a shared (though contested) identity and meaning system, an IISM may adopt a tactical repertoire already familiar to movement participants and targeted authorities. The meaning of "protest" adapts to the institutional space: what counts as meaningful protest (and, perhaps more importantly, what is dismissed) is refined to reflect institutional culture.

The foundational desire of VOTF to remain as faithful Catholics within the Catholic Church mandated a cautious tiptoeing around how much independence the organization had, the collaboration it permitted, the language it used to describe its intentions, and the strategies it deployed. The movement navigated both public, national tactics as well as more localized action to push for change from within the institution. These efforts resulted in persistent identity struggles and frequent resistance to be accepted as a legitimate decision-maker within the church. Acting within a religious institutional space, not only did the boundaries of the institution mold the repertoire of tactics available to movement actors, but the religious culture of the movement justified these boundaries theologically and threatened the legitimacy of movement identities.

Tactical accommodations also led VOTF to replicate the very institutional structures it sought to change. This was not entirely bad, as it provided a means of translating movement behavior and identity into a form recognizable to institutional authorities. But with the resource borrowing came compromises regarding available tactics and, more importantly, institutional practices that stifled some voices, privileged those in positions of power, and renewed the very structural dynamics that the movement had organized to change. The significance of this for IISMs in general and for our understanding of social movements, institutions, and religion is explored further in the next chapter.

9

Social Movements, Institutions, and Religion

The careful negotiations the VOTF movement made through mobilization, constructing a collective identity, defining leadership and membership, and selecting strategies provide considerable theoretical insight into the study of religion and social movements. Notably, the context within which the movement operated—a religious, institutional arena—offered its participants a repertoire of movement resources accompanied by a heightened awareness of boundaries around movement behavior. These boundaries can ultimately lead an IISM to replicate the form, tactics, and identity of the target institution. This chapter outlines these theoretical insights, drawing specific attention to the impact of the institutional context as well as to the understudied, multidimensional roles religion (and culture more broadly) can play in social movements.

Intrainstitutional Social Movements

Voice of the Faithful falls into the camp of "awkward movements" (Poletta 2006) in its mismatch to existing theoretical conceptualizations of social movements. Its examination demonstrates the usefulness of more expansive approaches to defining social movements. Most notably, research on VOTF affirms that social movements can emerge and operate within institutions. Only by expanding a definition of social movements beyond movements targeting the state can scholars begin to consider the many variants of challenges to authority.[1] The response to Zald and Berger's (1978) call to study social movements within organizations has been slow to emerge.[2] Institutional settings "not only represent contexts for identity formation, mobilization, and strategic action in the service of social movements, but they are themselves potential sites and targets of activism" (Clemens and Minkoff 2004:160). To discount VOTF as a social movement because it does not target the state would mean discounting an important realm of organized challenge to authority.

In chapter 2 I introduced the following definition for IISMs to address the need for terminology and clarity in this area of social movement scholarship:

> Intrainstitutional social movements (IISMs) are movements that
> target a specific, bounded institution (rather than the state or society
> at-large), primarily drawing participants from the institution's own
> established base (e.g., employees, adherents, or members).

Both the target of and participants in collective action identify with the institution. Activists, prior to and during their activism, maintain an insider relationship with the institution (which may or may not carry with it power in institutional decision making).

Though the bounds may be narrow or broad, the definition of institutions I employ here is limited to those with at least some degree of formalized boundaries on inclusion. IISM participants' institutional affiliation may be either ascribed or achieved, and as such is either permanent or mutable. In the case of VOTF, individuals' participation in the movement is wedded to their insider status as self-identifying Catholics. Although a religious identity is more malleable than other types of identities (one could feasibly "leave" the church), participants' adherence to the identity is an essential marker of their participation in the movement. By virtue of their identification as Catholic, they are insiders to the Catholic Church. The church is instrumental in shaping movement participants' self-identities and social experiences. Those for whom a Catholic identity is either not held or more loosely held might gravitate toward alternative movement options operating outside of the institutional church (as was the case with SNAP). Moreover, the collective identity of the VOTF movement emerged as one tied to not only identification, but also active participation in church life.

Social movements operating within institutions must deal with normative pressures produced by both internal and external sources. Because of their insider positioning, IISMs are also susceptible to the political and environmental opportunities that give rise to movements, or what Raeburn (2004) calls institutional opportunities. The theoretical model presented here suggests that any study of IISMs must take into account the impact of the target institution on the movement's form, strategy selection, and collective identity. Specifically, the target institution plays a central role in mediating the repertoire of tactics, forms, and identities available to the movement. IISMs are therefore *bounded movements*, restricted by the institutional environment within which they choose to operate. IISMs are largely driven by the cultural code of the institution they are targeting. Findings for VOTF reveal that this resulted in replication of the very institution the movement was trying to change.

Despite the absence of a name and definition for IISMs, empirical studies of this type have increased in recent years. Scholars have explored movements operating in a variety of institutional settings, including schools, corporations, the military, churches, and other settings (e.g., Binder 2002; Katzenstein 1998; Kniss and Chaves 1995; Lounsbury 2001; Moore 2008; O'Brien 2002; Raeburn 2004; Scully and Creed 1999; Scully and Segal 2002; Taylor 1996; Taylor and Raeburn 1995). But despite this increasing attention, no clearly elucidated definition for this variant on collective behavior has emerged. Only recently has a definition of social movements broadened to include movements targeting variants of authority beyond the state or society at-large. Even the American Sociological Association's Section on Collective Behavior and Social Movements describes its 1980 founding as intended to foster the study of "extrainstitutional social forms and behavior." It is time that all types of social movement challenges to authority be included in our theoretical toolkit.

The theoretical model presented here, evidenced by VOTF, provides a much-needed specification for movements operating within institutional spaces. It builds especially upon the conceptual tools offered by Mary Katzenstein (1998) to better understand activism within institutions. Katzenstein describes "institutional mobilization" or "institution-based organizations" acting within parent institutions as having financial or administrative ties to their targeted institutions. Her analysis of feminist mobilization within the Catholic Church and U.S. military revealed how insiders engage in institutional protest, seeking moderate policy change in the case of the military, or, within the church, more radical discursive shifts in the very meaning-making practices and norms of the institution.

Other scholars (notably, Binder [2002] and Raeburn [2004]) have expanded upon Katzenstein's work with considerations of the larger cultural system, political opportunities, and organizational practices that foster institutional opportunities for mobilization. Among the more promising recent directions in social movement scholarship that may accommodate an IISM definition and perspective is the "multi-institutional politics" approach proposed by Armstrong and Bernstein (2008). This approach offers a needed correction to more limited strands that assume movements target just one source of power (most often, the state) and that culture operates independently from structure.

Nonetheless, the base is still in flux: questions persist as to the specific nature (and name) of IISMs. Moreover, lost in this discussion is serious consideration of how central culture and collective identity are to the formation and activity of IISMs. This study of VOTF frames and refocuses our understanding of social movements operating within institutions, with particular attention to their cultural dimensions and bounded character. The sections that follow outline specific dimensions of IISMs: their stages in encountering institutional authorities, their form, strategy selection, and identity, the importance of culture (manifested here as religion), and, finally, the bounded character of IISMs.

Stages in Encountering Institutional Authorities

The mobilization of IISMs can be understood as a series of stages during which a movement encounters and responds to institutional authorities. This study of VOTF reveals five stages of IISM mobilization: (1) expressed commitment to the institution, (2) institutional authentication, (3) institutional receptivity or rejection, (4) movement response, and (5) absorption or replication. I will describe each of these stages in turn.

Early in the mobilization of an IISM, a pivotal stage is that of *expressed commitment to the institution*. It is this stage, when the movement emerges from among individuals who already identify with the institution, that defines a movement as intrainstitutional. Movement actors organize around and vocalize publically their institutionally based identities. This stated commitment may take various forms, depending on the nature of participants' relationship to the institution. If they are employees, as seen in mobilization among gays, lesbians, and bisexuals in the large corporations profiled by Raeburn (2004), this expressed commitment involves retaining one's employee status. Moore (2008) reveals this stage among scientists as they mobilized to shape scientific knowledge production while maintaining active ties to professional organizations and peers in the field. Parents and educational professionals described by Binder (2002) challenged American public schools, invoking arguments regarding what was best for the schools to which they, like their opposition, were committed. We see in VOTF how the movement released public statements and consciously voiced their Catholic identity and commitment to the Catholic Church. Unlike with other social movements, participants in IISMs express commitment to the targeted institution in the movement's formative stages. This commitment resonates with their identity as it is institutionally defined ("employee," "member," "Catholic") and carries immense consequences for subsequent movement decision making.

The second stage of IISM mobilization is *institutional authentication*. During this stage, institutional leaders and other insiders test the commitment claims made by movement participants. Activists are asked to authenticate their identity as institutional insiders, legitimately committed to the institution. As detailed previously related to identity within IISMs, movements must negotiate with institutional leaders to prove that they indeed have the right to (a) claim insider status, and (b) propose institutional critiques or suggestions for reform. In the case of the former, an employee status may be easier to authenticate than a religious one. This stage is important in its implication for subsequent stages and movement actions: Is the movement accepted by the institution as a legitimate voice for reform? Are movement activists invited to the decision-making table as authentic insiders, committed to the institution? Given the complexities demonstrated by VOTF's attempts to authenticate their Catholic identity and commitment to the church, it would seem that IISMs are likely to meet great resistance in this process.

From the intense institutional authentication stage (which may very well continue into subsequent stages), an IISM next moves into the third stage: *institutional receptivity or rejection*. Having authenticated (or further called into question) an IISM's institutional commitment, how does the institution respond? Are leaders receptive or resistant to the reform message of the movement? Do they invite movement participants into decision making and collaborative leadership or do they create barriers and further distance between them? It was in this stage that VOTF was banned by several diocesan bishops from meeting on church grounds. Although this did not stifle the movement's efforts (in fact, it increased interest among some Catholics), it did signal a clear rejection on the part of the institution to accept VOTF as an equal partner in responding to the crisis of child sexual abuse. Katzenstein (1998) describes an alternative institutional response in her study of feminist mobilizing within the U.S. military. Backed by the law, women were able to establish protected institutional spaces and the legal right to be "troublemakers" to advance their agenda within the military. This response, although still hindered by institutional resistance, exemplifies the receptivity response of an institution during this stage of IISM mobilization.

Facing institutional integration or rejection, an IISM enters the fourth stage of *movement response*. How does the movement proceed, knowing its stance vis-à-vis the institution it is targeting for reform? Does it seek to proceed from within the institution or, alternatively, forge a new path that parts from institutional allegiance in hopes of making real change from the outside?

Chapter 4 detailed the diverse paths of affiliates within the VOTF movement, echoing those identified by West and Blumberg (1990) in the women's movement (integration, parallelism, and independence). Affiliates embraced divergent responses to institutional rejection. Some sought to and succeeded in integrating into existing institutional modes for advocacy, meeting with institutional leaders and appropriating extant resources for voicing dissent. Other affiliates paralleled the institution by creating alternative structures for reform alongside the institution while simultaneously maintaining institutional commitment and supporting institutional survival. A third alternative, independence, breaks an IISM away from its founding premise of institutional commitment. Though none of the VOTF affiliates took this route, an IISM could feasibly choose this path if rejection leads them to also reject their original commitment and leave the institution (which may take the form of apostasy). Ample evidence of this exists among religious organizations that have emerged from within a parent institution but ultimately break away to form their own institution.

Finally, the fifth stage of IISM mobilization is that of *absorption or replication*. In this stage, we see movements reaching a point where they are either absorbed into the larger institution as a part of normal operations (perhaps indicating an internal policy change or participants' entry into positions of influence within the institution) or they maintain separate operations that begin to replicate those of the parent institution in form, identity, and strategy. Having met rejection, a movement might adapt its tactical repertoire such that it can pass within the institution despite perceived resistance. Although strategic, this also carries the risk of replication. VOTF provides numerous examples of institutional replication, as the movement tempered its protest strategies in order to be welcomed within institutional spaces. The cultural toolkit of the institution becomes a resource for reappropriation as a means of moving forward on movement aims in the face of resistance. Absorption and replication do not exactly paint a rosy portrait for IISMs in this last stage of mobilization, unless one considers that institutional change can indeed happen (perhaps even more effectively) as movement goals are seamlessly integrated into institutional practice and as movements bring new innovation to long-standing structural realities.

The Form of IISMs

Although the form of IISMs may vary substantially, this variation is constrained by the intrainstitutional context within which IISMs operate. By definition,

IISMs take on a form that intentionally aims to remain within the boundaries of the target institution. Movement participants emerge from among institutional insiders, thus ensuring an established link to the institution. This interconnectedness can be likened to the embeddedness that characterizes the institution itself (DiMaggio and Powell 1983; Fombrun 1986, 1988). An IISM has preestablished, formal ties through its participants to the environment within which it operates.

The embeddedness of an IISM may actually reduce the risk of movement demise. Organization scholars have highlighted the benefits of embeddedness, a characteristic that more typically increases with age, as enhancing an organization's survival chances (Hager, Galaskiewicz, and Larson 2004). Individual and collective engagement may also increase with embeddedness, as identified within studies of social movements and social networks (Passy 2001). Applied to IISMs, this would mean that the inherent embeddedness of an IISM will logically strengthen its viability, at least in the early stages. Furthermore, participants' already-established ties to the institution will increase and sustain their level of activity within the social movement.

Intrainstitutional social movements likewise benefit from appropriating a recognizable organizational form. By electing to operate within the bounds of a clearly defined space (the institution), IISMs can, at least to some extent, borrow the legitimacy afforded by that space. VOTF activists were able to use the recognition proffered by the label and space of the Catholic Church as a way of communicating their own agenda. Newer, less familiar organizational forms are less likely to elicit trust or legitimacy (Hannan and Carroll 1992). Organizational ecologists maintain that conforming to institutional norms and expectations and preserving sociopolitical legitimacy are vital to survival chances (Baum and Powell 1995; Meyer and Scott 1983). Moreover, when the target of collective action recognizes a social movement as a legitimate challenger, this in itself can be considered success (Gamson 1990). In other words, church leaders' very recognition of VOTF as a legitimate challenger is one marker of achieving movement goals.

Voice of the Faithful signaled conformity to the norms of its chosen institutional environment in several important ways. Notably, the movement selected from and replicated elements already available in the church. Affiliates incorporated prayer, Catholic songs, Masses, and other explicit markers of Catholic identity. The movement also distanced itself from doctrinal disputes, instead vocalizing a commitment to the teachings and authority of the church. Goal two, supporting priests of integrity, signaled a respect for the role of the ordained, even in company with the movement's goal for structural change related to authority in the church. Numerous attempts to dialogue and work together with bishops likewise reflected conformity to the standard institutional norms of the Catholic Church. These institutional affirmations and ties offered at least a preliminary—if temporary—approbation from a Catholic public.

As demonstrated by this example, intrainstitutional positioning can lead the movement to imitate the form of the institution. This can be likened to institutional isomorphism (DiMaggio and Powell 1991; Fennell 1980; Meyer 1983), whereby organizations begin to mimic others within their organizational field.[3] For IISMs, the institutional environment provides a model for operation and leadership. Mirroring the movement on this model can be incidental—a consequence of the close influence of the institution—or strategic—a way of further legitimizing the movement in the eyes of institutional authorities, infiltrating the institution, and orienting direct action.

Voice of the Faithful replicated the institutional model of the Catholic Church in a number of significant ways. Replication emerged primarily in approaches to authority and power. Board members were selected rather than elected. The representative council was not nationally representative. Affiliates expressed frustration with the lack of communication and direction from Boston leaders. Even while operating under the name "Voice of the Faithful," many complained that in fact not all voices were heard nor welcomed. Participants in many sites sought permission to gather from their pastor, thereby affirming the existing parish model of authority via ordination. VOTF regions were restructured to mirror the diocesan structure of the Catholic Church in the United States. VOTF also desired, yet resisted, national leadership over affiliate matters, mimicking the U.S. Conference of Catholic Bishops in its own hesitancy to dictate diocesan matters—a structure that led in part to the long delay for a national policy for responding to allegations of abuse.

In creating a movement form, VOTF leaders did not set out to replicate the model of the Catholic Church. Rather, they sought to reenvision the structural form of the church by incorporating VOTF movement goals of full participation and voice.[4] These ideological commitments led the group (at least initially) to employ consensus, elect officers, and create mechanisms for voice in decision making. However, when some of these attempts failed, members equated the VOTF movement to the Catholic Church and VOTF leaders (particularly those in national leadership) to the unresponsive hierarchy.

Even while the movement mirrored the institution in these ways, VOTF participants were overtly mindful and even fearful of replicating the church's hierarchical structure. This was in some ways paralyzing to the movement, particularly in its early stages. Leaders were elected for very short initial terms. Attempts at complete consensus fell apart during a pivotal vote to request

Cardinal Law's resignation. Original bylaws were skeletal, giving no one person or group a definitive say on movement activities. Despite appointing many leaders, none were given ultimate authority, leading to an inability to reach decisions on movement actions. The emotional energy of the movement was enough to sustain it in its early stages, but the lack of an agreed-upon, functioning structure nearly reached a crisis in year three. In a passionate letter to the chair of the board of trustees, three affiliate leaders then decried the "serious lack of strong leadership and direction by the Trustees and the Officers to complement the growing grassroots dynamics that have led to the recent election of a truly representative national council." The struggle for control was palpable, resulting in growing distrust internally.

Voice of the Faithful's positioning in the church yielded a paradoxical mix of replication and rejection of the institutional form of the church. Embeddedness strengthened the movement's viability and attracted participants, signaling conformity and legitimacy to both internal and external constituents. In rejecting components of the institutional form, however, the movement's inability to articulate its own authority crippled its organization and leadership. Boundaries introduced by VOTF's intrainstitutional positioning created nearly insurmountable barriers to effective organizational management.

As exemplified by VOTF, the form of an IISM is influenced heavily by its institutional environment. Advantages of embeddedness are accompanied by boundaries around form and limitations in authority for the movement, apart from the institution. The target institution models an organizational form that mediates those available to the movement. While an IISM may modify the institution's form, replication is likely nonetheless given the movement's institutional embeddedness.

The Tactical Repertoire of IISMs

As with the form of IISMs, tactics, too, are influenced and bound by the institution within which the movement operates. Past studies have illustrated that activism within institutions may rely upon previously-established institutional channels for effecting change. Strategies typically emerge from what participants know best (Taylor and Van Dyke 2004). Movement actors will therefore identify tactical options from among those in the cultural toolkit of the target institution to which they, too, belong.

Within VOTF, participants frequently relied upon known strategies within their parishes and dioceses to introduce conversations about abuse and increased accountability. The movement emerged over donuts and conversation in a church basement after Mass. VOTF members surveyed and joined parish councils, finance councils, parish-wide meetings, diocesan synods, and forums for adult education. Affiliates increased their membership levels by advertising to existing mailing lists of parishioners. Supportive priests and nuns attended and spoke at VOTF meetings. The movement also had a physical presence within churches: not only did VOTF participants attend services and partake as active parishioners in parish life, but affiliates commonly met on church grounds and strategized while sitting, literally, in their target's midst.

Voice of the Faithful's reliance upon existing institutional resources challenges the condition that social movements must, by definition, operate "primarily *outside* of institutional channels" (Snow, Soule, and Kriesi 2004, emphasis added). Rather, institutional channels can themselves become a resource, appropriated for movement aims. The opportunity structures of institutions are in fact strong predictors for strategy selection among IISMs (see Ferree and Mueller 2004). Close ties to the target of movement action can enhance the movement's survival chances because of this access to tactical resources.[5] Success is more likely when challengers have a "feel for the game" (Armstrong and Bernstein 2008). Furthermore, by using institutional resources for movement strategies, IISM participants contradict the notion that social movement participants are purely "noninstitutional actors" (see Freeman 1975; Gamson 1990; McAdam 1982; McCarthy and Zald 1977; Tilly 1978). Participants instead become "institutional activists" (Santoro and McGuire 1997) or "tempered radicals" who are committed to their organization and a seemingly contradictory cause (Meyerson and Scully 1995). VOTF participants aligned themselves with the Catholic Church while also advocating for structural change within it.

Strategy selection within IISMs is also bound by expectations and limitations on what constitutes acceptable movement behavior. Within VOTF, many common movement strategies were off-limits to activists because of their fear that such tactics would excise the movement from its desired internal and mainstream positioning. They critiqued other groups for engaging in strategies that were too abrasive or anger-based rather than aimed at "keeping the faith" (as stated in the VOTF motto). They experienced an institutional reprimand themselves after setting up the Voice of Compassion fund, through which VOTF attempted to raise charitable donations outside of diocesan control. Soon thereafter, church leaders admonished VOTF affiliates and banned them from meeting on church grounds. This presented clear boundaries for the movement regarding what strategies were acceptable.

In light of these boundaries around tactical options, VOTF leaders and participants made internal judgments regarding the appropriateness of particular tactics. The movement did not want to threaten its self-identified status and reputation as faithful Catholics in the church. Leaders selected strategies through the filter of what faithful Catholics "should" or "should not" do. Many members who suggested noncongruent strategies chose to leave the movement when their ideas were not accepted. For example, when leaders rejected one participant's idea of publishing publicly the names of every accused priest, he broke from VOTF and initiated his own organization targeting the church, but with fewer (and different) restraints on behavior.

Protest is therefore redefined within the intrainstitutional context to include only those strategies that can address movement aims while respecting extant institutional boundaries. Within VOTF, visible protest—marching with signs, for example—was rare. More common in the movement's tactical repertoire were prayer services, Healing Masses held in honor of victims of abuse, or lectures on Vatican II and the full participation of the laity in church life. Replicating known Catholic strategies also helped to construct VOTF's desired mainstream stance. The movement publicly avoided so-called hot button issues such as celibacy and female ordination in order to retain legitimacy as a group that did not challenge church teachings on these matters. Even when VOTF did broach these subjects, such as when the group responded to a papal document restricting homosexuals from entering the seminary, they did it in a subtle way: wearing green ribbons to Mass one weekend. They were thus able to be active, faithful Catholics, while also cautiously conveying dissatisfaction with the Vatican for focusing on homosexuality instead of the real structural causes of abuse.

An IISM's selection of strategies, then, has specific limitations based upon latent boundaries imposed by the institution. Certain protest tactics are deemed outside of acceptable behavior for internal movement activists. A certain conservatism—even fear—guides strategy selection within the institution. Consequently there is a natural alliance with already-existing avenues for reform within the institution: these resources have already earned the legitimacy of authority figures and are therefore more likely to gain ground as movement tactics. Replication characterizes IISM strategy selection, just as it characterizes the form of IISMs. Using existing institutional resources also feels familiar and comfortable to movement participants. In this way, strategy is tied to identity: as they acted out as Catholics within their church, VOTF participants used measures by which they have always understood change in the church. Their Catholic culture carried over into the culture of the movement.

Identity and IISMs

A third fundamental movement component influenced by institutional context (and closely wedded to form and strategy) is collective identity. By committing to effect change from within, movement participants are invested in remaining inside the institution. They define their movement in relation to the target institution, they take on a form that is recognizable to the institution, and they select strategies that align with their desired positioning within the institution. Given the movement's close connection to a particular identity (e.g., being Catholic) and positioning in a particular institutional location (e.g., within the church), identities are monitored carefully and debated both internally and publicly.

For VOTF to target the Catholic Church from within, the movement had to identify as Catholic and seek to be identified by others as Catholic. Their expressed institutional ties mattered: a movement would not be classified as an IISM within the Catholic Church if its collective identity denied entirely the institutionalized structure of the church toward which reform was aimed. The extent to which the culture of the institution permeates the movement will depend in part on how closely the IISM identifies with the institution. In the Catholic Church, groups such as Dignity USA (an organization supporting lesbian, gay, bisexual, and transgender [LGBT] Catholics), for example, embrace a Catholic identity and tradition while also separating from the institutional church by offering their own Masses and countering traditional church teachings on homosexuality.

In this way, identities within IISMs are *institutionally based*: driven and affirmed by a movement's relationship to the institution. VOTF participants are not just mobilized by their own Catholic identity, but (perhaps even more centrally) by their identity as Catholics *committed to the institution of the Catholic Church*, Catholics who wish to gain legitimacy and remain *within* the bounds of the church. Identities are therefore linked not only to the movement, but also to the institution. An IISM builds its collective identity by merging this *institutionally based* identity with a *change-oriented* identity. It is both Catholic and an advocate for change in the Catholic Church. Dillon (1999) writes of "pro-change Catholics" who similarly enact multiple overt loyalties in constructing seemingly contradictory identities. Leming (2006) describes the "religious agency" of Catholics who balance this paradoxical commitment.

The institutional context is therefore pivotal in shaping the collective identity of an IISM, even as participants forge a change-oriented movement identity. As also evidenced in form and strategies, the institutional context can lead the collective identity of the movement to replicate that of the institution. VOTF participants themselves critiqued the movement for acting "so Catholic"—members spoke of a collaborative, participatory environment, yet also wanted to be led. VOTF affiliates asked permission of priests to meet and cautiously guarded their desired mainstream Catholic identity. They interpreted their own authority as necessarily understood in relation to the authority of church leaders. Members noted frustration that movement participants were acting like "sheep," just like Catholics have always acted (and one of the very problems identified as a reason why the abuse had occurred).

The collective identity of an IISM (particularly its change-oriented component) will also challenge the identity of the institution.[6] A movement's identity might be interpreted by institutional authorities as a threat to the institution's own identity. VOTF's change-oriented identity threatened the Catholic Church in its desire to be unified as one collective body under one consolidated structure of authority. Church leaders made continual requests that VOTF participants work for reform as individual Catholics, not as the VOTF movement. Diocesan donations were welcome from individual Catholics, but not when organized collectively through an alternative fund. Diocesan responses to VOTF inquiries emphasized support for movement ideas only when separated from the movement's collective identity. This dynamic is not dissimilar to unionizing among employees within a corporation, where a company may feel threatened by requests made on behalf of employees operating as a movement rather than as individuals.[7] This is also strategic on the part of the institution; an individual request holds less power than that of an organized coalition.

An IISM's institutionally based identity can both attract and detract institutional insiders from participation in the movement. Institutional positioning may be a recruitment tool for the movement: individuals who have personal ties to an institution might be more willing to mobilize in the face of unsatisfactory conditions. Employees of a corporation, for example, will have a personal investment in the corporation's distribution of benefits and therefore might be more willing than others to mobilize for change within their institutional setting. Those within the institution may have privileged information regarding internal impropriety. Employees in certain institutional contexts, for example, may learn of illegal actions and become whistleblowers, mobilizing others internally. "True outsiders," as Armstrong and Bernstein (2008) point out, "lack the knowledge needed to identify the vulnerabilities of particular institutions" (p. 85). However, in the case of VOTF, most participants first learned of the problem via outlets external to the institution (e.g., extensive media coverage initiated by newspapers such as the *Boston Globe*).

On the other hand, an institutionally based identity can also dissuade mobilization. Those committed to an institution may not want to shake things up, to see the institution face public embarrassment, or risk failure. This, along with a fear of potential personal consequences (e.g., getting fired) could dissuade them from bringing contentious issues to the fore. In VOTF, the movement's institutionally based identity helped to recruit long-time committed Catholics who saw the possibility of improving and preserving their church for the future. On the other hand, an institutionally based identity made it difficult for VOTF to recruit supporters because many committed Catholics, though interested in seeing the church improve, did not wish to initiate or participate in public conversations surrounding the failings of their own church leaders.

The elite within an organization may be particularly well suited to balance both institutionally based and change-oriented identities.[8] Advocacy among the elite of an institution can pave the way for the success of IISMs, while also blurring the boundary between authorities and their challengers. Katzenstein (1998) and Smith (1991) found evidence of this in the Catholic Church when priests and bishops used their status through formalized, institutional means in order to advance a movement agenda supported by the powerless masses. While VOTF did forge alliances with some priests and establish a dialogue with some bishops, the movement was predominantly characterized by mobilization among the laity, most of whom did not hold official positions within the church but had ties through parish life and leadership. These connections had parallel effects, bringing the VOTF movement closer to local and more centralized authorities in the church.

It is also probable that the institutionally based identity of an IISM means that participants bring less experience with social movements. Participants' own affiliation with the institution is what brings the problem to their attention, not (necessarily) an established awareness of or experience combating injustice. The majority of VOTF participants had little or no previous experience with social movements.[9] They were not seeking out opportunities for activism; rather, it was their institutional positioning that introduced the opportunity to work for change internally. Said one participant, "I never thought I would get involved in anything like this. I was not a joiner." This connects again to the idea that mobilization can be provoked within the institution: it is a context with which movement participants are intimately familiar and in which they might feel a personal and pragmatic investment, perhaps to a larger extent than in other movement arenas. Within VOTF, many participants desired to create and preserve a better church for their own children and future generations of Catholics. They chose to move from within rather than disaffiliate from the institution.

Finally, given the centrality of identity to IISM mobilization, identity may itself emerge as a movement goal (Armstrong and Bernstein 2008). In navigating new interpretations of their institutional roles, legitimating their place within the institution, and forging new ways of doing and being (e.g., Catholic), IISM activists shift the very meaning of their identities. VOTF participants frequently highlighted as a success the opportunity that the movement gave them to express their Catholicism in a new way, to reconstruct their identity as lay Catholics without an automatic deference to church authorities. Acting within the institution mandated carving out a new space for a questioning, though committed, institutional identity.

Social Movements and Religion

Religion operates in multiple, complex ways within social movements. In the case of IISMs targeting religious institutions, religion can emerge in competing forms. Religious authorities may justify power arrangements theologically, movement participants may appropriate religious resources, and religious identities may become contested territory. Social movements operating within a religious structure may display "an intensity that is rarely seen in other organizations" given that the structure of the church is itself assigned sacred value (Zald 1982:333). Lessons from VOTF magnify the need to recognize religion as a central contributor to movement culture and, consequently, to collective identity and decisions regarding form and tactics.

The enduring institutional and cultural realities of religion—countering theories of secularization—have compelled (and required) social movement scholars to recognize the need for its closer study. Religious motivations cannot be explained away by other factors; religion *qua* religion is a causal force in mobilization and movement formation. A "cultural turn" in social movement scholarship has welcomed closer consideration of religion's relevance for movements. Religion, as both ideology and institution, can offer to social movements frames, resonance, legitimacy, and narratives for action and collective identity (Sherkat and Ellison 1999). Religion can mobilize resources (McAdam 1982; Smith 1991; Zald and McCarthy 1987), provide social capital and democratic skills (Greeley 1997; Putnam 1993, 1995; Verba, Schlozman, and Brady 1995; Warren 1995; Wood 1997, 2002), and sustain an open civil society (Casanova 1994; Cohen and Arato 1992).

Despite this important shift, scholars of social movements have been too narrowly focused on religion as structure and resource rather than as *culture* in social movements. Religion is also too often examined in light of its enabling mechanisms for social movements, without regard to the limitations religion may create for social movements. Religion emerges in IISMs not only as a resource for mobilization, but also as the very *reason* for mobilization. While the ability of religious beliefs to reveal worldly injustices and motivate action has been noted (see, e.g., Williams 2003), this has not been considered when injustice is revealed within the religious institution. Here, religion is reconceptualized as itself a site for injustice: in the case of VOTF, one of child abuse and insufficient institutional response to it. When the sphere of religious experience—the religious institution—is criticized, religion is parsed into multiple and potentially competing arenas. It operates as an institutional site for movement motivation, as a cultural code for negotiating movement approaches, and as a collective identity that is simultaneously shared and disputed.

Intrainstitutional social movements operating within religious institutional arenas present a complex manifestation of religion as multifaceted and contested. Movement activists share a cultural toolkit with the target of their reform. Extant resources within religious institutions can be appropriated and reenvisioned by movement actors for new goals. New functions and interpretations arise from a shared repertoire of resources. Thus not only do actors identifying with the same institution share a common set of ideas and symbols (Burns 1996), but also one of strategies and resources. This can lead to both innovation and replication within the movement. The movement culture of VOTF was marked by a competing desire among participants to remain Catholic and be seen as legitimately Catholic while demanding structural change within the institutional Catholic Church.

Religion can both cultivate and restrict a movement's collective identity. Identity politics may be particularly volatile within religious IISMs, given that religious institutions can assert authority over what constitutes an acceptable religious identity. In so doing, "religious institutions intervene to control the stock of identity narratives available to their participants" (Ammerman 2003:223). VOTF's collective identity reflected a dueling Catholic culture: both a product of its institutional environment and a reappropriation of the cultural toolkit proffered by the church. The religious culture of the movement, in effect, both constrained and enabled movement actors in collective identity and strategy selection. Religion is contested ground; identities become malleable and ownership contested.

Religion also operates within social movements to control and limit the resources available to adherents in their activist role. While the amorphous nature of Catholic identity offers flexibility in living out the faith (especially in a post–Vatican II era), established authorities within the church nonetheless narrow the options from which the faithful may select to secure movement success intrainstitutionally. Adherence to doctrine becomes a litmus test for an authentic Catholic identity. VOTF was rebuked when they aligned with other groups challenging the church, exemplified by refusals on the part of bishops to dialogue with VOTF leaders or participate in events that linked VOTF to other parties that did not embrace a doctrinal Catholic identity or commitment. A number of bishops denied VOTF affiliates the option of meeting on church property.

When religion becomes both unifier and divider in a movement, collective identities are debated and magnified internally. This complicates previous research that highlights the unifying character of religion in forging collective identity within a movement. IISMs operating within a religious institutional sphere retain elements of this shared identity: lay Catholics in VOTF and ordained Catholics in the hierarchy may share "common ground" (Davidson et al. 1997) on the major tenets of Catholic faith. However, each simultaneously draws upon different elements of that Catholic identity in order to promote a vision of what the Catholic Church ought to look like. VOTF emphasizes their commitment to the institutional church and shared identity as lay Catholics, while also highlighting the need for an increased recognition of their place in church decision-making. Neither the movement nor the authorities in contention aim explicitly to change a collective Catholic identity, but each come with different views of how that identity is expressed through the structural elements of the church.

Finally, religion intervenes in manifestations of power and claims of authority. Power is both institutionally and culturally bound, and as such will act differently in different institutional and cultural spaces (Armstrong and Bernstein 2008). In the case of religious IISMs, power has a divine twist: authority is conjured under the guise of spirituality and morality. Power commitments are justified theologically, and religion controls the scope of claimed authority.[10] As VOTF organizers read in the formal diocesan response to their fundraising offer, the refusal to accept VOTF-solicited funds stemmed from "a sincere effort to maintain the proper relationship between a bishop and the faithful." Ownership over who controls the religion and its institutional expression is debated on moral terms: bishops invoke the tradition of the church to legitimate their own authority; VOTF participants use the documents of Vatican II as justification for empowerment. In using religious texts and discourse as sources of legitimation, both sides affirm their commitment to sustaining religion as an institution with established norms of behavior and ordained positions of authority. As an IISM, VOTF challenges the institution while also reaffirming (and in many ways, replicating) it.

Bounded Movements

The framework that best fits the study of IISMs is one that brings into consideration multiple boundaries surrounding movement form, identity, and tactics. As the target of an IISM, the institution plays a central role in mediating what constitutes an acceptable repertoire in each of these areas. This occurs primarily through the shared meaning system embedded in both the institution and the emergent internal movement. IISMs engage in a heightened awareness of boundaries limiting their chosen form, identity, and tactics. As each of these movement elements links closely to the institution, this influence can result in institutional replication within the movement.

Boundaries arise in both explicit and implicit ways. Explicitly, boundaries emerge when certain institutional spaces are deemed off-limits to participants acting on behalf of the movement. Thus in VOTF, even while members were invited to worship and serve in their parish communities as individuals, these same individuals were banned in some dioceses from meeting on their own parish's property as a VOTF affiliate. Priests did not want to take the perceived risk of letting affiliates meet at their parish as VOTF. Implicitly, boundaries arise around tactical options as a result of the culture and socialization of the institution. As Catholics committed to the Catholic Church, VOTF members built symbolic walls around acceptable styles of protest based upon their own interpretation of appropriate Catholic behavior. These implicit boundaries drove out tactics (and even movement participants) that did not fit within institutional boundaries.

Intrainstitutional social movement boundaries are also malleable, particularly in the context of an institutional arena as expansive as the Catholic Church. Multiple and competing authorities at various levels of the institution may come to different conclusions regarding the acceptability of an internal movement, resulting in the permeability of some boundaries. Some dioceses and bishops were more receptive than others to dialogue and collaboration with VOTF. This emerged most commonly on the parish level, where individual priests would welcome or even encourage the mobilization of lay Catholics pushing for change within the church. VOTF members frequently spoke of loving their own parish and pastor, pointing to the existence of problems only beyond these immediate levels. Priests, however, risked personal admonishment in lending their support to the movement.

Boundary negotiations also enter into the public sphere. As a movement attempts to define itself in terms of the institution, external accounts (such as those made through print or online media) bring debates about movement identity into the public arena. The status of "insider" is negotiated internally as well as publicly. Both the movement and the institution make public plays for correctness, offering their own justification for action. The VOTF movement was well aware of this public communication in creating its public image. Their website emphasized faithfulness to church teachings, because leaders knew that they were being publicly questioned about this. Dioceses posted their own assessments of the movement's Catholic identity. The movement's entire emergence was tied closely to the role of the media (the *Boston Globe* in particular); VOTF and church leaders were very cognizant of the need to publicly project credibility.

Religion also plays a central role in boundary construction. Competing religious interpretations may intervene to determine what constitutes authentic participation and, more centrally, who authentically represents a religious identity. Movement participants acting within the bounds of a religious institutional space are keenly aware of this. They attempt to manage their own religious identity in the movement explicitly, advocating for the right to voice dissent as adherents. The movement is forced to reaffirm its own commitment to the institution, to outwardly accept the boundaries presented while also searching for ways to enact reform from within them. For IISMs targeting a religious institution, religion itself—operating as resource, identity, culture, and structure—enters the battle over what constitutes legitimate religious expression, ownership, and authority. Religious identities move from ascribed to achieved; movement actors are forced to prove their religious legitimacy and right to speak on behalf of the institution and its adherents.

Intrainstitutional social movements are centrally defined by the institutions within which they emerge and operate. IISMs function under a heightened awareness of boundaries around movement identity, form, and tactics, and are both limited and enabled by the resources proffered by the institutional setting. The culture of the institution permeates that of the movement within, thereby bounding the movement and increasing the likelihood that the movement will emerge as a reflection of the institution itself.

Conclusion

On the weekend of July 8–10, 2005, three-and-a-half years after the emergence of VOTF, approximately 560 people from thirty-three states gathered at the convention center in downtown Indianapolis for a VOTF-sponsored Convocation of Catholic Laity entitled "The Laity Speak: Accountability Now." Despite approximations that thousands of lay Catholics from all over would attend, reminiscent of the first convention in Boston at the peak of the abuse crisis, organizers' optimism for such a turnout waned in the months following the initial announcement. Focus shifted instead to gathering VOTF leaders, defined as all those who "made the commitment to speak up for change in our church" or who "used your voice, along with those of so many others."

The gathering invited yet another test of VOTF's acceptance within the institution of the Catholic Church, revealed in the local archdiocesan paper's refusal to run an announcement of the convocation. Indianapolis' Archbishop Daniel Buechlein wrote a letter to every pastor in the archdiocese, alerting area Catholics to VOTF and its questionable stance on structural change. In it, Buechlein wrote that VOTF leaders "have been unable to clearly articulate its meaning or implications" and "seem not to be aware of possible implications to changing the church's structure." The archbishop instructed his pastors to read the letter to all parishioners during Mass.

Voice of the Faithful's national leaders acted quickly to quell animosity in the weeks preceding the convocation. One leader recalled the exchange:

> [We] had a letter faxed back to [the archbishop], explaining the third goal and putting it in our own words about why we needed this goal, what we aspired to do, sending some material from the website about it. We were trying to head off a public conflict in Indianapolis which would have affected the media, would have affected local Catholics, and would have been picked up in Chicago. So, the letter was very strong in terms of clarity about his point. Either it worked or something else worked, but he didn't have his letter read from the pulpit on that following Sunday. So, I think we dodged a bullet on that one.

While the Indianapolis archbishop did not reach agreement with VOTF, he did recant his request to have the letter read at weekend Masses. VOTF was relieved to avoid a more public falling-out in the midst of their national gathering.

Speakers at the convocation (Figure 10.1) acknowledged the movement's loss of energy, slumping membership, burnout, lack of training, and frustration with the lack of change in the church. The agenda concentrated on training in affiliate leadership and grassroots organizing, reports of movement successes, and discussions aimed at determining a future agenda for VOTF. Speakers delivered spirited messages intended to revive the initial impetus behind the movement and reinvigorate the urgency for effecting change. At the heart of the convocation were nine breakout sessions addressing three larger themes of bishop accountability, financial accountability, and lay accountability. Nine resolutions emerged from the discussions, suggesting actions such as the creation of lay councils at all church governance levels, audits for all church-related entities, spiritual practices to foster healing, and legislation to hold bishops accountable for failures to protect children. Resolutions also included suggestions to initiate discussions about issues affecting women and a call for the election of bishops.

The convocation concluded with a promise to build the resolutions into a set of key strategies that would guide VOTF's agenda for the next few years, with the continued input of all participants. VOTF's President James Post shared in the closing gathering the reassurance that, although the movement had spent much of the last year working on internal problems, this process was now moving VOTF "toward a higher level of action, a more visible level of action, in the church." Speaking about what VOTF was doing, Post continued:

FIGURE 10.1.   VOTF Convocation, Indianapolis, Indiana, July 2005

> We know we're doing something that our parents would be shocked
> at. We've criticized our church, we've criticized our bishops. Those
> are not things that our parents probably would have done. But
> we're called to do that now. We leave Indianapolis now with a
> commitment . . . that we will be voices that challenge. And as always:
> keep the faith, change the church.

The process was under way to determine the future of the VOTF movement.

> Following the convocation, one leader reflected on its outcome:

> We had to come out of Indianapolis with a sharper sense of what
> we're going to be focusing on as we go forward . . . reflected in part
> in the resolutions, but not totally. We've got to cascade those ideas out
> through the rest of the organization. It's a real test of how we
> function as an organization. We say we are a grassroots organization.
> That requires us to go out to the grassroots to reach out and draw on
> them in some way. So, that's the work that's yet to be done.

The gathering was significant in that it affirmed a new model of governance reflecting VOTF's national presence and grassroots connections. The

movement had expanded its founding focus on sexual abuse into a larger discussion of how lay Catholics could participate actively in their own parishes and dioceses. It asserted its function as a voice for Catholic laity in the absence of existing structures for listening and participation in decision making. It contemplated needed changes to the structure of the church, emboldened by participants' own embraced identity as lay Catholics rather than by the stated permission of the Catholic hierarchy. VOTF had pushed against its own boundaries for demanding reform while remaining within the Catholic Church.

In December 2005, five months after the convocation and nearly four years after the day the *Boston Globe* published the headline that would ignite a lay Catholic movement, VOTF's President James Post announced that he would not be seeking reelection. Having held the position since early on, Post wrote to members that it was time to "encourage others to assume leadership roles in VOTF." Reflecting on the movement as a whole, he wrote:

> Four years ago, few would have imagined that an authentic Catholic lay movement could be formed, grow into a national and international network of members, and help introduce the ideas of "voice," "transparency," and "accountability" to the Catholic Church. Yet that is what we have done. Our efforts, coupled with those of thousands of other caring, committed Catholics, have made a difference as we have worked to "keep the faith, and change the church."

Indeed, the movement had moved thousands to apply their Catholic faith in new ways, transforming intense emotions after news of the scandal into a collective movement aimed at reforming the Catholic Church from within.

The scandal of child sexual abuse by clergy and its institutional cover-up created a cultural moment during which a critique of the Catholic Church was publicly accepted and expected. Harsh criticism of structural dynamics within the Catholic Church surfaced, reflected in psychologist Frawley-O'Dea's (2004) suggestion that "Bishops, priests, and Catholic laity were socioculturally and psychologically constructed to enable priests to abuse minors sexually and to cover up for them afterward" (p. 135). As revelations of abuse and concealment emerged in 2002, VOTF gained momentum as a Catholic voice that ran counter to the villain Catholic image painted in the media of pedophile priests and complicit bishops. In the absence of trustworthy leaders who could positively represent the Catholic religion publicly, lay leaders active at the grassroots level emerged as an alternative voice for the U.S. Catholic Church: a voice of the faithful.

When their church came under scrutiny, VOTF Catholics elected to retain their long-held loyalty to being Catholic while also reawakening the *aggiornamento* embraced by the church of their youth. They recalled promises elucidated in Vatican II documents regarding their rights in the church as baptized Catholics; they stood up to decry abusive behavior and advocate for internal structural change. VOTF presented new ways to be Catholic, combining a long-held acquiescent faith with the authority they felt in so many other realms of their lives. When requests to dialogue met with opposition from church leaders, the VOTF movement turned to grassroots mobilization in local parishes. Tapping into the anger and sadness of Catholics nationally, VOTF grew in numbers, attention, and power. Parish affiliates became sites for renegotiating religious agency. Participating lay Catholics began to foster a notion of religious identity that hinged upon responsibility for and ownership of their church, rather than on a passivity that they feared could result in further secrecy and abuse.

Absent early cooperation from church officials, VOTF pursued a model of reform based centrally on a Catholic identity that, while drawing strength from its institutional ties, was not fully wedded to them. Lay Catholics found new power in their church, separate from ordained leadership. This threatened traditional authority structures in the church and created a power struggle over what defined an authentic Catholic identity. Was ordination a requirement for decision making in the church? Or could an empowered Catholic identity include all those who self-identified, believed, and participated in the life of the church, regardless of ordination status? Could an authentic Catholic identity contain lay Catholics who questioned the internal operations of the church? Could it contain priests who had abused children, or bishops who had transferred them to parish after parish? The movement surged with momentum limited not to the crisis of sexual abuse, but fueled by new authority in the face of failed leadership, a long-awaited empowerment in decision making, and an urgent desire to preserve a church on the brink of losing its moral authority.

No mass exodus from the church occurred after the scandal of abuse was widely publicized in 2002, as some had predicted. The number of self-identifying Catholics in the United States remained consistent in the years immediately following the scandal, and polling data revealed only a slight dip (Gallup 2004) or no discernable change (CARA 2006) in Mass attendance. Self-reported financial giving to local parishes also remained consistent. There was, however, a reduction in financial giving at the diocesan level: the percentage of Catholics self-reporting contributions to diocesan financial appeals dropped ten percentage points from 2002 to 2004. Many Catholics' awareness of the scandal was also subject to inaccuracies. Although accusations were made against priests in every U.S. diocese, for example, only a quarter reported knowledge of abuse having occurred in their own diocese (CARA 2006).

On the legal front, statutes of limitations for criminal prosecutions or civil suits against child abusers have been revised in Delaware, Ohio, Virginia, New Jersey, Louisiana, and California. Changes have been debated in Colorado, Massachusetts, New York, and Pennsylvania. The legislation has often pitted members of VOTF against Catholic Church leaders, particularly in disputes regarding civil statutes. Civil suits have resulted in settlements for survivors topping a billion dollars, collectively. Common ground between VOTF and church leaders has been more frequently forged in cases related to criminal statutes of limitations, targeted at the individual perpetrator rather than the institutional church.

The psychological impact of the scandal is most poignantly evidenced by the inordinate number of suicides among individuals with ties to abuse by Catholic clergy, as either victim or perpetrator. Numerous victims of abuse have taken their own lives, some within months of learning it was too late to file criminal charges against their abuser. Many had been vocal and public about their abuse, active in survivor support groups, talking to the media, and participating in civil suits. Others first revealed their abuse in suicide messages. Janet Patterson of Conway Springs, Kansas, began advocating for victims of clergy abuse after her twenty-nine-year-old son, an abuse victim, killed himself in 1999. Wrongful death lawsuits have been filed by surviving family members against dioceses in several states.

Suicides have also occurred among clergy accused of abuse. Father Don Rooney, an associate pastor from the Cleveland Diocese, took his own life in April 2002 after being summoned to appear before officials about an accusation of abuse against a girl two decades prior. Father Alfred Bietghofer, sixty-four, hung himself in May 2002, a month after being stripped of priestly duties in light of allegations of abuse against him. A pastor in New London, New Hampshire, took his own life in December 2002 after learning he had been accused of abusing a minor more than thirty years earlier. Homicides have also been linked to clergy abuse. John Geoghan, whose own trial for abuse sparked the 2002 crisis, was strangled to death by a fellow inmate in August 2003 while serving time in a Massachusetts correctional center. In May 2002, a twenty-six-year-old man shot and wounded a priest in Baltimore whom he alleged had abused him nearly ten years earlier.

Since 2002 the Catholic Church in the United States has introduced changes to the way it addresses abuse by clergy. The U.S. Conference of Catholic Bishops (USCCB) approved the "Charter for the Protection of Children and Young People" (referred to as the "Dallas Charter") in 2002, establishing standards for responding to allegations leveled against priests and preventing future abuse. Passed after just two days of debates, the charter's mandates include swift inquiries into allegations, supervised by a lay-led National Review Board. Its zero-tolerance approach is reflected in a mandate to remove a priest from all ministerial duties after just one confirmed case of abuse, no matter how many years prior. The policy has also had the latent effect of introducing a culture of uncertainty and fear of false accusation among priests.

Along with the passage of the Dallas Charter, the USCCB established an Office of Child and Youth Protection. The newly established office was charged with creating safe environments for children in church activities, requiring an annual audit of dioceses to assess compliance with the Dallas Charter, and publishing an annual report for the public based on the annual audit. The USCCB also commissioned a study of the nature and scope of abuse among clergy, the results of which were released in 2004 and 2006. More thorough background checks have been implemented for church employees who work with children, as well as for entering seminarians. The majority of dioceses now have victim assistance coordinators and diocesan review boards to handle allegations, prevent abuse, and support victims. Despite these consolidated efforts, a survey five years later (CARA 2007) revealed that only 17 percent of Catholics knew of efforts by their diocese to prevent abuse and 34 percent were aware of policies created by the Dallas Charter to handle allegations.

Annual audits mandated by the Dallas Charter account for the number of new abuse allegations made against church employees, the amount of money spent in abuse-related costs (surpassing $2.3 billion), and individual dioceses' compliance with charter requirements. The methodology of these audits is limited, however, because dioceses self-report the data. Auditors do not have access to personnel files or other confidential materials. Dioceses also participate by choice. The Diocese of Lincoln, Nebraska, for example, has consistently refused to participate, without consequence. In addition, the audits measure implementation of charter mandates rather than their effectiveness. Recent audits have also revealed signs of "issue fatigue," including infrequent convening of diocesan review boards (USCCB 2008).

Boston's Cardinal Bernard Law was one of a handful of United States bishops who resigned in the wake of criticism related to the sexual abuse scandal. Subsequent to his December 2002 resignation, Law was appointed by Pope John Paul II to oversee a major basilica in Rome. He also presided at one of the public funeral Masses after Pope John Paul's death in 2005. Law's presence in Rome and participation on multiple Vatican committees, including one that helps select new bishops, has likely increased his influence in the Catholic Church, despite his unfavorable departure from Boston. VOTF has called for Law to resign from all positions in the Catholic Church.

In addition to calling for Law's resignation, VOTF leaders have advocated for the resignations of Bishop William Murphy of the Rockville Centre Diocese in New York, Bishop John McCormack of the Manchester Diocese in New Hampshire, Cardinal Francis George of the Chicago Archdiocese, Archbishop Daniel Pilarczyk of the Archdiocese of Cincinnati, and Cardinal Roger Mahony of the Archdiocese of Los Angeles. None have resigned in response, though some have or will soon reach the age of 75 at which all bishops are required to submit their resignation to the Pope. In April 2002, Bishop McCormack did resign his post as chairman of the USCCB committee on sexual abuse under mounting criticism and documentation that he had protected abusive priests.

Voice of the Faithful representatives have met with more than a dozen bishops and diocesan departments, which, although notable, is a small proportion of the total number of leaders in the U.S. church hierarchy. In August 2006, leaders from the Boston area VOTF met with Boston's Archbishop Cardinal Sean O'Malley, who replaced Cardinal Law. Although it was not the first meeting between archdiocesan leaders and representatives of the lay movement, it was touted by VOTF and the media as symbolic of increasing openness to dialogue and recognition that the movement's participants, though progressive, had not been relegated to the fringes of church decision making. On the table for discussion were legal statutes of limitations, a proposed registry for abusive priests who had served in the archdiocese, a program for protecting children from abuse, and the ban that had disallowed VOTF affiliates formed after October 2002 to meet in Boston's Catholic parishes.

A subsequent decision made by VOTF leaders not to reveal to the media what had transpired during this conversation with archdiocesan leaders signaled an important—and ironic—compromise. In its desire for acceptance among church leaders as authentic, loyal Catholics (rather than facing exclusion as external dissenters), VOTF had itself become inured to secrecy. Public transparency and accountability, it would seem, was a trade-off for the dialogue for which VOTF had so vehemently petitioned. While the VOTF–diocesan meeting solidified the sought-after movement status of institutional insider, it simultaneously replicated the boundaries between those with power and those without. The *Boston Globe*, whose very coverage made lay Catholics aware of abuse in the church, was not granted access to information about the internal negotiations to which VOTF had itself finally gained entry.

For many within the movement, this conversation with the church hierarchy constituted a proud success. However, it also exemplified an ironic contrast to the movement's founding cries for openness and discussion among all Catholics. In order to progress on reforming the church from within, the movement had in essence reaffirmed clearly established boundaries of the institution that excluded the full participation of all members. The movement had replicated the institution. These compromises left some pessimistic about the movement's ability to impart real change, as one participant's comments reflect:

> Even if VOTF accomplished its goals, and was able to establish an ongoing, collaborative relationship with the hierarchy, which I don't at all believe will happen in my lifetime, if at all, I think there's a need for a voice that steps outside that. Because the minute you become part of any organization, there is understandably, and predictably, a need to compromise and collaborate—you've got your interest, we've got ours.

Indeed, even as VOTF extended existing institutional boundaries, carving out a niche for a more inclusive power structure within the Catholic Church, it had simultaneously reinforced boundaries that differentiated between those empowered and those disempowered within the institution.

Movement Success

Success for any movement is difficult to identify. For IISMs, whose membership and positioning is so intertwined with the institutional target, it is difficult to parse movement success from initiatives introduced by institutional leaders themselves. Just as VOTF appropriated the resources available to them through their active participation and presence in the church, so, too, did church leaders appropriate the presence, participation, resources, and ideas of VOTF. Intimate links between a movement and its parent institution make it challenging to discern what should be attributed to the movement and what should be attributed to institutional elites already empowered within the church. Therefore it is difficult to link the specific actions of VOTF with measurable change in the church or broader culture of Catholicism.

Ambiguity in attribution aside, there is evidence of change in the Catholic Church—and in the meaning of being Catholic—since VOTF's emergence in 2002. The USCCB has created committees to address the scandal and its consequences. Dioceses have offered numerous Masses of Healing. Parishes have incorporated new measures to protect children, including background checks for those working with children and workshops on identifying inappropriate behavior. VOTF members have served on pastoral councils and lay-led boards. They have also been invited to serve on diocesan boards, including the council dedicated to managing church closings in Boston. VOTF leaders have lectured on Catholic college campuses, participated in panels on church life with other Catholic leaders and scholars, and written in numerous publications, effectively securing a place in public conversations about Catholic life. Regardless of who or what gets credit for these changes, they align with the goals of the VOTF movement.

The very recognition of VOTF by church leaders (whether through banning the movement or opening the doors for dialogue) is also a marker of success. Authorities in the Catholic Church knew about the VOTF movement early in its development. The VOTF website received page views from the Vatican during its first year. Some bishops saw VOTF's mobilization as enough of a threat to warrant diocesan bans or public reprimands. Priests made calculated decisions regarding whether or not to welcome affiliates in their parishes or attend VOTF meetings. The movement received coverage from local and national media outlets. Whether or not church leaders liked it, VOTF emerged as a public voice for Catholics and for the Catholic Church in the wake of the scandal.

Many in VOTF measured success not just by observable changes in the authority structures of the church, but by the very mobilization of a body of lay Catholics to whom integrity, voice, and change in the church mattered. VOTF became a means of networking with like-minded Catholics: those who had long felt alone in contemplating and laboring for a new realization of church. Although they attended the same Sunday morning service together for years, many who joined the movement did not know that others in their parishes were also eager for change (perhaps just fearful to admit it prior to the emergence of an organized voice). VOTF gave Catholics a space to express outrage at the scandal along with frustration and hope for the contemporary, post–Vatican II Catholic Church.

In this way, VOTF represented a generation of Catholics. The movement realized a model of Catholicism that emerged among baby boomers and the American ethos of the 1960s. VOTF participants were among the most upwardly mobile generation of Catholics in the United States to date. They used this new cultural capital to demand new responsibility and authority in the decision making of their church. The same questioning that had driven their generation to mobilize against the Vietnam War, for civil rights, and for women's rights had driven them to question the structure of their church. Although this generational legacy had given rise to power and success in corporate and civic spheres, come Sunday morning they had remained as powerless as children. The Second Vatican Council was also pivotal in forming this generation's Catholic identity. Through this collective memory of the church, they forged a new image of being Catholic in the wake of the scandal.

Evidence for the cultural consequences of the VOTF movement can be identified along individual, discursive, and larger cultural levels.[1] On the individual level, tens of thousands of Catholics found an avenue through which they could affirm their Catholic identity while simultaneously asserting the intelligence and professionalism they had carried with them into other areas of their lives. They commiserated in sorrow and fear that their own complicity or negligence could have contributed to the abuse of children at the hands of priests. In contemplating contributing factors, they began to recognize their own disempowerment and envision a church within which they, too, had a voice. VOTF raised questions and posed new models for the lived experience of Catholicism for all lay Catholics. The movement changed the values and meanings individuals carried of lived Catholicism.

Discursively, VOTF changed the conversation in the Catholic Church. They introduced discussions in parishes, dioceses, and collective bodies of Catholic leaders regarding sexual abuse, power, authority, and the rights and offerings of the laity. They refused to let the issue of abuse and secrecy surrounding it go unspoken any longer. They publicized stories of those victimized by clergy abuse. They spoke out through national media outlets and showed up at planning meetings of Catholic leaders. They changed the practice of many church boards that were neither democratic nor lay inclusive. They reawakened conversations about Vatican II that had lain dormant for decades. Although they maintained that doctrine was outside the purview of their reform efforts, the movement used it selectively to advocate for structural change in the church. VOTF helped to write and tell the history of the scandal, and helped shape the agenda of the Catholic Church after 2002. A movement's contribution to constructing the historical narrative is one marker of its success, as "those who win in the writing of history shape the future" (Meyer 2006).

In a larger cultural sense, VOTF shifted the very meaning of Catholic identity. The cultural code of the Catholic Church was instrumental in shaping the form, discourse, and tactics of the VOTF movement. But VOTF, in turn, shaped the culture of the church. They broadened the "we" within Catholicism to include not just the ordained, not just the silent masses obedient to existing structures of authority. They created new communities in local parishes emphasizing the leadership and abilities of lay Catholics. Gatherings drew thousands of attendees. VOTF presented a Catholic identity that could contain both faithfulness and challenge to the institution. Mainstream Catholics suggested that it was okay to, as stated in the VOTF motto, "keep the faith and change the church." When Catholic identity was tenuous, VOTF found a receptive audience to engage a new public image. Ownership of the church shifted. Success can be measured in part, then, in VOTF's ability to carry its message to a broader audience, thereby prompting cultural shifts in the meaning of Catholicism and ownership of a religious identity.

Murmurs of sexual abuse among clergy in the U.S. Catholic Church have settled in public conversation. The director of the USCCB's Office of Child and Youth Protection told reporters in March 2008 that the sense of urgency is easing. It is probable, however, that future opportunities will arise to again mobilize lay Catholics. Mobilization at the grassroots level has already stirred in response to parish closings, removed pastors, and papal encyclicals. As with VOTF, each of these movements will test the limits of Catholic identity, institutional boundaries, and the meaning of authority within the church. The Catholic Church—both its ordained leadership and its lay adherents—will continue to debate the extent to which a Catholic identity can maintain its religious distinction, legitimacy, and salience while harboring internal diversity and dissent. Thus far, at least, the Catholic Church has shown strong institutional resilience despite the magnitude of tremors that have murmured from within.

Appendix: Research Methodology

I began this study in fall 2002 among a large crowd gathered at a Southern California parish to discuss the formation of a local VOTF affiliate. Though initially conceived of as an exploratory field visit, I began feverishly taking notes once I realized the magnitude of what was transpiring in the stucco and stained glass meeting room adjacent to the main church. Seeing Catholics grabble visibly with the tension of faithfulness and anguish at revelations of abuse revealed an element of religion that was unfamiliar to me. It was a story that needed to be told, a window into a larger dynamic of a malleable and contested Catholic identity.

Unfolding from this moment was my three-year ethnography of an emergent Catholic movement that introduced countless candid illustrations of lived religion. Given the real-time development of VOTF during my study, I selected ethnography as the method best suited to capture the richness of movement activity and participants' experiences. Participant observation, in-depth interviews, and discourse analysis provided a means by which I could construct a movement narrative and introduce a conceptual framework for what was happening during this meaningful moment in church history.

Participant observation led me to local, regional, and national VOTF events in settings throughout the country. I conducted two years of observation in Santa Barbara, California, followed by a year of observation at several VOTF affiliates in the greater Washington, D.C. area. I attended VOTF gatherings in New York, New York, San Francisco, California, Worcester, Massachusetts, Washington, D.C., and Indianapolis, Indiana. An extended research trip to Boston in June 2005 allowed me to see firsthand the environment that sparked and sustained the VOTF movement, from the basement of St. John the Evangelist to twenty-four-hour vigils at closing parishes. Participants and leaders willingly cooperated with my research inquiries throughout this process. They consented to my attendance at public forums, regular meetings, and planning sessions. VOTF's president announced my presence at the national convocation in 2005, encouraging everyone to answer my questions and tell me their stories. In field settings I recorded speeches, conversed with movement participants, gathered literature, and took extensive field notes on environment, people, and behavior. Being there for both the spectacular and the mundane meant that I was privy to participants' attempts to structure the movement, frame their message, encounter dissent, and make tactical decisions about movement direction. Participants came to recognize, acknowledge, and welcome me at VOTF gatherings. The familiarity and trust I built with participants granted me entree into their honest reflections on the challenges that accompanied reforming the church.

Semistructured interviewing contributed to my understanding of context, meaning-making, identity construction, and agency within VOTF. Through conversations with fifty individuals involved in the movement (including VOTF founders, affiliate leaders, clergy, survivors of abuse, and ex-VOTF participants), I gathered personal stories and organizational histories that allowed me to paint a portrait of Catholics committed to preserving while changing their church. My selection of interviewees was based upon nonprobability techniques, guided by theoretical concerns in addition to representativeness. Nearly all whom I asked agreed to be interviewed. Ranging between 41 and 137 minutes, interviews took place in coffee shops, offices, restaurants, and private homes, or were conducted via telephone. They were recorded digitally and later transcribed in full. Each interviewee signed a letter of consent and was assured anonymity unless speaking in the capacity of a public representative. It is for this reason that I include very few real names in this book, unless otherwise noted.

My interview sample reflects diversity proportionate to VOTF membership patterns. Forty-two percent of interviewees were male; 58 percent were female. Two percent identified as people of color. Their ages ranged from twenty-six to seventy-three, with an average age of fifty-eight. Seventy-five percent of respondents were married. A quarter were retired, and nearly 20 percent had spent some time in seminary (although only two had been ordained). Almost all respondents had at least a college degree (96 percent) and had been raised

Catholic (93 percent). Of those who aligned themselves with a political party, 58 percent identified as Democrat.

Recognizing that what any movement or organization says about itself can matter as much as what it does (see, e.g., Bruce 2006), I also incorporated discourse analysis into my study of VOTF. Unlike purely text-based content analysis, a discursive approach empirically assesses texts and symbols for their greater cultural import. Symbolic and textual artifacts of VOTF (including online postings, press releases, annual reports, logos, e-mails, and letters to bishops), combined with extensive media coverage of the movement and textual artifacts from dissenters, constituted my units of observation. Combined with data from participant observation and interviews, this proved essential in understanding the movement's collective identity negotiations and public struggles to institute reform as committed Catholics.

I straddled insider and outsider status in the field as a sociologist-researcher with a Catholic upbringing. I knew the cultural code of Catholicism from which VOTF participants drew, albeit one learned entirely post-Vatican II. This familiarity likely presented access to places, conversations, and ideas that other researchers would not have had. The rarity of my youth (mid-20s while in the field) attracted much attention and frequent inquiry ("Where are all the young people?! How can we recruit people your age?"). Though I primarily just observed at movement gatherings, on one occasion I delivered a summary report of a regional VOTF conference to a local affiliate. In all settings, I was open about my role as a researcher and avoided normative statements about the church or the movement.

As with most qualitative research, the challenge lies less in gathering data and more in winnowing it down to present a narrative that is representative, informative, and true. To the extent possible, I have allowed participants themselves to tell the story of VOTF, how it is changing the church, and how this matters for what it means to be Catholic. Nevertheless, in creating this account I am myself shaping the historical narrative and collective understanding of Voice of the Faithful. I am confident in the validity of my account and am hopeful that others will see it as having fairly relayed the movement's essence, import, and intrigue.

Notes

INTRODUCTION

1. "Will," along with nine others abused by the same perpetrator, participated in a lawsuit against a Catholic diocese that resulted in a settlement allocation for each victim. The accused priest now resides in a retreat house which he is not permitted to leave without supervision.

2. This data was compiled by the John Jay College of Criminal Justice for their USCCB-commissioned study of child sexual abuse in the church, 1950–2002. Most abuse reports were made via phone calls and letters to diocesan or parish representatives. Public media coverage of abuse increased sharply in 2002.

3. "Eparchy" refers to a diocese of the Eastern (rather than Latin) Catholic Church, in communion with the Bishop of Rome.

4. In addition to the financial pressures related to the scandal, other factors such as a severe shortage of priests and changing attendance patterns across geographies have also contributed to parish closures.

5. See, for example, the contentious politics approach of McAdam, Tarrow, and Tilly (2001).

CHAPTER 1

1. Name has been changed here and for all study participants, unless noted otherwise.

2. I use Muller's real name here given that he is well established in the public record as having been central to the formation and early leadership of the VOTF movement. With the assistance of Charles Kenney, Muller authored a book on the movement's emergence entitled *Keep the Faith, Change the Church* (2004).

3. This statement was published on the Voice of the Faithful website, http://www.votf.org.

CHAPTER 2

1. Zucker (1977) defines an institution as characterized by organized patterns of activity and formal, structural embeddedness. Institutions are denoted by a shared culture that includes norms, beliefs, and ideas about what the institution stands for (though this might be contested internally). Examples include families, schools, corporations, and churches. Institutions may contain a single or numerous organizations. Institutions help individuals orient their daily lives, interpret their experiences, and govern their social relationships (see Nee and Ingram 2002). Beyond administering the sacraments and codifying a belief system, the Catholic Church as an institution is also instrumental in shaping the self-definition and social experiences of Catholics.

2. Studies of social movements often attribute insider status to those with decision-making power. Katzenstein (1998) cautions against assuming a strict boundary between institutional insiders and outsiders, instead examining the lines of accountability along the three dimensions: financial (who funds whom), organizational (who reports to whom), and discursive (whom activists identify with). Binder (2002) emphasizes the need to consider the type of power insiders hold (political or institutional). My use of "insider" is more cultural, in that one who merely identifies as "Catholic" is inside the institution of the church, regardless of the decision-making power they may (or likely do not) have.

3. For a more thorough description of VOTF founding leaders and participants' commitment to the Catholic Church and parish life, see D'Antonio and Pogorelc (2007).

4. Diocesan priests (also called "secular priests") are under the direct jurisdiction of their local bishop. Religious priests, by contrast, are under the jurisdiction of the superiors of their religious order (e.g., the Paulists or the Benedictines). In 2000, of the 45,700 priests in the United States, approximately two-thirds were diocesan priests and one-third were religious priests.

5. The VOTF President's real name is used here, as he is speaking publicly in the capacity of his VOTF position.

CHAPTER 3

1. This policy changed in 2006; girls may now serve as altar servers.

2. Scholarship in new social movements has drawn special attention to the search for identity in movement formulation, replacing the function previously served by class consciousness (Hunt and Benford 2004).

3. Classic sociological theories hinted at notions of collective identity under the guise of "class consciousness" (Marx and Engels 1970), "collective effervescence" (Durkheim 1965), and "party" action (Weber 1946).

CHAPTER 4

1. Flinn's (2007) *Encyclopedia of Catholicism* defines a diocesan synod as a gathering of "clergy, religious, and laity who meet to offer advice and opinion to the bishop ordinary," noting also that "such local synods are not mandated but are allowed" and "have often served as an outlet for the articulation of dissent and negative judgments" (p. 587).

2. This runs counter to Katzenstein's (1998) claim that "in the case of the church, the law is simply absent" (p. 146). She elaborates that court actions against the church do force punitive restitution, but ultimately do not hold it "accountable to existing constitutional or legal standards of justice and equality" (p. 148). VOTF's deployment of legal strategies introduces creative ways in which insiders can leverage legal tactics to impart structural change. Hence the law is both present and useful in mobilization.

3. D'Antonio and Pogorelc (2007) summarize some of the historical and contemporary differences that are reflected regionally in VOTF affiliates.

4. In their comparative study of the Archdiocese of Omaha and the Diocese of Des Moines, Harper and Schulte-Murray (1998) found that the Archbishop of Omaha exemplified a tighter supervision style and "was a master at avoiding and defusing potential conflict," while the Des Moines bishop's more charismatic and permissive leadership style led to greater autonomy among priests and laity in the diocese (p. 107). The authors concluded that such differences led to "powerful impacts on both the social dynamics and religious ethos of the two dioceses" (p. 115).

5. West and Blumberg (1990) introduce this framework to classify women's mobilization in social protest. Gender-independent movements feature the work of women and men in separate organizations, with little overlap. Gender-parallel movements feature separate structures and activities for women that parallel those for men (e.g., the Knights of Columbus and the Catholic Daughters). These movements, as West and Blumberg point out, are frequently asymmetrical (and patriarchal) in power. Gender-integration movements include both women and men within the same structures engaging in joint action toward shared movement goals.

CHAPTER 5

1. It is important to note that more than half of the respondents in the D'Antonio and Pogorelc survey were not members of a VOTF affiliate and two-thirds had never attended any VOTF meetings.

2. See D'Antonio and Pogorelc (2007) for a detailed comparison of VOTF members and the Catholic population nationally.

3. For a thorough exploration of the Second Vatican Council's process and resulting changes, see Melissa Wilde's *Vatican II: A Sociological Analysis of Religious Change* (2007).

4. Pope John XXIII died during the second session of Vatican II. His successor, Paul XI, elected to continue with the council's efforts in *aggiornamento*.

5. Not all Catholics interpret this shift in the locus of authority the same way. Some equate the notion of the "People of God" to a democratic "we the people"; others see it more as "obedient harmony with Church authority" (Weaver 1999:88).

6. Among all diocesan leadership positions, women constitute 47 percent (USCCB 2004).

7. Gamson (1997) and others have emphasized the need to examine collective identity construction in social movements as a gendered process.

CHAPTER 6

1. Thanks to an anonymous reviewer for this insight and phrasing.

2. Swidler (1986) wrote of the "toolkit" function of culture as it "shapes the capacities from which such strategies of action are constructed" (p. 277), particularly during "unsettled" periods.

3. For a discussion of distinctions between official religion, nonofficial religion, and individual religiosity, see McGuire (2001).

4. The American Society for the Defense of Tradition, Family, and Property (http://www.tfp.org).

5. Chaves (1993) identified a similar "dual structure" within Christian denominations: a religious authority structure that controls access to the supernatural and an agency structure engaged in more concrete, administrative tasks.

6. On the contrary, scholars of social movements have actually noted that the existence of radicals within the broader movement field can have a positive impact on movement outcomes (the "radical flank effect") (Haines 1984). The presence of radicals will highlight and affirm the more moderate stance of nonradicals, increasing their chances for dialog and negotiation with authorities in power. For VOTF, this would mean that groups like Call to Action and SNAP made VOTF look more mainstream and therefore more attractive for dialog with church leaders.

7. For a discussion of the complexities surrounding Jewish identity, see, for example, Hartman and Kaufman (2006).

8. See West and Zimmerman (1987) for a discussion of "doing gender."

9. Isomorphism refers to the tendency of organizations to mimic others in their organizational field (DiMaggio and Powell 1983).

10. Melucci (1996), in line with Taylor and Whittier (1992, 1995), underscores the necessarily politicized nature of collective identity in social movements. A perceived "they" group possessing unjust authority will encourage politicization of the "we" group (Gamson, Fireman, and Rytina 1982; Hirsch 1990).

CHAPTER 7

1. Source: Religion Newswriters Association.

2. Tensions frequently emerge when a leader is selected from outside of an original challenging group, leading to potential factions and jealousy (Marx and Useem 1971; McAdam 1988).

CHAPTER 8

1. See, for example, Williams (2004) for a more thorough discussion of this phenomenon.

2. For one exploration of regional differences in the culture of the Catholic Church in the United States, see Mario T. García et al., "Religious Geography: The Significance of Regions and the Power of Places," *U.S. Catholic Historian* 18, no. 3–4 (2000).

3. Scholars of social movements have found that the strategies enacted by movement participants are largely predictable and limited to a repertoire of tactics with which they are already most familiar (see Taylor and Van Dyke 2004).

4. For social movements operating within institutions, the movement's structure, beliefs, tactics, and discourse have been shown to resemble that of the institution. Movement strategies may conform to those of the "parent" institution, as Scully and Segal (2002) observed among workplace activists. In the institutional arena of religion, Kniss and Burns (2004) noted that the form taken by intrareligious movements "will depend upon the polity structure within which they must operate" (p. 705).

5. The term "MA-NY" was also used to represent affiliates in Massachusetts and New York who embarked on the first action initiatives.

CHAPTER 9

1. Although the subject of continuous debate, there is general agreement that social movements necessarily challenge or defend existing authority. The meaning of "authority," however, may be expanded or limited depending upon the theoretical lens employed. Those within the "contentious politics" camp, for example, have largely viewed social movement activity as necessarily involving a government entity (e.g., McAdam, Tarrow, and Tilly 2001). The proliferation of current scholarship on social movements, however, has emphasized, by its diversity, the need to locate authority in a much broader realm of understanding.

2. Zald and Berger (1978) described three types of movements within organizations, varying along six dimensions. Movement types include organizational coups, bureaucratic insurgencies, and mass movements.

3. Organizational scholars have noted that activists who most closely mirror institutionally legitimated actions have a better chance of success than those who choose other tactics (Meyer and Rowan 1977, Powell and DiMaggio 1991).

4. The ideology and goals guiding a movement can have a significant impact on the form the movement takes (Breines 1989; Downey 1986; Poletta 2002; Staggenborg 1989).

5. Increased success has been reported among organizations that establish networks with those controlling resources (Pfeffer and Salancik 1978).

6. Organizations can themselves exhibit an identity built around enduring characteristics (Albert and Whetten 1985).

7. Walmart, for example, has long discouraged unionizing among its employees and instead emphasizes an open-door policy for any individual employee to express his or her concerns to a direct supervisor.

8. Much of the research on institutional insiders has drawn attention to mobilization among the political elite, meaning those holding power and access within the institution (Binder 2002; Epstein 1996; Katzenstein 1998; Moore 1999; Smith 1991; Taylor 1996). Smith (1991) points out that oftentimes the initial stages of an internal movement are "not carried out by powerless, excluded masses using nonconventional means, but by theological elites in the context of a powerful, well-established organization using largely institutionalized means" (p. 234).

9. D'Antonio and Pogorelc (2007) found that about a quarter of VOTF members and more than 40 percent of leaders had prior involvement in a "Catholic social movement"; however, the authors defined social movement broadly to include more individually oriented religious activities such as marriage encounter and Cursillo.

10. Anson Shupe, in Spoils of the Kingdom (2007), identifies five characteristics of the manifestation of power within religious institutions: (1) "hierarchies of unequal power," in which the elite of religious institutions (2) "possess a greater power of moral persuasion," which may include the ability to "deny laity access to privileges of membership" and even the hope of salvation. Religious institutions are also unique in their tendency to encourage followers to (3) "trust or believe in the benevolent intentions, fiduciary reliability, selfless motives, and spiritual insights/wisdom of their leaders." This can in turn create (4) "opportunity structures" for resource abuse by church leaders and (5) systematic "opportunities and rationales for such deviance" (p. 7).

CONCLUSION

1. Following Earl's (2004) application of Hart's (1996) definition of culture, the cultural consequences of social movements can be measured on the social-psychological level (through changes in values, beliefs, and opinions), the level of cultural production and practice (through media, discourse, etc.), and the level of worldview and community (through collective identity and subculture).

Works Cited

Albert, S., and D. A. Whetten. 1985. Organizational identity. In *Research in Organizational Behavior*, ed. B. M. Staw and L. L. Cummings, 263–95. Greenwich, CT: JAI Press.

Ammerman, Nancy T. 2003. Religious identities and religious institutions. In *Handbook of the Sociology of Religion*, ed. Michele Dillon, 207–24. New York: Cambridge University Press.

———— 2008. Whose voice? *Boston College Magazine*, March 2008.

Armstrong, Elizabeth A., and Mary Bernstein. 2008. Culture, power, and institutions: A multi-institutional politics approach to social movements. *Sociological Theory* 26(1):74–99.

Aucoin, Don. 1992. New bishop reaches out to the abused. *Boston Globe*, June 17, 1992, p. 29.

Aymond, Bishop Gregory. 2007. Conversation with Bishop Gregory Aymond. Speech, Woodstock Forum, Georgetown University, Washington, DC, March 20.

Baum, Joel, and Walter W. Powell. 1995. Cultivating an institutional ecology of organizations: Comments on Hannon, Carroll, Dundon, and Torres. *American Sociological Review* 60:529–38.

Berry, Jason, and Thomas C. Fox. 1993. As nation discusses pedophilia, even pope admits it's a problem. *National Catholic Reporter*, July 2, p. 2.

Binder, Amy. 2002. *Contentious Curricula: Afrocentrism and Creationism in American Public Schools*. Princeton, NJ: Princeton University Press.

Bonavoglia, Angela. 2005. *Good Catholic Girls*. New York: HarperCollins.

Bourdieu, Pierre. 1977. *Outline of a Theory of Practice*. Cambridge: Cambridge University Press.

Breines, W. 1989. *Community and Organization in the New Left, 1962–1968.*
New Brunswick, NJ: Rutgers University Press.

Bruce, Tricia C. 2006. Contested Accommodation on the Meso Level: Discursive
Adaptation Within Catholic Charities Immigration and Refugee Services.
American Behavioral Scientist 49:1489–1508.

Burns, Gene. 1996. Studying the political culture of American Catholicism. *Sociology
of Religion* 57:37–53.

Cadge, Wendy, and Lynn Davidman. Ascription, Choice, and the Construction of
Religious Identities in the Contemporary United States. *Journal for the Scientific
Study of Religion* 45:23–38.

CARA[Center for Applied Research in the Apostolate]. 2004. *Annual Survey of
Allegations and Costs.* Washington, DC: USCCB.

———. 2005. *Annual Survey of Allegations and Costs.* Washington, DC: USCCB.

———. 2006. *Catholic Reactions to the News of Sexual Abuse Cases Involving Catholic
Clergy.* Washington, DC: USCCB.

———. 2007. *Five Years Later: Many Catholics Lack Awareness of Steps Taken by the
Church to Deal with and Prevent Abuse.* Washington, DC: USCCB.

Casanova, Jose. 1994. *Public Religions in the Modern World.* Chicago: University of
Chicago Press.

Chaves, Mark. 1993. Denominations as dual structures: An organizational analysis.
Sociology of Religion 54(2):147–69.

Clemens, Elizabeth S., and Debra C. Minkoff. 2004. Beyond the iron law: Rethinking
the place of organizations in social movement research. In *The Blackwell Companion to Social Movements,* ed. David A. Snow, Sarah A. Soule, and Hanspeter Kriesi,
pp. 155–70. Malden, MA: Blackwell Publishing.

Cogley, John. 1973. *Catholic America.* New York: Dial Press.

Cohen, Jean L., and Andrew Arato. 1992. *Civil Society and Political Theory.* Cambridge,
MA: MIT Press.

D'Antonio, William V., James D. Davidson, Dean R. Hoge, and Katherine Meyer. 2001.
American Catholics: Gender, Generation, and Commitment. Walnut Creek, CA: Alta
Mira Press.

D'Antonio, William V., and Anthony Pogorelc. 2007. *Voices of the Faithful: Loyal
Catholics Striving for Change.* New York: Crossroad.

Davidson, James, Andrea S. Williams, Richard A. Lamanna, Jan Stenftenagel, Kathleen
Maas Weigert, William J. Whalen, and Patricia Wittberg. 1997. *The Search for
Common Ground: What Unites and Divides Catholic Americans.* Huntington, IN:
Our Sunday Visitor.

Dillon, Michele. 1999. *Catholic Identity.* Cambridge: Cambridge University
Press.

DiMaggio, P. J. and Powell, W. W. 1983. The iron cage revisited: Institutionalism
isomorphism and collective rationality in organizational fields. *American Sociological Review* 48:147–60.

———. 1991. *The New Institutionalism in Organizational Analysis.* Chicago, IL:
University of Chicago Press.

Downey, G. L. 1986. Ideology and the clamshell identity: Organizational dilemmas in the anti-nuclear power movement. *Social Problems* 33:357–71.

Durkheim, Emile. 1912/1965. *The Elementary Forms of Religious Life*. New York: Free Press.

Eagan, Margery. 2002. Watch out, Law: The church ladies are now after you. *Boston Herald*, July 21, 2002, p. A4.

Earl, Jennifer. 2004. The cultural consequences of social movements. In *The Blackwell Companion to Social Movements*, ed. David A. Snow, Sarah A. Soule, and Hanspeter Kriesi. Malden, MA: Blackwell.

Ebaugh, Helen Rose. 1991. Vatican II and the revitalization movement. In *Religion and the Social Order. Vatican II and US Catholicism*, ed. Helen R. Ebaugh, pp. 3–19. Greenwich, CT: JAI Press.

Edwards, Bob, and John D. McCarthy. 2004. Strategy Matters: The Contingent Value of Social Capital in the Survival of Local Social Movement Organizations. *Social Forces* 83:621–651.

Epstein, S. 1996. *Impure Science: AIDS, Activism, and the Politics of Knowledge*. Berkeley: University of California Press.

Fennell, Mary L. 1980. The effects of environmental characteristics on the structure of hospital clusters. *Administrative Science Quarterly* 25:484.

Ferree, Myra Marx, and Carol McClurg Mueller. 2004. Feminism and the women's movement: A global perspective. In *The Blackwell Companion to Social Movements*, ed. David A. Snow, Sarah A. Soule, and Hanspeter Kriesi, pp. 576–607. Malden, MA: Blackwell.

Finke, Roger, and Patricia Wittberg. 2000. Organizational revival from within: Explaining revivalism and reform in the Roman Catholic Church. *Journal for the Scientific Study of Religion* 39:154–70.

Flinn, Frank K. 2007. *Encyclopedia of Catholicism*. New York: Facts on File.

Fombrun, Charles J. 1986. Structural dynamics within and between organizations. *Administrative Science Quarterly* 31:403–21.

———. 1988. Crafting an institutionally informed ecology of organizations. In *Ecological Models of Organizations*, ed. G. R. Carroll, pp. 223–39. Cambridge, MA: Ballinger.

Franklin, James L. 1993. Porter says church to blame; memory of crimes hazy, ex-priest says. *Boston Globe*, December 8, 1993, p. 33.

Frawley-O'Dea, Mary Gail. 2004. Psychosocial anatomy of the Catholic sexual abuse scandal. *Studies in Gender and Sexuality* 5:121–37.

Freeman, Jo. 1975. *The Politics of Women's Liberation: A Case Study of an Emerging Social Movement and Its Relation to the Policy Process*. New York: McKay.

Friendly, Jonathan. 1986. Roman Catholic Church discusses abuse of children by priests. *New York Times*, May 4, 1986, p. 26.

Gallup, George H. 2004. Religiosity levels stabilize among Catholics. http://www.gallup.com.

Gamson, Joshua. 1997. Messages of exclusion: gender, movements, and symbolic boundaries. *Gender and Society* 11:178–99.

Gamson, William. 1990. *The Strategy of Social Protest*. Belmont, CA: Wadsworth.

———. 1992. *Talking Politics*. New York: Cambridge University Press.

Gamson, William A., Bruce Fireman, and Steven Rytina. 1982. *Encounters with Unjust Authority*. Homewood, IL: Dorsey.

Gramsci, Antonio. 1990. Culture and ideological hegemony. In *Culture and Society: Contemporary Debates*, ed. Jeffrey C. Alexander and Steven Seidman, pp. 47–54. NewYork: Cambridge University Press.

Greeley, Andrew M. 1972. *The Denominational Society*. Glenview, IL: Scott Foresman & Co.

———. 1997. The other civic America: Religion and social capital. *American Prospect* 32:68–73.

Hager, Mark A., Joseph Galaskiewicz, and Jeff A. Larson. 2004. Structural embeddedness and the liability of newness among nonprofit organizations. *Public Management Review* 6:159–88.

Haines, Herbert. 1984. Black Radicalization and the Funding of Civil Rights: 1957–1970. *Social Problems*, 32:31–43.

Hannan, M. T., and G. R. Carroll. 1992. *Dynamics of Organizational Populations: Density, Competition, and Legitimation*. New York: Oxford University Press.

Harper, Charles L., and Rebecca K. Schulte-Murray. 1998. Religion and the sociology of culture: Exploring the organizational cultures of two midwestern Roman Catholic dioceses. *Review of Religious Research* 40:101–19.

Hart, Jordana. 1992. Law raps ex-priest coverage. *Boston Globe*, May 24, 1992, p. 23.

Hart, Stephen. 1996. The cultural dimension of social movements: A theoretical reassessment and literature review. *Sociology of Religion* 57:87–100.

Hartman, Harriet, and Debra Kaufman. Decentering the Study of Jewish Identity: Opening the Dialogue with Other Religious Groups. *Sociology of Religion* 67:365–385.

Hirsch, Eric L. 1990. Sacrifice for the cause: The impact of group processes on recruitment and commitment in protest movements. *American Sociological Review* 55:243–54.

Hirschman, Albert O. 1970. *Exit, Voice, and Loyalty*. Cambridge, MA: Harvard University Press.

Hoge, Dean R. 2005. Center of Catholic Identity. *National Catholic Reporter*, September 30, 2005, p.11.

Hunt, Scott A., and Robert D. Benford. 2004. Collective identity, solidarity, and commitment. In *The Blackwell Companion to Social Movements*, ed. David A. Snow, Sarah A. Soule, and Hanspeter Kriesi, pp. 433–57. Malden, MA: Blackwell.

Investigative Staff of the *Boston Globe*. 2002. *Betrayal: The Crisis in the Catholic Church*. Boston: Little, Brown and Company.

Isely, Paul J., and Peter Isely. 1990. The sexual abuse of male children by church personnel: Intervention and prevention. *Pastoral Psychology* 39:85–99.

John Jay College of Criminal Justice. 2004. *The Nature and Scope of the Problem of Sexual Abuse of Minors by Priests and Deacons*. Washington, DC: USCCB.

————. 2006. *2006 Supplementary Report: The Nature and Scope of Sexual Abuse of Minors by Catholic Priests and Deacons in the United States, 1950–2002.* Washington, DC: USCCB.

Jones, Arthur. 2003. Making distinctions: A bishop defends his actions. *National Catholic Reporter,* March 21, 2003, p. 6.

Katzenstein, Mary. 1998. *Faithful and Fearless: Moving Feminist Protest Inside the Church and Military.* Princeton, NJ: Princeton University Press.

Kinney, Bishop John F. n.d. *Op Ed Piece.* http://www.usccb.org/comm/kit5.shtml.

Kniss, Fred, and Gene Burns. 2004. Religious movements. In *The Blackwell Companion to Social Movements,* ed. David A. Snow, Sarah A. Soule, and Hanspeter Kriesi, pp. 694–715. Malden, MA: Blackwell.

Kniss, Fred, and Mark Chaves. 1995. Analyzing interdenominational conflict: New directions. *Journal for the Scientific Study of Religion* 34:172–85.

Leming, Laura M. 2006. Church as contested terrain: Voice of the Faithful and religious agency. *Review of Religious Research* 48:56–71.

Lounsbury, Michael. 2001. Institutional sources of practice variation: Staffing college and university recycling programs. *Administrative Science Quarterly* 46:29–56.

Marx, Gary T., and Michael Useem. 1971. Majority involvement in minority movements. *Journal of Social Issues* 27:81–104.

Marx, Karl, and Friedrich Engels. [1845] 1970. *The German Ideology.* New York: International.

McAdam, Doug. 1982. *Political Process and the Development of Black Insurgency 1930–1970.* Chicago: University of Chicago Press.

————. 1988. *Freedom Summer.* New York: Oxford University Press.

McAdam, Doug, Sidney Tarrow, and Charles Tilly. 2001. *Dynamics of Contention.* New York: Cambridge University Press.

McCarthy, John D., and Mayer N. Zald. 1977. Resource mobilization and social movements: A partial theory. *American Journal of Sociology* 82:1212–41.

McGreevy, John. 2004. The sex abuse crisis: The view from recent history. In *Governance, Accountability, and the Future of the Catholic Church,* ed. Francis Oakley and Bruce Russett, pp. 136–42. New York: Continuum.

McGuire, Meredith B. 2001. *Religion: The Social Context,* 5th ed. Belmont, CA: Wadsworth.

McNally, Michael J. 2000. The universal in the particular: The new regional history and Catholicism in the United States. *U.S. Catholic Historian* 18:1–12.

Melucci, Alberto. 1996. *Challenging Codes: Collective Action in the Communication Age.* Cambridge: Cambridge University Press.

Meyer, David S. 2006. Claiming credit: Stories of movement influence as outcomes. *Mobilization* 11(3):281–98.

Meyer, John. W. 1983. Institutionalization and the rationality of formal organizational structure. In *Organizational Environments: Ritual and Rationality,* ed. J. W. Meyer and W. R. Scott, pp. 260–82. London: Sage.

Meyer, John.W., and Rowan, Brian. 1977. Institutional Organizations: Formal Structure as Myth and Ceremony. *American Journal of Sociology* 83:340–363.

Meyer, John. W., and W. R. Scott. 1983. *Organizational Environments: Ritual and Rationality*. Beverly Hills, CA: Sage.

Meyerson, Debra E., and Maureen A. Scully. 1995. Tempered radicalism and the politics of ambivalence and change. *Organization Science* 6:585–600.

Minkoff, Debra C. 2002. Macro-organizational analysis. In *Methods of Social Movement Research*, ed. Bert Klandermans and Suzanne Staggenborg, pp. 260–85. Minneapolis: University of Minnesota Press.

Moore, Kelly. 1999. Political protest and institutional change: The anti-Vietnam War movement and American science. In *How Social Movements Matter*, ed. Marco G. Giugni, Douglas McAdam, and Charles Tilly, pp. 97–115. New York: Oxford University Press.

———. 2008. *Disrupting Science*. Princeton, NJ: Princeton University Press.

Mueller, Carol McClurg. 1994. Conflict networks and the origins of women's liberation. In *New Social Movements: From Ideology to Identity*, ed. Enrique Larana, Hank Johnston, and Joseph R. Gusfield, pp. 234–63. Philadelphia: Temple University Press.

Muller, James E., and Charles Kenney. 2004. *Keep the Faith, Change the Church*. New York, NY: Rodale Books.

Myers, Daniel J., and Daniel M. Cress, eds. 2005. *Authority in Contention*. Oxford: JAI Press.

Nee, Victor, and Paul Ingram. 2002. Embeddedness and beyond: Institutions, exchange, and social structure. In *The New Institutionalism in Sociology*, ed. Mary C. Brinton and Victor Nee, pp. 19–45. New York: Russell Sage.

O'Brien, Jodi. 2002. How big is your God? Unpublished manuscript, Department of Sociology, Seattle University.

O'Dea, Thomas F. 1961. Five dilemmas in the institutionalization of religion. *Journal for the Scientific Study of Religion* 36(2):30–41.

Passy, Florence. 2001. Socialization, connection, and the structure/agency gap: A specification of the impact of networks on participation in social movements. *Mobilization: An International Journal* 6:173–92.

Paulson, Michael. 2002a. Catholic lay leaders urge board reforms ask for rethinking of ministry, secrecy. *Boston Globe*, March 10, 2002, p. A1.

———. 2002b. In his first meeting with Voice of the Faithful, Law seeks answers. *Boston Globe*, November 27, 2002, p. B1.

Perl, Paul. 2005. Are former Catholic women over-represented among Protestant clergy? *Sociology of Religion* 66:359–80.

Perl, Paul, Jennifer Z. Greely, and Mark M. Gray. 2006. What proportion of adult Hispanics are Catholic? A review of survey data and methodology. *Journal for the Scientific Study of Religion* 45:419–36.

Pfeffer, J., and G. Salancik. 1978. *The External Control of Organizations: A Resource Dependence Perspective*. New York: Harper & Row.

Poletta, Francesca. 2002. *Freedom is an Endless Meeting: Democracy in American Social Movements*. Chicago: University of Chicago Press.

———. 2006. Awkward movements. *Mobilization* 11:475–8.

Pope John Paul II. 1993. Veritatis splendor. http://www.vatican.va.

Putnam, Robert D. 1993. *Making Democracy Work: Civic Traditions in Modern Italy*. Princeton, NJ: Princeton University Press.

———. 1995. Bowling alone: America's declining social capital. *Journal of Democracy* 6:65–78.

Raeburn, Nicole. 2004. *Changing America from Inside Out: Lesbian and Gay Workplace Rights*. Minneapolis: University of Minnesota Press.

Robnett, Belinda. 2002. External political change, collective identities, and participation in social movement organizations. In *Social Movements: Identity, Culture, and the State*, ed. David S. Meyer, Nancy Whittier, and Belinda Robnett, pp. 266–85. New York: Oxford University Press.

Rogers, Mary F., and Phillip B. Lott. 1997. Backlash, the matrix of domination, and log cabin Republicans. *Sociological Quarterly* 38:497–512.

Santoro, Wayne A., and Gail M. McGuire. 1997. Social movement insiders: The impact of institutional activists on affirmative action and comparable worth policies. *Social Problems* 44:503–19.

Scully, Maureen, and W. E. Douglas Creed. 1999. Restructured families: Issues of equality and need. *Annals of the American Academy of Political and Social Science* 562:47–65.

Scully, Maureen, and Amy Segal. 2002. Passion with an umbrella: Grassroots activists in the workplace. In *Research in the Sociology of Organizations: Entrepreneurs, Organizations, and Social Change*, ed. Michael Lounsbury and Marc Ventresca, pp. 125–68. New York: Elsevier.

Seidler, J., and K. Meyer. 1989. *Conflict and Change in the Catholic Church*. New Brunswick, NJ: Rutgers University Press.

Sherkat, D. E., and C. G. Ellison. 1999. Recent developments and current controversies in the sociology of religion. *Annual Review of Sociology* 25:363–94.

Shupe, Anson D. 2007. *Spoils of the Kingdom: Clergy Misconduct and Religious Community*. Urbana and Chicago: University of Illinois Press.

Smith, Christian. 1991. *The Emergence of Liberation Theology: Radical Religion and Social-Movement Activism*. Chicago: University of Chicago Press.

Snow, David A. 2001. Collective identity and expressive forms. In *International Encyclopedia of the Social and Behavioral Sciences*, ed. N. J. Smelser and P. B. Baltes, pp. 196–254. London: Elsevier Science.

———. 2004. Social movements as challenges to authority: Resistance to an emerging conceptual hegemony. In *Research in Social Movements, Conflicts and Change: Authority in Contention*, ed. Daniel J. Myers and Daniel M. Cress, pp. 3–25. New York: Elsevier.

Snow, David A., Sarah A. Soule, and Hanspeter Kriesi. 2004. Mapping the terrain. In *The Blackwell Companion to Social Movements*, ed. David A. Snow, Sarah A. Soule, and Hanspeter Kriesi, pp. 3–16. Malden, MA: Blackwell.

Staggenborg, Suzanne. 1989. Stability and innovation in the women's movement: A comparison of two social movement organizations. *Social Problems* 36:75–92.

Stammer, Larry B. 1993. Pope targets 'scandal' of sex abuse by clergy. *Los Angeles Times*, June 22, 1993, p. 1.

Sutton, John R., and Mark Chaves. 2004. Explaining schism in American Protestant denominations, 1890–1990. *Journal for the Scientific Study of Religion* 43(2): 171–90.

Swidler, Ann. 1986. Culture in action: Symbols and strategies. *American Sociological Review* 51:273–86.

Taylor, Verta. 1989. Social movement continuity: The women's movement in abeyance. *American Sociological Review* 54:761–775.

Taylor, Verta. 1996. *Rock-a-by Baby: Feminism, Self-Help, and Postpartum Depression.* New York: Routledge.

Taylor, Verta, and Nicole C. Raeburn. 1995. Identity politics as high-risk activism: Career consequences for lesbian, gay, and bisexual sociologists. *Social Problems* 42:252–73.

Taylor, Verta, and Nella Van Dyke. 2004. "Get up, stand up": Tactical repertoires of social movements. In *The Blackwell Companion to Social Movements*, ed. David A. Snow, Sarah A. Soule, and Hanspeter Kriesi, pp. 262–93. Malden, MA: Blackwell.

Taylor, Verta, and Nancy Whittier. 1992. Collective identity in social movement communities: Lesbian feminist mobilization. In *Frontiers in Social Movement Theory*, ed. Aldon D. Morris and Carol McClurg Mueller, pp. 104–29. New Haven, CT: Yale University Press.

———. 1995. Analytical approaches to social movement culture: The culture of the women's movement. In *Social Movements and Culture*, ed. H. Johnston and B. Klandermans, pp. 163–87. Minneapolis: University of Minnesota Press.

Tilly, Charles. 1978. *From Mobilization to Revolution.* Reading, MA: Addison-Wesley.

———. 1995. Contentious repertoires in Great Britain, 1758–1834. In *Repertoires and Cycles of Collective Action*, ed. Mark Traugott, pp. 15–42. Durham, NC: Duke University Press.

USCCB. 2002. *Sex Abuse Committee Releases Survey Results.* Washington, DC: USCCB.

———. 2004. *Women in Diocesan Leadership Positions: Progress Report, 2003.* Washington, DC: USCCB.

———. 2008. *Report on the Implementation of the Charter for the Protection of Children and Young People.* Washington, DC: USCCB.

Van Dyke, Nella, Sarah A. Soule, and Verta A. Taylor. 2004. The targets of social movements: Beyond a focus on the state. In *Authority in Contention*, ed. Daniel J. Myers and Daniel M. Cress, pp. 27–51. Oxford: Elsevier.

Verba, Sidney, Kay Lehman Schlozman, and Henry E. Brady. 1995. *Voice and Equality: Civic Volunteerism in American Politics.* Cambridge, MA: Harvard University Press.

Warren, Mark R. 1995. Social capital and community empowerment: Religion and political organization in the Texas Industrial Areas Foundation. PhD dissertation, Harvard University.

Weaver, Mary Jo. 1999. Resisting traditional Catholic sexual teaching. In *What's Left?: Liberal American Catholics*, ed. Mary Jo Weaver, pp. 88–108. Bloomington: Indiana University Press.

Weber, Max. 1946. *From Max Weber: Essays in Sociology.* Trans. H. H. Gerth
    and C. Wright Mills. New York: Oxford University Press.
West, Candace, and Don H. Zimmerman. 1987. Doing gender. *Gender and Society*
    1(2):125–51.
West, Guida, and Rhoda Lois Blumberg. 1990. Reconstructing social protest from a
    feminist perspective. In *Women and Social Protest,* ed. Guida West and Rhoda Lois
    Blumberg, pp. 3–35. New York: Oxford University Press.
Whittier, Nancy E. 1995. *Feminist Generations: The Persistence of the Radical Women's
    Movement.* Philadelphia, PA: Temple University Press.
Wilde, Melissa. 2007. *Vatican II: A Sociological Analysis of Religious Change.* Princeton,
    NJ: Princeton University Press.
Williams, Rhys H. 1995. Constructing the public good. *Social Problems* 42:124–44.
———. 2003. Religious social movements in the public square: Organization,
    Ideology, and activism. In *Handbook of the Sociology of Religion,* ed. Michele Dillon,
    pp. 315–30. Cambridge: Cambridge University Press.
———. 2004. The cultural contexts of collective action: Constraints, opportunities,
    and the symbolic life of social movements. In *The Blackwell Companion to Social
    Movements,* ed. David A. Snow, Sarah A. Soule, and Hanspeter Kriesi, pp. 91–115.
    Malden, MA: Blackwell.
Williams, Rhys H., and Timothy J. Jubal. 1999. Movement Frames and the Cultural
    Environment: Resonance, Failure, and the Boundaries of the Legitimate. *Research
    in Social Movement, Conflicts and Change* 21: 225–48.
Williams, Rhys H. and Gira Vashi. 2007. Hijab and American Muslim Women:
    Creating the Space for Autonomous Selves. *Sociology of Religion* 68:269–287.
Wood, Richard. 1997. Social capital and political culture: God meets politics in the
    inner city. *American Behavioral Scientist* 40:595–605.
———. 2002. Faith in Action: Religion, Race, and Democratic Organizing in America.
    Chicago: University of Chicago Press.
Yearbook of American and Canadian Churches. 2008. Ed. Eileen W. Lindner. New York:
    Abingdon Press.
Zald, Mayer. 1982. Theological crucibles: Social movements in and of religion. *Review
    of Religious Research* 23:317–36.
Zald, Mayer, and Michael Berger. 1978. Social movements in organizations: Coup
    d'état, insurgency, and mass movements. *American Journal of Sociology* 83:823–61.
Zald, Mayer, and John McCarthy. 1987. Religious groups as crucibles of social
    movements. In *Social Movements in an Organizational Society,* ed. Mayer N. Zald
    and John D. McCarthy, pp. 67–96. New Brunswick, NJ: Transaction Books.
Zucker, Lynne G. 1977. The role of institutionalization in cultural persistence.
    American Sociological Review 42:726–43.

Index